RIVER COTTAGE gluten free

RIVER COTTAGE
gluten free

NAOMI DEVLIN

foreword by **HUGH FEARNLEY-WHITTINGSTALL**

photography by LAURA EDWARDS

BLOOMSBURY

LONDON · OXFORD · NEW YORK · NEW DELHI · SYDNEY

All recipes are gluten free. Recipes marked ❋ are freezable, and those marked 🥛 are dairy free, provided dairy free ingredients are always chosen when there is an option.

foreword

by HUGH FEARNLEY-WHITTINGSTALL

Some people choose a gluten free diet because they have no option, because eating gluten makes them feel desperately ill. Others follow this path for slightly less dramatic reasons: gluten doesn't actually leave them unwell, but they undoubtedly feel better without it. For some, it's simply an intuitive step – the modern diet is stuffed, swollen and bound together with tonnes of this stuff; can that possibly be a good thing?

For reasons that fall somewhere between these last two, I myself now eat less gluten than I used to. I regard wheat bread as an occasional carb option, rather than a daily filler and I have reduced my reliance on pastry, pasta and flour thickened sauces. This shift has paid dividends. I have more energy; I feel better, sharper, healthier.

To me, it makes sense to regard with some suspicion the monopoly that glutinous grains have over our diets. It simply isn't wise to let any ingredient have a dominance in our systems. And when you look into the scientific history of modern wheat, the way our bread making practices have changed and the insidious manner in which gluten finds its way into countless processed foods, the fact that so many people now seem to have a problem with it isn't really surprising.

Naomi Devlin discusses those issues in these pages, taking a succinct look at how we've found ourselves in a world where food intolerance and dietary problems are so rife. But what she really focuses on is the way forward. This is a joyful book. Not only does it contain dozens of recipes that I, for one, want to go home and cook right away, but her writing encapsulates what I think is a crucial belief: that cutting out or cutting down on gluten can be, rather than a sacrifice, a truly positive and life enhancing step.

Whatever your reason for choosing to eliminate or reduce gluten, you will doubtless come up against the view that doing so is a penance, a relinquishing of pleasure. You may even feel yourself that you are taking, if not a step backwards, then a step away from nourishing, delicious food. I have noted that adopting a vegetarian diet can sometimes be seen in the same way – as a sad thing, a reductive choice. But in both cases, this thinking is all wrong. Just as meat is simply one ingredient, so gluten-containing grains represent just a small slice of the carbohydrates available to us. Removing these elements should simply shift one's focus to the thousands of other fantastic foods that are still very much on the menu.

It's not all plain sailing, of course. It would be glib to suggest that giving up gluten is easy; its ubiquity has had us all under its spell for a long time, and learning how to cook without it is a challenge. But I have found that challenges in the kitchen – and I have set myself many over the years – nearly always lead to creative and delicious solutions.

In the West, our reliance on gluten (and on wheat in particular) is a case of almost arbitrary favouritism. We feel that gluten-containing flours are the best for all jobs because they are the ones we are familiar with. But, in reality, our cooking has evolved to accommodate them, not the other way round. There is no reason why it can't evolve

further – and cookery is always evolving – to accommodate different foods. Indeed, in many cultures, gluten free ingredients such as buckwheat, chickpeas and corn already are starchy staples and have been for a very long time – for centuries, if not millennia. Gluten free cooking isn't always about innovation: sometimes, it means turning back to time honoured, traditional recipes.

Of course, gluten free food is not always good – I'm thinking particularly of the products that fill the 'free from' shelves in so many supermarkets. And it's an unfortunate fact that many people first come to gluten free cooking via the experience of ill health. When you take these factors into account, it is no surprise that gluten free eating is so often associated with negativity. But that is exactly why we need colourful, life affirming, celebratory, downright delectable books like this one. In these pages, Naomi, whose wonderful teaching at River Cottage has delighted, reassured and inspired so many of our visitors, turns the regretful 'no' of giving up gluten into a glorious, greedy 'yes!' to delicious, simple, health enhancing food.

When I wrote a book of wheat free recipes myself a while ago, my approach was the same: to enthusiastically embrace the new ingredients I was discovering and the fresh ways of cooking they inspired – to positively celebrate this rather new way of putting food on the table. I was determined never to bemoan the lack of anything, or to reinforce the sense that without wheat, we deny ourselves. And I found it easy: I had a blast testing and trying those recipes and many of them are now regular staples in my kitchen.

I am quite certain the same will be true of the fantastic recipes in this book. Naomi is a hugely creative and inventive cook, but also a reliable and thorough one. Of course choux pastry or chocolate chip cookies made without gluten won't be the same as their glutinous counterparts. But they can be equally good, or better. I have come to the firm belief that gluten free brownies, for instance, are often superior to wheaty ones: the chocolatey corkers you'll find on pages 242–5 prove my point.

Naomi is not just an inspiring cook and expert teacher, but a lovely writer too. She has a gift for clarifying the sometimes rather complex world of nutrition, neatly and elegantly teasing out the facts that are truly useful and relevant. And the *joie de vivre* you see in her recipes is there in the writing too, because this is not some dour health food tome – it's a bright, lively celebration of good food.

HUGH FEARNLEY-WHITTINGSTALL
november 2015

going gluten free

I have been living gluten free for over twelve years now and I feel fantastic for it, but it took a long while to discover exactly what food made me thrive. I'd been struggling for years with a kind of unease in my gut and increasing lethargy, then when I became pregnant with my son Finn, this acted as a catalyst for food intolerance. I began to react to so many different foods that I wasn't sure what I could safely eat anymore, so I started to follow a very restricted diet to avoid being in pain. Eventually I came to understand that gluten was the problem. Back then, coeliac disease was much less widely known, and the experience of my hard-won diagnosis taught me how difficult it can be to identify exactly what is making you ill.

I grew up in West Dorset but headed to London for university, as so many do. After a few years of working as a costume designer, I retrained as a homeopath when Finn was still tiny. When my husband Nick and I were able to return to the soft hills and pebbly beaches of my youth, I knew I'd come home again. I set up a practice and focused on getting myself well by eating clean and wholesome gluten free food. I started to blog about the experience of going gluten free and shared recipes with other people around the world in the same situation. Blogging was a new and novel thing back then and I had a wonderful sense of being a pioneer.

As a newly qualified homeopath, I came to realise that nearly every client I saw had some issue that could be related to their diet and lifestyle. The experience of finding a solution to my own health issues (and eventual coeliac diagnosis) has been an invaluable tool for advising others in the same situation. It can seem like an overwhelming task to cook and eat when you have to cut out gluten or dairy. My job is to help people rediscover a joyful relationship with food. No matter what you prefer to eat, you can always find something gluten free that's thrilling and delicious!

I help people decide what to eat, how to cook it and when to fit all this cooking and eating into a busy lifestyle. I can also explain food in scientific terms when it helps people to understand how it all works. However, like everyone else at River Cottage, I am really just a food enthusiast, someone who loves to cook with good produce – eggs with orange yolks, seasonal vegetables, whole grains and wild meat. I use my scientific knowledge purely to explain why we could all do with eating less processed food and cooking more from scratch (and this applies whether you have a food intolerance or not). Our connection to the land and the produce that comes from it means that my colleagues and I prize freshness and quality over convenience.

If, like me, you hanker after the wholemeal flavour of a digestive biscuit, or long to slather butter on a deeply flavoured slice of sourdough, this is the book you have been longing for. A whole larder of incredible inherently gluten free produce awaits – you just need to grab a wooden spoon and say 'yes'.

the evolution of wheat

Modern Western diets are liberally sprinkled with wheat, so if you suffer when you eat gluten it is important to know where you might find it. However, before looking at gluten in detail, a little history can help to explain why people around the world might be increasingly wheat sensitive. We have been cultivating wheat for about 10,000 years in Europe, which on the face of it seems an awfully long time. Yet humans were hunter-gatherers for about 200,000 years before they settled down to an agricultural way of life. At first, they just ate what seeds they could find, and gradually began to find that some were better than others. They eventually cultivated the ancestors of juicy modern wheat from tough, wild grasses with small, hard seeds. Some relatives of these early grains such as einkorn, emmer, spelt and durum wheat are still grown around the world, but the wheat that we consume in the West is, almost exclusively, common wheat (*Triticum aestivum*), a cultivar that contains chromosomes from all these ancient relatives.

Common wheat has been selectively bred by farmers from a combination of the ancient wheat strains into a grain with a very complex genetic structure. Earlier versions were lower in gluten, higher in protein and had a close-fitting hull that made threshing difficult. Common wheat has been bred to increase the grain size, gluten content and starchiness, and to make for easier threshing. The issue with all this selective breeding is that the type of wheat our bodies got used to, which had stayed roughly similar for thousands of years, changed quite radically over the course of a couple of hundred years as farmers became more skilled at plant breeding.

With a more complex genetic structure, there are new elements in common wheat that our immune systems can react to, which may explain why some people react adversely to common wheat and yet can eat some spelt or emmer bread without any issues. Interestingly, common wheat also has a greater tendency to raise blood sugar levels than ancient varieties. Coeliac sufferers would still react to ancient varieties of wheat, as they contain gluten, but others may find that seeking them out is worthwhile. It is possible to find einkorn and emmer flour for sale, and spelt is now widely available.

As grain evolved, so did baking methods. All whole grains naturally contain the wild yeasts and lactic bacteria necessary to start fermentation; breads and pastries made using these, rather than cultivated yeast, are known as 'sourdough'. When the grain is mixed with water, the yeasts start to digest the starch in the grain, while the bacteria digest the various anti-nutrients that can interfere with digestion and absorption of nutrients. For thousands of years, people around the world have been using this type of fermentation to make porridges, puddings and breads that are easy to digest, with a deeply savoury flavour.

All European breads were sourdough loaves until the nineteenth century, when we discovered how to isolate the most aggressive yeast strain, baker's yeast (*Saccharomyces cerevisiae*), and we embraced it wholeheartedly to make lighter, sweeter breads. When sourdough was the norm, it was seen as a sign of social status to eat fluffy white bread, so we aspired to leave our heavy sourdough loaves behind as we climbed the social ladder. In the late nineteenth century, when bicarbonate of soda became commercially available, bakers were also able to make soda bread: this is the least digestible of all bread types – gluten free or not – as it eliminates the need for any sort of fermentation at all.

The problem with this quantum shift in bread making is that by taking out the bacteria, and cultivating yeast for speed and growth, we lost the most beneficial aspect of the sourdough process: the removal of anti-nutrients and hydrolysis (breaking down) of gluten. Modern bread is fluffy but often, paradoxically, difficult to digest. Made from genetically complex wheat, it contains all the things that our ancestors had managed to remove through years of experimentation.

Happily, sourdough is enjoying a much-needed renaissance and can now be bought in many bakeries and supermarkets. Recent studies of sourdough have shown that after a long ferment, most of the gluten has been digested and broken down by the bacteria into a form that is much less likely to trigger reactions. Coeliac sufferers, however, should wait to see more evidence before chomping through a slice of standard sourdough!

coeliac disease and gluten intolerance

You could imagine gluten sensitivity as one of those paint colour charts, ranging from deep blue to 'bluebell white'. Where you are on that chart will depend on lots of factors: your genetic heritage, DNA, stress levels and general health. At one end are people who don't have to avoid gluten but notice that they feel lighter and more energetic if they do. At the other end are those who have autoimmune reactions to gluten, and possibly many other substances too. Gluten proteins can be difficult to digest for everyone, so unless you have a cast-iron constitution, chances are that you show up somewhere on the paint chart.

Gluten is a protein complex found in the following grains: wheat (and all wheat relatives such as spelt, emmer, einkorn, kamut and farro), rye and barley. There is also a type of gluten found in oats that is called avenin, which some people react to and others do not. People may react to all gluten proteins (gliadin in wheat, secalin in rye, hordelin in barley and avenin in oats), or they may react to some, depending on their particular intolerance.

With coeliac disease, gluten proteins cause an autoimmune reaction in the gut, destroying the little villi that absorb nutrients and thus often resulting in malnutrition. Symptoms can be wide ranging, from fatigue and joint pains to painful gastrointestinal issues and skin conditions. The treatment is to avoid gluten for the rest of your life (no great hardship, in my opinion). Many coeliac sufferers can tolerate oats that have been screened for gliadin contamination from wheat (even though oats naturally contain avenin); these are called gluten free oats.

If you have coeliac disease, it is important that your flours and other ingredients are not contaminated with gluten during their processing. Some flour may have been contaminated in the field, mill or processing plant, although it comes from an inherently gluten free source. Aim to use ingredients that you know are 100 per cent gluten free. When buying flours, look for the crossed grain symbol (see page 26) or evidence of Elisa testing for gluten contamination.

Although distinctions are often drawn between those who have coeliac disease and those who do not, I am wary of lumping everyone into the same camp, because it appears that someone without coeliac disease can also have autoimmune reactions to grains and gluten. For example, the tests for coeliac disease don't work for people with a newly discovered condition called 'non coeliac gluten sensitivity' (NCGS), even though they may react to even smaller amounts of gluten than those with coeliac disease. The symptoms appear to be more neurological than the gastrointestinal issues that are common with coeliac disease. If you suspect this might be you, even if you do not have a diagnosis, it's worth eliminating gluten for a while to see if you feel better, and finding a doctor who understands the condition.

For those who can eat a bit of gluten and feel fine, but find that increased quantities trigger bloating and tiredness, this book will open up a world of alternative flours and baking methods to extend your repertoire of recipes. You are lucky, in that you won't need to be so careful about obtaining your ingredients from a certified gluten free source. Increasing the number of grains you eat reduces over-reliance on the same few that make up the modern diet and this can help with intolerance issues. Make a sourdough starter (see page 24) and bake your own bread, soak your porridge oats overnight to reduce anti-nutrients (see page 23) and eat as many vegetables as you can – you'll soon feel the difference.

where gluten sneaks in

The table opposite gives a general guide to where you might find gluten in commercial food. Fresh produce such as meat, fish, fruit and vegetables, as well as milk and butter and drinks such as wine, coffee and tea, are always a safe bet; for anything else, make sure you check the packet for gluten content. Gluten free (GF) options are available for most products.

Spirits such as whisky, vodka and gin are fine for coeliac sufferers to consume, as there is no gluten left after the distilling process. It has been shown, however, that alcohol can make the walls of the gut become more permeable ('leaky gut syndrome') and allow particles of undigested food through, causing immune reactions such as rheumatoid arthritis, chronic fatigue and allergies. So if you have a damaged gut or experience irritable bowel symptoms or arthritis, be cautious with all alcohol.

staying safe
If you have coeliac disease or non coeliac gluten sensitivity, it's important to make sure no gluten sneaks into your food when you're eating out or baking at home. For those of you who are just avoiding gluten for other health reasons, you probably don't need to

which foods contain gluten?

	definitely contains gluten	check for gluten (gluten free options available)
grains	wheat, barley, rye, kamut, spelt, triticale, farro, emmer, einkorn, semolina, farina, orzo, bulgur wheat, couscous, bran	oats, buckwheat, flours such as sweet rice, gram or jowar (sorghum) from Asian food shops
meat	breaded ham, corned beef, stuffing	sausages, burgers, meatballs, sausagemeat, pre-cooked poultry
fish	battered fish, breaded fish	crab sticks
drinks	beer, coffee substitutes, Barleycup, malted drinks such as Ovaltine and Horlicks, oat milk, barley water	hot chocolate, instant coffee
sauces	béchamel, bread sauce	brown sauce, salad dressings, gravy
vegetables		oven chips, vegetables in sauce, canned beans and peas, soups, stews
condiments and spices	soy sauce, malt vinegar	rice syrup, pickles, mustard, white pepper, miso, marinades, spice mixes
dairy	yoghurt with whole grains	blue cheese, low fat yoghurt
snacks	dry roasted nuts, Japanese rice crackers	flavoured crisps, tortilla chips, crackers, muesli bars, fruit bars, Bombay mix, wasabi peas
sweets	wafer chocolates, biscuit bars, malted fillings, liquorice	marshmallows, caramels; sweets that contain wheat glucose syrup are acceptable for coeliac sufferers, but may not be for those with a wheat allergy
other	seitan	quorn, veggie burgers and sausages, stock cubes, bouillon powder, suet, vegetable suet, baking powder

be quite so fastidious. This section will help you identify where gluten might be hiding in your kitchen and give you a plan for eating out.

at home

Rolling pins, pastry brushes, wooden spoons and chopping boards all come into contact with gluten in the kitchen. If you are a completely gluten free household, simply replace these items to create a 100 per cent gluten free zone! If you share your kitchen with gluten eaters, you can nominate certain items as gluten free and mark them with a painted handle. Otherwise, use metal utensils, as these won't absorb gluten.

● Roll pastry between two pieces of parchment or cling film, lightly dusted with tapioca starch. This will protect the pastry from any stray crumbs containing gluten.

● Grill toast on a piece of foil, or have your own gluten free toaster, to prevent cross contamination.

● Have a gluten free butter dish, or cut your butter packet in half and clearly label one half gluten free, to make sure that no crumbs sneak into your butter.

● Don't store ingredients containing gluten next to gluten free ones in the cupboard – this is particularly important with flour.

● Label everything in the freezer, to avoid confusion. Plastic containers or bags are a great help with things like bread, cookie dough and leftovers that you need to freeze.

eating out

Make your waiter aware that you have dietary requirements as soon as they come to your table. I usually say that I have coeliac disease, which means I can't have any gluten, then I ask the waiter if I may check with them which things are suitable for me to eat. Do it with a smile and nobody will mind that your meal needs a little extra care. If you have a long list of ingredients to avoid, you can print this out and hand it to them, so they can consult the chef without needing to remember everything. Although many foods are inherently gluten free, let the waiter know that you need a strictly gluten free meal and you shouldn't be surprised by croûtons that weren't mentioned on the menu.

● Anything fried in oil is likely to come into contact with crumbs or bits of batter from something else. Check whether chips are from a dedicated chip fryer, or if you can have yours fried separately. If in doubt, choose potatoes cooked another way. Some fish and chip shops have a dedicated gluten free night, the day after they clean the fryers.

● Spices and dried fruit can get contaminated with gluten in commercial kitchens, as they tend to be kept in large containers. If you want to eat something spicy on the menu, ask whether this is the case – the chef may be conscious of the problem and have taken steps to prevent contamination.

- Sauces can contain flour, so always check. Even sauces made with cornflour may have a small amount of gluten. Most people will be fine with a sauce thickened with a little standard cornflour, but if you know you are sensitive, go for hollandaise or mayonnaise, or ask for some meat juices with your meal. If in doubt, a knob of butter is always good!

- Soups and stews should be fine, as long as they do not include pearl barley or macaroni.

when going gluten free doesn't work

Many people still experience symptoms after going gluten free. Some even develop new and strange food intolerances over time, until they can barely eat a thing without a reaction. Food becomes an anxious subject when it should be a source of pleasure. Some issues can occur as a result of eating commercially available gluten free alternatives, because these contain emulsifiers and modified starches that can irritate the gut.

However, even a gluten free diet full of home cooked food and nutritious whole grains can cause problems because of anti-nutrients – components in grain that have nothing to do with gluten. Those who have issues with gluten often have poor digestion, so it's important to make food that is as easily absorbed as possible. Below, I outline some of the elements of grains and pulses that can cause problems if you are eating them in any great quantity.

fodmaps

Although not anti-nutrients, FODMAPs (an acronym for fermentable oligosaccharides, disaccharides, monosaccharides and polyols) are fermentable short-chain carbohydrates and alcohols that can cause intestinal distress for some people. Wheat, fruit, cabbage, beans, onions and sugar free sweets are some notable culprits. Irritable bowel syndrome (IBS) sufferers tend to benefit from reducing the quantity of FODMAPs they eat. So if you think this might be you, look up a list and try to avoid including too many of the problem foods in each meal.

lectins

Lectins are sticky proteins that are found in all plant matter. Eaten in large quantities, they can bind to the gut lining, causing it to leak and allow small particles of undigested food to enter the bloodstream. Leaky gut syndrome is associated with many different autoimmune conditions. Some plant foods are higher in lectins than others: the most concentrated sources are grains (particularly wheat), pulses (especially soya), nuts and seeds, dairy and veg from the nightshade family (potato, pepper, tomato and aubergine). Fermenting or sprouting (see phytic acid, overleaf) reduces or even totally eliminates lectins, so this is the best treatment for grains, nuts and seeds, dairy and pulses. If you suffer from joint pains or headaches, it might be worth eliminating nightshades from your diet for a period, to see whether they are affecting your immune system.

phytic acid

This acid is found in the bran part of grains and the protein part of pulses. In the gut, phytic acid binds to minerals such as calcium, iron and magnesium to form phytates that are excreted rather than absorbed, potentially contributing to mineral deficiencies. However, phytic acid is also an antioxidant, so the goal should be to minimise its binding qualities, whilst retaining its benefits. Eating small amounts of meat or fish and lots of fresh veg with your grains can aid absorption.

You can also reduce the binding effect of phytic acid by soaking or fermenting your grains and pulses before using them; sprouting can help too.

To sprout dry grains or dried pulses, first soak them in water for 24 hours, then drain and put into a large clean jar. Cover with muslin and secure with a rubber band. Fill up the jar with water and then immediately drain it off through the muslin. Repeat the filling and draining process twice daily until small green shoots start to grow, about 2–4 days. Cook as usual, or eat raw in small quantities.

saponins

Bitter saponins occur naturally in pulses, amaranth and quinoa. Small amounts appear to reduce cholesterol, support immunity and reduce the risk of cancer. However, they can also make the lining of the gut more prone to reacting to certain foods. Soaking and rinsing pulses, amaranth and quinoa should remove most of the saponins, leaving just enough to be beneficial.

fermenting makes everything better

Unfortunately for anyone who is sensitive to gluten, the flour used in most commercial gluten free baked goods is starchy, refined and somewhat lacking in flavour. In fact, most commercially produced gluten free food has the same effect on blood sugar as eating pure sugar. Because most of the nutrients and fibre are removed during processing, it makes sense for everyone to avoid refined flours in order to be healthy, not just those who need to eat gluten free.

Fortunately for us home bakers, there are now a fantastic number of gluten free wholegrain flours available, all bursting with flavour and nutrients. In order to make your breads, pancakes and whole grains even more nutritious and delicious, I would suggest that you try fermenting them in some way to help break down any anti-nutrients they may contain. Fermenting has also been shown to reduce some of the starch in flour, making it a good option for regulating your blood sugar.

You can ferment your grains by introducing some friendly bacteria to them in the form of sourdough culture or yoghurt. You can also use acid from lemon juice or vinegar to soak whole grains, such as rice or quinoa, although this is less effective. Fermenting can seem daunting to the uninitiated, but it is simply a case of introducing some friendly bacteria to your flour or grain and letting time do the work.

what is fermentation?

Fermentation is a metabolic process by which yeasts or bacteria digest sugars or starches and produce acids, alcohols and gasses. In beer making, yeasts feed on the sugars in the grain and produce alcohol, carbon dioxide and acid as a result, making a drink that is slightly fizzy, pleasantly sour and intoxicating. In sourdough bread making, the natural yeasts present in wholemeal flour (gluten free or otherwise) are allowed to flourish in a warm, humid atmosphere and feed on the starch contained in the flour; as a by-product they produce carbon dioxide, which gives bread its holey structure.

A sourdough starter also naturally contains lactic bacteria (the same kind that you have in your gut). These bacteria digest the anti-nutrients in the flour, producing acids that give the dough a savoury flavour, as well as keeping the yeasts from growing too much. Yoghurt is produced by fermenting milk with lactic bacteria, which feed on the lactose sugars in the milk, curdling and souring it. By adding yoghurt to a pancake batter, or a bowl of oats, you allow the lactic bacteria to digest some of the anti-nutrients in the grain, without the need for a sourdough starter.

The following key ingredients can benefit from fermenting:

gluten free oats

Make sure you choose a brand that is gluten free, as oats are quite often contaminated with wheat while they are growing. Cover the oats with tepid water and stir in 1 tsp live yoghurt. Cover and set aside at room temperature for 12–24 hours. Either eat as muesli by adding fresh fruit, seeds, nuts and yoghurt, or make porridge by adding some more water or milk and cooking gently for a few minutes.

pulses

All dried pulses need to be soaked prior to cooking, even most lentils, as they need to be fully rehydrated in order to be digestible (the only exception to this is red lentils, which should be well rinsed). Cover with plenty of water, add 2 tsp lemon juice (or any vinegar except malt) and leave at room temperature for 24 hours. Rinse and cook in plenty of clean water until soft (with a pinch of bicarbonate of soda for beans). You can add a strip of kombu seaweed to the water to tenderise the outer skin of the bean; it will also add useful trace elements, including iodine. When cooked this way, beans can be frozen for a convenient ready supply. Avoid tinned pulses as they often contain firming agents.

quinoa, millet, buckwheat and amaranth

To ferment and cook 200g of grain, cover with twice the volume of water, add 1 tsp lemon juice, or any vinegar except malt, or 1 tbsp live yoghurt and leave covered at room temperature for 24 hours. Rinse thoroughly, drain and put into a saucepan with 200ml water. Bring to the boil, cover tightly and lower the heat. Cook for 10–15 minutes, until all the water is absorbed and the grain is soft. Leave covered for 5–10 minutes, then fluff with a fork. The grain can now be frozen or kept in the fridge for up to 3 days.

rice

Cover your wholegrain rice with twice the volume of water and add 1 tsp lemon juice (or any vinegar except malt) or 1 tbsp live yoghurt. Leave covered at room temperature for 24 hours. Drain, rinse and cook as usual, with a pinch of sea salt.

sourdough starters and yoghurt ferments

Most of my bread recipes use the sourdough method because the flavour and texture are improved and the loaf is more digestible. The sourdough method has three stages: first a 'starter' is made, kept dormant in the fridge and fed with flour and water to wake it up before baking; next a 'sponge' is made with some of the flour, all of the liquid and some of the starter; and finally the dough is made by adding the remaining flour and ingredients that inhibit the further development of the yeast, such as egg, salt or fat. The process is slower than making a loaf with baker's yeast, but the result is infinitely more complex and interesting. Try adding some of your sourdough starter to pancakes, batters, muffins and fruit cakes, for added depth of flavour and digestibility.

Live yoghurt will also help to remove anti-nutrients if you add some to breads, cakes and batters, with the added bonus that the milk proteins will give a softer crumb.

eating well gluten free

Cooking from scratch is the key to eating well for anyone, but busy lives can make that pretty daunting. A little forward planning is all that is needed to make meals effortless.

breakfasts

If you get into the habit of deciding on breakfast ahead – at least the evening before – there are no end of possibilities:

● Soak gluten free oats overnight with a spoonful of live yoghurt so that you can cook them quickly the next morning; it makes your oats more digestible too.

● Make a big batch of almond breakfast risotto (see page 52) or 'pumpkin pie' porridge (see page 50) and freeze in portions. Just take out of the freezer the night before and heat through in the morning.

● Make some sourdough muffins (see page 66) and freeze – two trays will make enough for a month. Eat with a pot of live yoghurt, seeds and berries. Kids love making these.

● Bake two or more loaves of gluten free sourdough at a time. Slice once cooled and lay on a board covered with cling film, in layers, placing cling film between the layers and on top. 'Open freeze' the slices like this on the board, then bag up and label. Take individual slices out as needed. Toast from frozen, then butter and top with eggs, tinned sardines, smoked salmon or gravadlax, or spread with nut butter or cream cheese and berries...

● Cook extra veg the night before, to heat up and eat with scrambled eggs. It may not be the most elegant breakfast, but it's delicious and sustaining, and ups your veg intake.

lunches

Few of us can set aside time to cook lunch during the working week, but thoughtful shopping and a few planned leftovers will give you a variety of almost instant options:

● Soak and cook a large batch of quinoa or organic brown rice and freeze in individual portions. Flatten each portion in its bag and stack up in the freezer, so that your grain will defrost in minutes for a quinoa or rice salad (see page 145).

● Cook extra veg and protein at supper and add this to your lunch the next day. You can throw together a great packed lunch from a bit of shredded leftover meat or fish, a large handful of grain, some cooked or raw veg, fresh herbs and dressing. Keep jars of olives, peppers, sun-dried tomatoes and artichoke hearts on hand to pep up salads. Let children choose their own additions and they are more likely to eat the resulting salad.

● Make a large batch of pasties (see page 107) and freeze. Just take a pasty straight from the freezer when you leave for work and it will defrost in time for lunch, as long as you don't put it in the fridge.

● Cook a batch of soup and freeze in portions – include some protein to keep you going until supper. Think about adding a little rice or quinoa, or have a slice of gluten free bread and butter, crackers or gluten free oatcakes too.

suppers

I always make sure that I have enough roast meat and cooked grains to hand to make suppers from scratch in minutes:

● Roasting a large joint of meat or an extra bird at the weekend can give you several quick suppers during the week. Add shredded meat to a quinoa or rice salad (see page 145), or slice some cold meat and eat with boiled new potatoes and a couple of handfuls of leaves. You can even make an impromptu stew with leftover roast chicken or slow-cooked lamb shanks on the bone and chopped veg. Simply put everything in a saucepan, add just enough water to cover, put the lid on and simmer gently for about 20 minutes until the veg is tender, then season and serve with a splosh of olive oil.

● Make ready meals for yourself and stash them in the freezer in portions. Lasagne (see page 194), fish pie (see page 184), cottage pie, stews and hearty soups are all good choices. Just add steamed veg or salad leaves to make it a meal.

● Make thin omelettes (see page 179) or crêpes (see page 62). Slice up any leftover meat, heat up a curry, grate some cheese, put vegetables preserved in oil and slices of cured meat on the table and let everyone make their own wraps. This also works with large lettuce leaves instead of wraps.

- Make a tortilla (see page 180) or frittata with cooked veg or some cold potatoes and throw in a few frozen peas if you like. Any left over makes a great lunch the next day.

treats and snacks

While I don't advocate snacking in general, there are times when you just need a little something to tide you over to your next meal. Try the following:

- Make sea salt crackers (see page 140) and dip into courgette hummus (see page 142), roast carrot dip (see page 143) or Greek yoghurt flavoured with fresh herbs and garlic.

- Slather a piece of sourdough toast with butter or olive oil and top with cheese, avocado, cold meat or some nut butter.

- Make fruit and nut bars. Blitz a handful of pitted dried dates, prunes or raisins and 2 handfuls of raw nuts in a food processor until they resemble coarse crumbs. Flavour with ½ tsp ground cinnamon or cardamom, the grated zest of an orange or 1 tbsp cocoa powder. Mix in 2–3 tsp coconut oil, butter or melted chocolate and whiz until the mixture forms a ball. Press into a small parchment lined tray. Chill and then slice into bars. Keep in an airtight container in the fridge and eat within a week.

- Keep a roll of cookie dough (see page 252) in the freezer so that you can bake up a few at a time and enjoy freshly baked cookies with your afternoon tea.

- Bake some muffins (see pages 70, 71 and 248) or banana bread (see page 249) and freeze, or make a batch of digestive biscuits (see page 258). These snacks are treaty, yet won't unbalance your blood sugar.

storecupboard

The bulk of your diet should revolve around fresh produce that is inherently gluten free, but there are some storecupboard items that are good to have on hand. Always look for the crossed grain symbol: an ear of wheat inside a circle, with a cross through it, which can only be used on a product that has been certified as gluten free.

flours

Gluten free white flour, rice flour, buckwheat flour, sorghum flour, teff flour, chestnut flour, ground almonds, cornflour, tapioca starch.

baking ingredients

Gluten free baking powder, bicarbonate of soda, sea salt, muscovado sugar, ground or whole linseed, psyllium husks, liquid pectin, whole and ground spices.

grains

Fairtrade quinoa, organic arborio rice, organic basmati rice, wild rice, gluten free oats.

gluten free flours

Whether you want to avoid gluten or you are simply curious about the world beyond wheat, a huge range of inherently gluten free flours is out there, just waiting for you to experiment. Because I like to tinker about in my own kitchen, I tend to use combinations of individual flours rather than commercial mixes.

Through experimentation, I have learnt the different properties that enable me to tailor the flour mix to suit a particular recipe. To help you do this yourself, the flours that are most widely available are described below, grouped according to their performance in a flour mix. For a basic flour mix, try to include something from each of the groups in roughly equal proportions, such as a mix of sorghum flour, rice flour, cornflour, tapioca starch and ground almonds.

If you are converting a recipe to gluten free, you need to know what qualities you are looking for in the flour mix, and to understand how the recipe works, before you can make a good substitution. Cake and biscuit recipes are easy to convert, because they don't rely heavily on gluten for their structure (in fact gluten can even be a problem). Bread and pastry, on the other hand, need careful assessment, so stick to reliable gluten free recipes at first, and tinker with these before you strike out on your own.

flavour flours

This group of flours are wholesome and nutritious, adding flavour and depth to breads, batters and pastry.

amaranth flour

Amaranth is digested slowly because it is high in protein and fibre. However, since it contains anti-nutrients, which are removed by the sourdough process, the flour is at its best in a sourdough loaf. Amaranth is usually found as a grain in health food shops; you can grind this into flour in a dedicated gluten free electric coffee grinder (with blades). Dilute this flour with other, mild tasting flours, because whilst incredibly nutritious, it has a distinctly peppery tang that can overwhelm delicate flavours.

Amaranth flour should be kept in the fridge, because it has a high oil content.

buckwheat flour

Buckwheat sounds as though it should be closely related to wheat, but it is actually a distant cousin of rhubarb. It is slowly digested owing to a high protein and fibre content, but ideally should be fermented in a sourdough loaf or yoghurt ferment to remove anti-nutrients that can interfere with digestion.

Used alone, buckwheat flour has an earthy, slightly sour and sometimes musty flavour, which tends to polarise people a little like Marmite does! In cakes, brown sugar brings out a floral, grassy note in buckwheat. It gives breads a chewy texture similar to rye and a little added to a flour mix helps to bind the dough and aids rising. The groats can be sprouted and added to breads or salads, eaten cooked like rice, or ground in a dedicated gluten free electric coffee grinder (with blades) to make coarse flour. Always check that you are buying certified gluten free buckwheat flour.

carob flour

A sweet, slightly chocolatey flour can be made from the carob pod (the carob beans, meanwhile, are used to make carob gum). Roasted carob is more bitter and coffee flavoured, while raw carob has a sweeter, caramel flavour with a fruity edge.

High in calcium and a host of other essential minerals, carob flour can be used as part of the flour content for chocolate cakes or dark breads. You can also combine it with nut flours to make delicious, naturally sweetened cookies. Owing to the high natural sugar content, carob flour will burn at lower temperatures, so take 20°C off the suggested oven temperature if you are converting a recipe.

hemp flour

This greenish grey 'superfood' flour is a rich source of omega fatty acids, calcium, iron and magnesium. The downside is that it has a strong earthy, grassy taste that can overpower everything else and it turns rancid very quickly. However, if used in a ratio of 1:10 with other flours, it will boost the nutritional profile and bring a deep nuttiness to breads.

Hemp flour should be kept in the freezer, owing to its high oil content, or you can grind hemp seeds to order in a dedicated gluten free electric coffee grinder (with blades).

pulse flours (bean, dried pea, lentil and peanut)

You can buy flours made from chickpeas (gram flour), peanuts, adzuki beans, mung beans, red lentils and soya beans (but do be aware that the types normally stocked in Asian food shops are unlikely to be certified gluten free). Although high in protein and fibre, pulse flours tend to contain high levels of phytic acid, which can interfere with digestion and the absorption of nutrients.

These flours can be added to the sponge stage of a sourdough, but really benefit from at least 24 hours' fermentation to make them more digestible, so give your sourdough sponge a longer ferment period than usual – 20–22 hours is ideal.

Fermenting pulse flours (as a sourdough loaf or yoghurt ferment) also reduces the strong beany flavour and dry gritty texture.

Cooked beans and pulses can be mashed and added to breads, pancakes, muffins and even brownies in place of some, or all, of the flour content.

quinoa flour (and quinoa)

An almost perfect source of protein from the vegetable kingdom, this grain is useful for athletes, as it helps rebuild muscle and is good for maintaining even blood sugar levels. Quinoa is called a 'pseudo grain', as it is actually classified as a vegetable, rather than a grain. People following an otherwise grain free diet do often eat quinoa, as the pancreas seems to tolerate it better than other grains. It has a mild, slightly grassy taste that's a great foil for other, stronger flavours in dishes such as tabouleh (see page 152), quinoa salad (see page 145) and banana bread (see page 249).

You can either buy quinoa flour (for suppliers, see pages 261–3) or make your own, by grinding the grain in a dedicated gluten free electric coffee grinder (with blades). It has a nutty, earthy, slightly sweet flavour and works well in baked goods that have a fairly robust flavour, such as muffins. It can also be used to thicken soups and stews.

sorghum flour

Sorghum is one of the major cereal crops grown around the world. A little like millet, it has a mild, malty flavour, a wholemeal texture and good binding properties. It is very nutritious and eaten as the main source of carbohydrate in many African countries – mostly as a fermented porridge. Sorghum flour makes a great pastry when combined with ground almonds, and good bread when mixed with millet flour. It is expensive to obtain certified gluten free sorghum flour in the UK and although it is widely sold in Asian food stores as jowar flour, this is commonly contaminated with wheat, so is only acceptable if you are wheat intolerant rather than coeliac. Make your sorghum go further by pairing it with cheaper staples like rice flour.

teff flour

Eaten widely in Ethopia, teff flour is traditionally used to make a delicious sourdough flat bread with a spongy texture called injera, which is used to scoop up spicy stews. Even though it is one of the smallest grains, teff is five times richer in calcium, iron and potassium than any other grain. It also contains substantial amounts of protein and fibre, making it excellent for everyday breads and pancakes.

Teff flour has a wholesome, slightly smoky, malty flavour reminiscent of rye, and a silky texture that helps to bind a mixture together. The flavour can be quite strong, but not unpleasantly so, and it is brilliant for breads, fruit cakes, carrot muffins and chocolate or carob flavoured cakes.

Teff flour is available in a few varieties, but in the UK we mostly find wholegrain white teff flour (milder and sweeter) or brown teff flour (maltier, darker and nuttier). These flours should be refrigerated, due to their high oil content.

short and crumbly flours

'Shortness' describes the dry, crisp texture of shortbread or shortcrust pastry. The flours described here don't hold much water, and therefore give a short quality to biscuits and pastry. They are also neutral flavoured, though not flavourless, making them a perfect backdrop for flavour flours and the binding flours that absorb water and keep a dough or batter moist. Pastry made with these flours will benefit from an overnight rest.

If you soak these flours as part of the sponge for a bread dough, pancake batter or sourdough starter, then much of the sandy shortness is reduced.

coconut flour

If you like the flavour of coconut, you'll love this coarse textured, creamy tasting flour. Made from dehydrated coconut flesh, it is very high in fibre (for this reason, some people will find it hard to digest). Coconut products are high in healthy short-chain saturated fats, which stimulate the metabolism and immune system.

Coconut flour gives your baking shortness and bulk, but it can be very dense, so it's good to use as part of a flour mix (add an extra egg or two to any recipe that you are converting). You can use coconut flour in place of ground almonds in many recipes if you wish, with denser results.

I make my own flour from desiccated coconut – grinding it in a dedicated gluten free electric coffee grinder (with blades) – at a fraction of the price; just be sure to check that it is gluten free. Coconut flour should be stored in the fridge or freezer due to its very high oil content; the flour can be used straight from the freezer.

maize flour, polenta and masa harina

Custard yellow and finely ground, with a delicate popcorn flavour, maize flour is widely available from gluten free suppliers. It's great for soaking up liquid in a tart crust or a loose bread mix. You could make your own coarse maize flour from polenta using a dedicated gluten free electric coffee grinder (with blades), but you will need to buy the fine polenta specified in the recipes for this. (Maize flour is made from a type of starchy sweetcorn and contains a type of carbohydrate that can quickly raise blood sugar levels, so it's advisable to use it as part of a flour mix with wholemeal or nut flours.)

Ground corn comes in several different forms: polenta is a coarsely ground version of maize flour, while masa harina is a flour made from white corn, used frequently in Mexico and South America. Masa harina is treated with lime (nixtamalized) in order to make the nutrients absorbable, and this gives it the classic corn tortilla flavour. You can buy masa harina in delicatessens and online, though certified gluten free masa harina is very hard to find, so do remember to check. (Cornflour is also made from maize, but this is a pure starch – see page 32.)

millet flour

Millet is one of the world's most widespread grain staples, familiar to many people as the tiny yellow seeds in birdseed. There are many types of millet grown across Asia and Africa, but pearl millet is the most common type in the UK. The grains look similar to quinoa, with a blonde colour and a mildly sweet, corn-like flavour, and they can be used in the same way as oats to make a fermented porridge (see page 23).

Millet flour is particularly good for adding shortness to a bake and I often use it as a substitute for maize flour when I need to make a recipe corn free. If you have bought the flour ready made, then you should keep it in the fridge, because it has a high oil content and will deteriorate at room temperature – or make it fresh each time by blitzing millet grain in a dedicated gluten free electric coffee grinder (with blades).

rice flour

Rice comes in a wide variety of shapes and sizes, and flour can be made from lots of different types. The most common are white rice flour, which has a completely neutral flavour, and brown rice flour, which has a slightly nutty taste.

Rice flours tend to give a sandy texture to your baking. Resting a rice flour dough or batter will moderate the sandiness by allowing the flour to hydrate. I tend to use rice flour either as part of a mix of flours, or partnered with ground almonds if I want a very short texture. Most rice flour will keep for a long time in the cupboard, though brown rice flour needs to be used up a little more quickly than white.

starchy and crisp flours

These flours are either pure starch, or have a fine texture that makes them ideal for adding lift or crispness to a bake.

chestnut flour (and chestnut purée)

Made from ground sweet chestnuts, this flour is traditionally used by the French to make deeply flavoursome crêpes and rustic breads (combined with wheat flour). It has a warm, sweet flavour, with smoky caramel tones. Although the flour feels quite heavy, it makes surprisingly light and moist breads and cakes when combined in a flour mix. Whilst French and Italian chestnut flour is reasonably easy to find, a certified gluten free version is relatively difficult to come by. Once you've tracked it down, keep the flour in the freezer due to the high oil content.

You can also use chestnut purée in some recipes that call for chestnut flour, but if you're measuring it out by weight, be aware that it will contain about 50 per cent more liquid, so you will need to experiment. Chestnut purée is great for crêpes and breads, where there is a liquid component to the recipe.

cornflour

Cornflour is a fine, white, flavourless flour made from the starchy part of maize. Root starches, such as tapioca and arrowroot, can be substituted for cornflour in recipes with a high liquid content such as sauces and puddings, or in biscuits, but will become gummy in breads and cakes. They seem to have a less dramatic effect on blood sugar levels than cornflour, although they all lack fibre and protein in the same way.

Cornflour does not absorb water as well as tapioca and arrowroot, so it tends to give drier or harder results in baking – this can be useful when you want crispness. It is also good for thickening sauces.

potato starch

Potato starch is very fine and can be used to lighten cakes, breads and biscuits. When it is introduced to water and heat, it expands quickly – making it perfect for fluffy breads. Potato starch is white and fine. You can also buy potato flour, which is creamy coloured and coarser in texture (see page 34 for how to use this). Nutritionally empty, potato starch is processed like rocket fuel in the body once it has been cooked, so use it sparingly. It has a long shelf life, as do all starches.

binding flours

These flours absorb water and hold it in the dough, making them ideal partners for short and crumbly flours, or in breads where you want stretch. However, too much binding flour can create a gummy or dense texture, so use with restraint.

arrowroot powder

Traditionally used to calm an upset stomach and provide some easily absorbed calories, arrowroot powder is a pure starch made from the root of the maranta plant. It can also be used for baking where a light starch is required, though it has a slightly chalky taste if used in quantity. Tapioca starch works as a cheaper substitute in baking, although the particles are not quite as fine as true arrowroot.

Many prefer arrowroot powder to cornflour for thickening sauces, as it thickens at a lower temperature, is not weakened by acidic ingredients, and is not affected by freezing. It makes particularly shiny sauces for glazing. However, arrowroot doesn't mix well with dairy products, since the combination creates a slimy mixture.

linseed, ground

Whole or crushed linseeds (or flaxseeds) can be added to the sponge component of bread dough to help bind the mixture, whilst imparting a seedy texture to the loaf. Ground linseed is best used as a small part of a recipe to help bind the mixture together, but it can also be used rather like a flour to make low carb breads and crackers when mixed with ground almonds or coconut flour.

Full of the omega 3, 6 and 9 fatty acids that are essential for good health, ground linseed is a great thing to add to your porridge or sprinkle over a salad (don't eat whole linseeds, unless they have been soaked).

oat flour

I have largely avoided using oats in this book as they are tolerated by some but not others – I can't tolerate them myself. The culprit is a type of gluten called avenin that occurs naturally in oats. Always choose certified gluten free oats if you are sensitive to wheat gluten, as oats can easily become contaminated with wheat or barley in the field.

It is easy to make your own oat flour from rolled oats using a dedicated gluten free electric coffee grinder (with blades) or a food processor. Oats have a lovely hint of caramel flavour and make a brilliant supporting partner for many gluten free flours. Oats help make bread stretchy and cakes moist and they give cookies a pleasing density. You can also use oat flour as a stand-in for ground almonds in many recipes – be cautious about adding water too early though, or the oat flour will become gummy.

potato flour

Made from dehydrated potato, this flour is slightly creamy coloured, dense and heavy. Adding a little potato flour to soda bread or sourdough gives a wonderful chewy texture. You can also use the flesh from a floury baked potato in place of part of the flour in a recipe, which will give the same chewy texture as found in potato farls.

sweet rice flour

Sweet rice (or glutinous rice) flour is made from the starchy rice that is used to make sushi. Also known as mochi flour in Japan, it has a super-fine texture, excellent binding qualities and a delicate flavour.

Use sweet rice flour as part of a flour mix for choux pastry, puff pastry and Yorkshire puddings, and for binding cakes and muffins in place of starches. Beware of adding too much, or you will end up with a very sticky mix that will never cook all the way through. Sweet rice flour also makes an excellent thickener for sauces. It's hard to find certified gluten free sweet rice flour in the UK, although Asian food shops do often sell an uncertified version.

tapioca starch

As a child you may have been put off eating tapioca by tapioca pudding, a frogspawnish porridge made from tapioca pearls and milk, though I have to confess that I love it. Tapioca starch (or tapioca flour) is quite different. It is a very fine, highly absorbent flour made from cassava (manioc) root. You cannot use it alone, as it makes very chewy baked goods, but it is an excellent lightener and binder. Due to its lack of nutrients, it is best paired with nutritious whole grains and nut flours. It can also be used to thicken stews and sauces: simply mix with a little cold water and stir into the boiling liquor.

Tapioca starch will keep for a long time in a cool kitchen cupboard.

nut flours and seed flours

All nuts and seeds can be ground to make richly flavoured, nutritious flours. The oil content of the seed or nut and the type of grind will have a bearing on the finished product. These flours can be used alone, or as part of a flour mix.

almonds, ground

Ground blanched almonds can be used as a type of coarse, low carb flour with a mild marzipan flavour. Almonds contain a high amount of healthy monounsaturated fat and vitamin E; they also increase the protein and fibre content of your baking. Adding almond flour to cakes and muffins gives moistness and an open texture, while in cookies and pastry it can help give a crisp finish.

You can make completely grain free breads, cakes, biscuits and muffins by using only almond flour – they are incredibly rich though, so eat them sparingly. If you're converting a recipe from standard flour, lower the oven setting by 20°C (as nuts burn easily).

Ground almonds should be stored in the fridge or freezer due to their very high oil content, or used within a couple of weeks. They can be used straight from the freezer.

If you have coeliac disease, check that ground almonds are gluten free, as they may be processed on a production line contaminated with gluten. Buying a 10-kilo box can be the best way to ensure that they are safe, as this quantity won't have been packed into bags. However, the ground almonds won't have been Elisa tested, so if you are very sensitive, contact the mill you are buying them from, to establish how likely they are to be contaminated. Bag up into 1-kilo batches, squeeze out all the air and store in the freezer for up to 6 months.

nut meals and seed meals

Nut and seed meals are just ground whole nuts or seeds, with a coarser texture than ground blanched almonds. They contain all their natural oils, which is a consideration when swapping them into a recipe. Use nut meal to make moist, dense cakes and muffins, or as part of the flour content of pastries and breads. If you are converting a recipe from standard flour, bake at a lower temperature as nuts burn easily – about 20°C lower than the recipe states.

You can make your own nut and seed meals in a food processor or dedicated gluten free electric coffee grinder (with blades); use either raw or roasted nuts or seeds. My favourites are pecan (malty and sweet), walnut (savoury, rich and good with cheese, banana or coffee), roast hazelnut (sweet, toasty and excellent in chocolate recipes) or cashew (very mild and creamy, and can be ground very fine to produce very light baked goods). Store in the fridge or freezer.

useful ingredients

If you need to avoid gluten completely then it is important to make sure that all your ingredients are safe to consume.

baking powder

Some brands of baking powder use wheat starch or wheat flour as a carrier. Make sure you buy a gluten free one, or make your own baking powder by mixing two parts cream of tartar, one part bicarbonate of soda and one part cornflour or tapioca starch.

butter and lactic butter

I always specify whether butter is salted or unsalted in my recipes. Choose organic butter if you can; it will contain fewer toxins and more beneficial fats. I love to bake with lactic butter, which is made from cream that has been lightly soured with friendly bacteria and then churned. It has an extra buttery flavour and is more flexible in pastry than standard butter. It won't be labelled 'lactic butter', so look for butter made in the Charentes region of France, such as Lescure, Elle and Vire, or Beurre D'Isigny.

I have developed a dairy free butter (see page 136) for my puff pastry, as it is one of the few recipes that just doesn't work with a dairy free, pure fat such as coconut oil or lard. I would only use this for puff pastry, since coconut oil, lard and duck fat work well for other pastries.

chilli flakes

When I want a seasoning with a sweet peppery flavour and only a little heat, I tend to use Turkish dried chilli flakes (also called pul biber). Mild, sweet red aleppo chillies that have been dried with sea salt to make delicious, tender chilli flakes with a similar level of heat to black pepper, you can use them exactly as you would pepper, to give a hint of warmth. You could also use urfa biber – smoky, mild dried chilli flakes with a darker red colour.

You can use standard dried chilli flakes instead of the Turkish chilli flakes I suggest in the recipes, but do go cautiously with them unless you want a lot of heat in the dish. Turkish dried chilli flakes are available online and in good delicatessens or Middle Eastern food shops.

chocolate

Unless otherwise specified, I use chocolate with 70 per cent cocoa solids in all my recipes. If you use milk chocolate, things may often turn out differently. If you are adding chips or chunks of chocolate to a recipe, however, you have the choice because the chocolate won't melt into the other ingredients. Check that your chocolate is gluten free if you are sensitive, as chocolate can be handled on a production line with gluten.

eggs

I buy organic eggs that are ungraded and have learnt over the years to judge what size they are. The weight of egg can be crucial to the success of some gluten free baking recipes. Where it is critical, I have specified the weight of egg out of its shell, or if it is less so, I have specified the size of egg required. Where the size of egg really doesn't affect the end result, I generally use medium eggs.

fats and oils

When frying or roasting something, it is important to use a fat that is stable and won't be adversely affected by high temperatures. Vegetable oils, olive oil and cooking sprays are all damaged by heat and I therefore do not use them to fry or roast food. My cooking fats of choice are listed in the section on cooking fats (see page 40), but if in doubt, roast or fry in animal fats such as lard, dripping or duck fat; vegetarians can use coconut oil, ghee, clarified butter, groundnut oil or sesame oil.

Where I have suggested duck fat or lard in a baking recipe, you could use any other solid fat of your choice. For recipes where lard or duck fat are suggested for frying just substitute your frying oil of choice if you would prefer not to use them, bearing in mind that vegetable oils and olive oil can be damaged by high temperature frying.

gluten free flour blends

Most of the recipes in this book use a combination of inherently gluten free flours (see page 27 for a guide to the different types). However, where I have specified a pre-made version (listed simply as 'gluten free white flour'), choose a brand with no xanthan gum in it, or the texture of your recipe will be wrong.

The recipes assume that your pre-made flour will be a blend of rice flour, potato starch, tapioca starch, maize flour and buckwheat flour (as in the Doves Farm version); this will contain a high proportion of finely milled white rice flour. If you choose a flour blend that has a high proportion of maize flour or sorghum flour instead, the recipes will turn out differently but they may still work.

linseed

I use ground linseed (also known as flaxseeds) in some of my recipes to mimic gluten and bind things together. Golden linseeds are preferable to brown for baking. Pre-ground linseed is expensive and tends to go rancid very quickly, due to the abundance of omega fatty acids it contains, so the best thing is to grind your own linseed in a dedicated gluten free electric coffee grinder (with blades). Store the ground linseed in a jar in the fridge.

milk

Whole milk is always preferable to skimmed milk, because the butterfat helps you to absorb calcium. Most milk is homogenised to reduce the size of the fat particles in it, so that the cream does not rise to the top; however, the fat can then become rancid in the milk and cause inflammation in the body, so choose unhomogenised milk if you can. Choose wholemilk yoghurts rather than reduced fat versions too.

If you can't tolerate milk, there are a host of dairy free alternatives available. Avoid sweetened dairy free milks and those with emulsifiers such as carrageenan, guar gum and xanthan gum. For more information, see the section on dairy alternatives on page 43.

pectin

Liquid pectin is useful in gluten free baking, because it forms a stretchy gel that keeps things moist. It can also help to support the starch structure of breads and choux pastry. However, the commercially available pectin in the UK contains sulphur dioxide, so if you know that you are sensitive to this food preservative, don't use it. Powdered pectin is also available: you will need to dilute it with nine parts water to one part pectin to get the right concentration for the recipes in the book. You can also look into making your own pectin from apples.

psyllium husks

Psyllium is the common name for a plantain-related plant, which you might find in your garden. The fibrous outer husks of psyllium seeds absorb a huge amount of water, creating a sort of gel that helps to stabilise and hydrate gluten free dough. In bread dough, it's fine to use whole psyllium husks, but for pastry you may prefer to grind them in a dedicated gluten free electric coffee grinder with blades (although whole will still work OK). Psyllium may seem expensive to buy, but a little goes a long way.

salt

It is important to use salt in gluten free baking because it helps dough retain moisture and balances sweetness, giving a rounder flavour. It also helps to brown crusts – pale crusts can otherwise be an issue, owing to the low protein content of gluten free flours.

I always use finely ground sea salt in these recipes, unless otherwise specified. The sea salt I prefer is the coarse grey type that comes from the Atlantic coast of France, which is more salty than standard white sea salt flakes, so you may want to add another pinch if you use a different salt.

sugar and sweeteners

I mostly cook with light and dark muscovado sugars for their rich flavour, and because they tend to make a bake more moist – always helpful in gluten free cooking! If you would like to use an alternative, choose rapadura (evaporated cane juice), palm sugar or coconut sugar; these should work wherever muscovado is used. In muffins and heartier cakes and cookies, ground dates (date sugar) can be used with similar results. If a recipe calls for caster sugar, then you can use either the golden or white kind.

I often sweeten dishes with dates, date syrup, maple syrup, carob molasses, honey, molasses, fresh fruit and even vegetables. You can buy date syrup in health food shops, and both date syrup and carob molasses in Middle Eastern food shops or online. You can also make your own date syrup by cooking up some dried dates in water until they collapse to a mush, adding a little molasses to get the treacly depth of traditional date syrup. I would not advise you to use agave syrup, xylitol, stevia granules or sweeteners – your body knows what to do with sugar in its natural forms, so it is best to stick to unprocessed sweeteners and use them sparingly.

yeast

Sourdough bread is raised with the wild yeasts inherent in the dough, but I do love fresh yeast for the fragrant bready flavour it gives to baking. While yeast is sometimes grown on wheat, it does not contain any gluten. However, if you buy your yeast from a baker, there is a good chance that it will have been contaminated at some point. Buy fresh yeast online, or from a supermarket that stocks it in the chiller cabinet and if in doubt, undertake some due diligence and ask exactly where it has come from. Alternatively, you can use a gluten free dried yeast; in my recipes that use fresh yeast, I have given the alternative quantity of quick (active) dried yeast in brackets.

Be aware that some people react to baker's yeast (*Saccharomyces cerevisiae*) in the same way that they react to gluten, because the protein can appear similar to the body. If in doubt, stick to sourdough.

xanthan gum and guar gum

These emulsifiers are often used in gluten free baking to mimic the binding and hydrating qualities of gluten. I try to use as little xanthan gum as possible in my baking because it is highly processed and some people react adversely to it, with symptoms ranging from a little embarrassing wind to full-blown gut cramps or joint pains similar to a gluten 'poisoning'.

Most people are fine with a little bit, although you may be one of the few who have a real sensitivity to xanthan and just need to avoid it completely. As sensitivities can build up with a lot of exposure, the sensible thing is to eat it only occasionally. In this book, xanthan gum is used only in the puff pastry recipe on page 132, which is a treat rather than an everyday staple.

I do not use guar gum at all because it is poorly tolerated by many people.

cooking fats

If you have gluten intolerance or coeliac disease, it is important to focus on avoiding gluten for your health, but fats also have a large part to play in healing your body, by aiding cell repair, promoting mineral and vitamin absorption, and maintaining hormone production. Food intolerance and autoimmune conditions such as coeliac disease are associated with inflammation that can be soothed by the omega fats contained in seeds, nuts, grass fed meat, oily fish and dark greens.

Naturally occurring saturated fats that are found in dairy products, meat fat and coconut oil are used by the body to strengthen and repair cell walls. Fat also helps you to digest both carbohydrate and protein, so it is important to include some in every meal in order to make your diet as nourishing as possible.

Population studies have shown that people who consume the fat that naturally occurs in their milk and meat are less prone to diabetes and heart disease than people eating low fat alternatives. Those eating high fat junk food, on the other hand, are much more likely to develop these diseases of modern life.

Damaged fats, such as heat-expelled vegetable oils and trans fats, are likely to be responsible for many of the dangers that are often attributed to saturated fat. After all, we have been eating the fats that occur naturally in meat and dairy products for many thousands of years without major increases in heart disease. It is only since we started to eat lots of processed food that heart disease has become more common. Try eating some of the fat that comes with your meat and you may find you need to eat less meat overall.

We manufacture our vitamin D and steroid hormones (essential for body functions) from the saturated fat cholesterol. It is always preferable to get this cholesterol from your diet, rather than produce it in your liver. We need to have a high ratio of 'good' (HDL) to 'bad' (LDL) cholesterol in order to be healthy, but bad cholesterol increases when we experience stress and consume refined carbohydrates, sugar and alcohol. Rather than cutting out sources of dietary cholesterol, try to minimise the things that increase bad cholesterol, whilst aiming to include lots of fresh veg and unheated virgin olive oil in your diet to reduce the level of bad cholesterol in your body.

Vegetarians and vegans need to be particularly careful to ensure they have enough saturated fat and cholesterol in their diet, as these are mostly obtained from animal sources. Sources of good cholesterol include beef, pork, liver, butter, eggs, cheese, crab, prawns and lobster.

Only consume vegetable oils that claim to be 'cold pressed' or 'virgin'. Other oils should be avoided, as these are heated and chemically processed, destroying the delicate structure of polyunsaturated fats. Margarine, vegetable oil spreads and even olive oil spreads and vegetable shortening should also be avoided for this reason. Choose butter, olive oil or coconut oil for spreading on bread and anointing your vegetables – they will help you absorb the minerals in your meal too.

The table below will help you choose the right fats for frying, sautéeing and dressing salads. The fats suggested for high temperatures are chemically stable when heated, meaning the high heat needed for fast frying or roasting does not damage them and they are good choices for these cooking methods. Those in the second category should only be used for a gentle sauté or in a low oven, or used for non cooking purposes. You should avoid cooking those in the third category, as the fragile polyunsaturates they contain will be damaged by heat and may cause inflammation (our cellular response to irritating substances, which can result in joint and muscle pain, digestive discomfort and increased reactions to allergens).

which cooking fats to choose?

temperature	type of fat	cooking method
for high temperatures	Beef dripping, lamb fat, coconut oil, palm oil, lard, goose fat, duck fat, bacon fat, chicken fat, sesame oil, groundnut oil	Stir-frying, roasting meat or potatoes, frying eggs, searing meat, cooking steak
for gentle heat (up to 140°C)	Olive oil, ghee, clarified butter, unsalted butter	Slow-roasting vegetables or meat, softening onions without colour
avoid cooking	The following cold pressed oils: hazelnut, almond, avocado, rapeseed, sunflower, macadamia, argan, hemp, borage, walnut, evening primrose	Salads, adding to vegetables after cooking, aïoli and vinaigrettes, dipping bread, on toast

dairy alternatives

Many people who experience adverse symptoms from eating gluten also have issues with dairy. If this is the case for you, it's important to find healthy substitutes for milk, cheese and butter, so that you aren't compounding the problem by eating something non beneficial. In my experience, many people who can't tolerate milk, yoghurt, cream or cheese can still tolerate butter, because it is almost pure fat, with only tiny amounts of the casein or lactose that may cause problems.

Clarified butter and ghee are purified and therefore contain no lactose or casein, so they may be worth trying in small amounts too. You will know if you react to butter; if this is the case, there are alternatives to choose from (see below).

Most of the recipes in this book use cow's butter, unless they are specifically dairy free. You can substitute goat's butter, but note that it melts at a lower temperature. Bear this in mind if you are using it to make puff pastry and keep everything chilled.

The other fat substitutes I use for butter are: coconut oil, duck fat, goose fat or lard, but not margarine (for the reasons given on page 41). If you are converting the butter in a recipe to one of these substitute fats, then you will need to use 20 per cent less. This is because butter contains about 80 per cent fat, whilst the substitutes contain 100 per cent fat. Your substitute fat will perform differently from butter, and it depends on the other ingredients in the recipe as to how successful this will be. It is possible to use olive oil, nut oils or rapeseed oil as a substitute for butter, but only where the butter is melted, as in choux paste (see page 131).

Many commercial dairy free milks contain emulsifiers such as guar gum, carrageenan, xanthan gum and soya lecithin to stop the product from separating during storage. Recent studies have shown that emulsifiers could have a negative effect on gut flora and may increase your chances of becoming obese or developing leaky gut syndrome, where the gut walls become permeable to undigested food particles. Emulsifiers are present in many 'free from' foods, as well as in processed food. If you don't have the time to make your own milk alternative, try to find one that doesn't contain emulsifiers.

To convert the recipes in this book to dairy free you will need to choose a milk alternative for cow's milk, and use coconut milk, cashew cream or another non dairy cream in place of cream.

nut or seed milk (and cream)

All nuts and seeds can be made into a creamy milk with a subtly nutty flavour; almonds, cashews, macadamia nuts and sunflower seeds are the most neutral tasting choices, while sesame seeds, pumpkin seeds and walnuts make strongly flavoured milks. Nut and seed milks are high in good fats and low in carbohydrates. If you buy nut milk, choose an unsweetened one and check for stabilisers and emulsifiers.

You can also make your own nut or seed milk by whizzing soaked nuts in a blender with their soaking water and then straining through muslin. A high-speed blender will generally blend finely enough to eliminate the need to strain the milk.

Cashew nuts make a thick velvety cream that can be used in desserts. Soak a handful of cashews with a pinch of sea salt and enough water to cover for a few hours, then blend until silky smooth and sweeten with a little raw honey.

coconut milk and oil
Rich and nourishing, coconut milk contains lauric acid (found in abundance in breast milk) and has metabolic and immune stimulating qualities. It is available in cartons for use in tea or tins as a cream substitute. Organic coconut milk tends to have fewer stabilisers in it. You can use coconut oil as an excellent substitute for butter in baking, or for frying at higher temperatures.

goat's milk and sheep's milk
Although technically dairy products, the fat and protein molecules in goat's milk and sheep's milk are smaller than those in cow's milk, and for this reason some people find them easier to digest. If you are lactose sensitive, the best way to try this out is to start with a small quantity of goat's or sheep's yoghurt, as this has been partially digested by lactic bacteria and is lower in lactose than milk. (You can also make or buy a type of yoghurt called 'kefir' to try, as it has a broader range of friendly bacteria than standard cow's yoghurt and can help restore gut flora.)

Always choose whole milk, preferably unhomogenised. Goat's and sheep's butters are also available.

hemp milk
Nutty and mildly creamy, with a grassy aftertaste, hemp milk is high in omega 3 and healthy monounsaturated fats, but try not to boil it as this will destroy the delicate polyunsaturates. You can make it yourself, or buy it sweetened, fortified and emulsified.

lactofree milk
There are lactose free milks on the market that have the enzyme lactase added to them, in order to remove the lactose. Choose a fresh variety if you would like to try one of these, as any that are not sold from the fridge will be ultra-pasteurised, which damages the proteins and nutrients in the milk.

The process of making yoghurt and cheese reduces lactose in milk naturally and partially digests the proteins, so you may tolerate live yoghurt or hard cheese even if you are lactose sensitive – try fermenting your yoghurt for 24 hours if you make your own.

rice milk and amazake
Rice milk is high in carbohydrate, thin and sweet tasting. There are concerns over the arsenic content of some rice milks, due to environmental pollution in countries where the rice is grown, so it should not be used as a sole milk alternative for children. Go for an organic brand to reduce the likelihood of it containing problematic levels of arsenic.

Amazake is a sweet and creamy Japanese alternative to rice pudding, fermented using koji culture to turn the carbohydrate into simple and easily digested sugars. You can find amazake in health food shops.

soya milk and soya cheese

Soya beans contain very high levels of phytic acid, which remains intact even when made into products like soya milk, soya flour and soya cheese. This can lead to mineral and vitamin deficiencies over time as the phytic acid binds with nutrients in the gut. Soya is a powerful goitrogen, inhibiting the thyroid, and therefore it is important to avoid it during the menopause or if you suffer from chronic fatigue.

Soya also contains high levels of phytoestrogens, which are present in smaller amounts in many of the plant foods we eat. This means soya products can exacerbate the oestrogen dominance suffered by many women, with symptoms including bloating, water retention, Premenstrual Syndrome (PMS), sore breasts and irregular periods.

In countries where soya is part of the diet, it is fermented with a culture – as in miso, tempeh, natto, fermented (stinky) tofu and tamari – to transform the anti-nutrients into beneficial compounds. Unfermented soya is a modern phenomenon and one that is best avoided unless large quantities of mineral rich foods, such as seaweed and bone broths, are included in the diet.

yeast flakes

Made from a similar type of yeast to baker's yeast, these flakes have a distinctly cheesy, nutty taste and a creamy texture. They can be used in place of grated cheese to make a dish more savoury. They are high in B vitamins and protein, but it's worth noting that some people react to yeast as they would to gluten, and yeast flakes can sometimes also induce wind.

yoghurt

Yoghurt can be made from any milk that has a reasonable protein content: coconut, almond, hemp, soya, goat's and sheep's milk all work well, but rice milk does not. The milk alternatives will produce a thinner yoghurt than goat's and sheep's milk, though you can buy commercial varieties that may be thickened with emulsifiers.

You can make dairy free yoghurt yourself, using a yoghurt starter culture – make sure that the starter culture is dairy free, as some contain dried milk powder.

For a dairy free alternative in recipes that use a yoghurt ferment, such as buckwheat blinis (see page 61), chestnut and buckwheat cheaty sourdough (see page 88), or crêpes (see page 62), you can use live dairy free yoghurt or a probiotic capsule and a milk alternative, to partially digest the anti-nutrients in the mixture. The texture will not be exactly the same as usual because the milk proteins in cow's, sheep's or goat's yoghurt normally soften the crumb and help to hold the structure, but the results will still be pretty good, especially if you can find coconut yoghurt.

breakfast

Breakfast is the most important meal of the day, sending a signal to your body to ramp up the metabolism and burn some fuel. Find a way to fit it into your schedule, ideally within a couple of hours of waking. Your first meal of the day should be like any other – satisfying and delicious. If you skimp on breakfast, you often have to play catch up for the rest of the day.

Because there are many tasty gluten free cereals available, it is tempting to eat a swift bowl of flakes in the morning. The recipes in this chapter aim to turn your breakfast into something more like a meal, full of the nutrients that boxed cereals do not provide. If you have some gluten free bread in the freezer, there are a host of toppings that will sustain you until lunchtime: tinned sardines, poached eggs and spinach, or peanut butter and banana will all provide the protein and healthy fats that slow down the release of carbohydrate from the bread.

If you're likely to be in a rush in the mornings, prepare breakfast in advance – make a batch of muffins and freeze them or cook up a big pot of pumpkin porridge. The tomato base of huevos rancheros can be made well ahead, so that all you need to do in the morning is add a couple of eggs and a slice of gluten free toast to infuse your day with a little Mexican colour. Stash some brioche in the freezer so you can serve up French toast of a weekend. If porridge is your thing, buy some gluten free oats, millet seed or quinoa, soak overnight with a spoonful of yoghurt and just enough water to cover, and cook up in next to no time the following morning.

'pumpkin pie' porridge serves 3

This porridge recipe contains no grains. Instead, it makes great use of the velvety texture of squash and the caramelised sweetness that root veg take on when they are braised slowly. It's almost like starting the day with a delicious bowl of pumpkin pie. Make the porridge the day before and just heat it up in the morning.

for the pumpkin porridge
2 sweet eating apples
2 tsp butter or coconut oil
3 medium carrots, peeled and chopped
½ small squash, peeled and deseeded
  (about 200g prepared weight)
½–1 tsp ground cinnamon
A pinch of ground allspice or mixed spice
½ tsp vanilla extract
A drizzle of honey (optional)

for the crumble topping
120g pecan nuts or flaked almonds
6 tsp ground linseed
10–12 dried dates, pitted and roughly
  chopped
1 tsp ground cinnamon

to serve
Full fat Greek yoghurt or coconut milk

Peel, core and roughly chop the apples into chunks. Melt the butter or coconut oil in a large saucepan. Add the apple chunks and sauté over a medium heat until they start to soften, about 10 minutes.

Add the carrots to the pan, lower the heat and cook, stirring every now and then, for about 10 minutes until they start to soften. Meanwhile, cut the squash into 2–3cm chunks. Add the squash to the pan and cook over a low heat, stirring from time to time, for about half an hour, until everything is soft and starting to colour.

Meanwhile, make the crumble. Put all the ingredients into a food processor and blitz until finely ground. Add a few drops of water (no more or you'll end up with a paste) and blitz again until the mix just starts to form crumbs. (Or, finely chop the ingredients together by hand, then mix with a few drops of water.) This crumble will keep for a few days in the fridge.

Pour enough boiling water over the softened veg in the pan to just cover, then sprinkle on the spices. Cover and simmer for about an hour, topping up the liquid during cooking if necessary, but don't add too much – you can always thin it down at the end.

Allow to cool a little, then tip the veg and their liquid into a blender. Add the vanilla and process until velvety smooth. Sweeten with honey to taste, if you like.

Either chill overnight and heat up the porridge in the morning or return to the pan and heat up again, stirring constantly to prevent sticking. Serve topped with some yoghurt or coconut milk and a few spoonfuls of the crumble topping.

almond breakfast risotto serves 3–4

When you wake up feeling tired and in need of comfort, try this original breakfast risotto. A little like porridge, but without the gloopiness of oats, it has a creamy nuttiness that sings with fresh fig, ripe banana or blackberries. You might think that stirring a pot of risotto for a while in the morning would be a chore but it can be very therapeutic. Think of it as a morning meditation, with a delicious breakfast at the end!

25g salted butter or coconut oil
125g arborio or other risotto rice
60g ground almonds
1 litre almond milk, plus extra to serve
Light muscovado sugar or honey,
   to taste

A few drops of vanilla extract, to taste
   (optional)

to serve
30g flaked almonds
A drizzle of almond milk or cream

Melt the butter or coconut oil in a saucepan over a low heat and add the rice, stirring to coat the grains completely. Add the ground almonds, turn up the heat to medium and stir constantly for a few minutes, until the almonds start to smell nutty and a little toasted. Don't let the butter burn – you just want a little nuttiness.

Add just enough almond milk to loosen the rice (about 150ml) and stir until it is all absorbed. Continue adding almond milk in this way, waiting for each addition to be fully absorbed by the rice before adding the next, stirring almost constantly and keeping the pan at a low simmer. When the rice is cooked through but still with a bite, about 20 minutes, take the pan off the heat.

Stir in a little sugar or honey and check for sweetness – err on the side of savoury and have a bowl of sugar or honey on the table so people can add a little more if they like. Add some vanilla extract if you like, but be delicate – too much will overwhelm the almond flavour.

Spoon into bowls and top with flaked almonds and a drizzle of almond milk or cream.

variation: hazelnut risotto
Use ground hazelnuts and hazelnut milk in place of the almonds and almond milk. Serve sprinkled with chopped hazelnuts and a little maple or date syrup.

scrambled eggs with courgette serves 2

I eat eggs of some sort most mornings and a quick rootle about in the fridge yields the veg that form the base of a dish we call 'revueltos' at home, after the Spanish dish of scrambled eggs with a few veg and maybe a little chorizo thrown in. This is the sort of recipe that you can vary according to the seasons, replacing tomato and courgette with squash and kale in the winter, or whatever leftover veg you have at your disposal. A little piquant sausage is a great addition too.

2 medium or 4 small courgettes
Butter or duck fat, for cooking
½ red onion, finely sliced
A sprig of thyme or marjoram, leaves picked
1 beef tomato or a large handful of cherry tomatoes

4 large eggs
A handful of chives, chopped
Olive oil to drizzle
Sea salt and black pepper

Dice the courgettes (if the skin is tough, peel them first).

Heat a knob of butter or 1 tsp duck fat in a heavy-based frying pan over a medium heat until melted, then add the red onion, courgettes, thyme or marjoram and a pinch of salt. Sweat until the vegetables have just started to take on a little colour and sweeten, about 5–6 minutes.

Meanwhile, cut the beef tomato into chunks, or slice the cherry tomatoes in half.

Beat the eggs in a bowl with lots of black pepper and a large pinch of salt.

Turn the heat under the frying pan right down. Scrape the veg to one side of the pan and add the egg to the empty side. Cook over a medium heat for just over a minute, scraping the egg into curds – take off the heat while there is still a bit of runny egg left.

Stir everything together until the egg is creamily scrambled and dish up straight away, before the egg has a chance to overcook. Top with the tomato, chives, a grinding of pepper and a drizzle of olive oil.

huevos rancheros serves 3

One-pot breakfasts are my idea of heaven. Tomato takes on a new identity when it is simmered slowly with sweet onion and pepper, the juices mingling with chorizo fat to form a piquant, velvety sauce for the eggs. Adjust the spiciness to your liking, and provide extra chilli flakes at the table for those with a penchant for heat. You can serve these burrito style, wrapped in a crêpe (see page 62), or with shredded lettuce and gluten free corn tortillas.

2 x 400g tins peeled plum tomatoes
1 large red onion, roughly chopped
1 red (or Romero) pepper, halved, cored, deseeded and roughly chopped
400g gluten free chorizo cooking sausages (or plain gluten free sausages)

A few pinches of Turkish dried chilli flakes
A splosh of extra virgin olive oil
3 large eggs
Sea salt and black pepper
Flat leaf parsley, roughly chopped, to finish (optional)

Roughly chop the tinned tomatoes and tip them with their juice into a large sauté or frying pan (suitable for use under the grill). Half-fill one of the tins with water and then tip it into the pan. Heat until just boiling.

Add the onion, red pepper, whole chorizo sausages, chilli flakes, a good pinch of salt, a grinding of pepper and splosh of olive oil. Turn the heat down to a simmer and place a lid on the pan, slightly off centre, so that some steam can escape. Simmer until the liquor has reduced to a velvety sauce, about 45 minutes. Taste for seasoning and chilli heat, and adjust as necessary.

Preheat the grill to medium-high. Remove the sausages from the sauce, chop into chunks and return to the sauce.

Make 3 indentations in the sauce to make spaces for the eggs. If the sauce is very thick, add a little more water as you need some liquid to poach the eggs in, but not so much that it becomes soupy.

Crack the eggs into the hollows and simmer until the edge of the white is opaque, but the yolk and white surrounding it is still uncooked. Then pop the whole pan under the grill just long enough to cook the white but leave the yolk runny.

Serve as soon as the eggs are cooked, scattered with chopped parsley, if you like.

turkish eggs with garlic toast serves 2

Spicy, smoky, sharp and buttery, these poached eggs nestled in yoghurt and drizzled with paprika butter are a feast for the eyes as well as the taste buds. Garlic toast, ideally made with a lighter sourdough (see page 86) or focaccia (see page 92), provides the crunch that brings the whole thing together. This is also lovely for lunch, with a crisp garden salad on the side.

for the paprika butter
25g salted butter
1 garlic clove, squashed in its skin
½ tsp hot smoked paprika
½ tsp sweet paprika

for the turkish eggs
4 large eggs
A few drops of vinegar or lemon juice
About 125g full fat Greek yoghurt

for the garlic toast
4 slices of gluten free bread
2 garlic cloves, peeled and halved
Extra virgin olive oil to drizzle

to finish (optional)
Turkish dried chilli flakes
Flat leaf parsley or mint leaves

For the paprika butter, melt the butter in a small saucepan, add the garlic clove and cook over a medium heat, stirring, until you can see the sediment in the bottom of the pan start to turn golden. Immediately plunge the bottom of the pan into cold water to arrest the cooking process. Remove the garlic clove and then stir both types of paprika into the butter. Taste and add a little extra of either, if you like, but don't overdo it. Set aside.

Next, poach the eggs (to do so my way, have ready a bowl of warm water to keep the cooked eggs warm). Bring a small saucepan of water to the boil and add a few drops of vinegar or lemon juice. Swirl the water to create a whirlpool, add one egg and then turn the heat down to a gentle simmer. Poach gently for a few minutes until almost done. To check, lift the egg out with a large spoon: the white will be opaque but the yolk should still feel completely runny if you press it gently with your finger. Transfer to the bowl of warm water where it will continue to cook to runny yolked perfection.

Toast the bread on both sides, then rub all over with the cut surface of the garlic cloves and drizzle with olive oil. Place on one side of each plate.

Spread half the yoghurt on the other side of the plates and top with two eggs per person. Drizzle paprika butter over each serving. Finish with a sprinkling of chilli flakes and some parsley or mint leaves, if you like (or you could just put the chilli flakes on the table).

prosciutto mini quiches makes 6

These crustless quiches are great for breakfast. They will keep in the fridge for a couple of days – have them for lunch or a quick supper, with buttery steamed veg or a salad on the side. Vary the ingredients according to what you have to hand: try wilted spinach, caramelised onions, spring onions, roasted peppers, sun-dried tomatoes, artichoke hearts in oil, grated Cheddar on top... the possibilities are endless. For a veggie version, instead of prosciutto, line the moulds with crêpes (see page 62, making them smaller).

10g butter
6 slices of prosciutto ham or speck
   (or 6 small crêpes)
120g frozen peas
4 large eggs
A glug of milk
A large slice of feta

2–3 spring onions, trimmed and finely
   sliced
Black pepper

equipment
6-hole muffin tray

Preheat the oven to 200°C/Fan 180°C/Gas 6.

Lightly butter and line the hollows of a 6-hole muffin tray with rounds and collars of non-stick baking parchment. (This isn't essential, but it does hold up the prosciutto and makes it easier to lift out the quiches.)

Carefully lay a slice of prosciutto in each of the lined muffin tray holes, leaving the long ends draping over the edge – try not to break it as you lay it in. (Don't worry if there are small gaps round the edge.) Sprinkle in the frozen peas, dividing them equally.

In a jug, beat the eggs well with a balloon whisk, add a glug of milk and season with black pepper (there is no need for salt – the prosciutto provides enough). Pour the mixture into the prosciutto cases, leaving just enough room for some feta and spring onions.

Crumble in the feta, sprinkle in the sliced spring onions and grind a little pepper over the top. Bake for 10–12 minutes, until risen and starting to turn a little golden.

Leave the mini quiches in the tray for a few minutes and then run a knife around the edge to loosen them before carefully removing from the tins. Eat hot or cold.

buckwheat blinis makes 16–18

Beaten egg whites make the lightest of pancakes and yet these blinis have a pleasingly wholesome, bready quality too. Soaking helps to develop flavour and hydrate the flours so that they fluff up well in the pan – you could do this part overnight in the fridge if you want to have blinis for breakfast. I like to eat blinis topped with smoked salmon, crème fraîche and a little finely sliced red onion, but they are also delicious with eggs as part of a cooked breakfast, or with roast pears and yoghurt in the autumn.

70g gluten free white flour (or a mix of
   35g rice flour and 35g tapioca flour)
60g buckwheat flour
2 eggs, separated
100g full fat Greek yoghurt

140ml whole milk
10g fresh yeast (or 3g quick dried)
1 tsp psyllium husks
3 pinches of sea salt
Unsalted butter for cooking

Put all the ingredients except the egg whites and butter into a large bowl and beat with a wooden spoon until smooth. Cover and set aside to prove in a warm place for 2 hours, or in the fridge overnight.

If you prove the mixture in the fridge, take it out half an hour before making the blinis to allow it to come up to room temperature.

When you're ready to fry the blinis, whisk the egg whites until stiff and fold them gently into the batter, just until no white is showing.

Heat a heavy-based frying pan and grease with butter, using a heatproof brush or a folded wad of kitchen paper to spread the butter around and give a nice thin coating.

Drop tablespoonfuls of batter evenly around the pan, leaving space in between to turn them. Cook for 40–50 seconds until golden brown on the bottom and just starting to set on top.

Flip the blinis over carefully, using a palette knife and your fingers. Cook on the other side for 30 seconds until just set underneath. Check to see if they are done by tapping with your fingertips – there should be no squidge. (If they feel very solid, however, they might be overdone – you'll get used to judging them after you've cooked a batch.)

Keep your blinis warm in a low oven while you cook the rest of the mixture. Serve as soon as they are all cooked.

crêpes with banana and greek yoghurt serves 4

This crêpe batter includes some yoghurt, which makes the flour more digestible when the batter is left to stand overnight; it also makes for silky textured pancakes. They are a little more delicate than wheat based crêpes, so don't be disheartened if your first one isn't perfect. Sorghum makes a malty, slightly wholemeal crêpe, but you could substitute other single flours or use a mixture: teff and buckwheat will give a darker, more flexible crêpe, whilst millet, maize and rice flour will give mild flavoured, slightly stiffer pancakes.

for the crêpes
130g sorghum flour
300ml whole milk
2 tbsp full fat Greek yoghurt
2 large eggs
A large pinch of sea salt
Unsalted butter, coconut oil or duck fat
  for frying

for the filling
4 ripe bananas (or other fruit)
1 lemon
50g flaked almonds or shredded coconut
About 100g Greek yoghurt

to serve
Honey or maple syrup

About 6–12 hours before you plan to cook your crêpes, whisk the flour, milk and yoghurt together in a bowl. Cover and leave at room temperature for up to 24 hours.

For the filling, slice the bananas thickly on an angle. Place them in a bowl and squeeze in enough lemon juice to coat the slices, turning them gently. Lemon zest is a delicious addition too, so grate some in if you like.

Toast the flaked almonds or coconut in a dry pan and add to the bananas, giving a final gentle turn (or add untoasted if you prefer).

When you are ready to cook the crêpes, whisk in the eggs and salt – the consistency should be like double cream, so add a little more milk if needed.

Heat a heavy-based frying pan over a medium heat. Brush lightly with butter, using a heatproof brush or a folded wad of kitchen paper.

Pour a small ladleful of batter into the pan and swirl it around to give you a thin crêpe. (If there are lots of bubbly holes, you have the pan a little too hot.) When the underside is golden brown, loosen gently with a palette knife and flip over to cook the other side briefly. Keep warm in a low oven while you cook the rest, interleaving the cooked crêpes in the oven with pieces of baking parchment to stop them sticking together.

Spread each crêpe with some Greek yoghurt and add a spoonful of bananas. Fold in half and fold again into quarters. Drizzle with a little honey or maple syrup to serve.

squash drop scones makes 15

Drop scones are little fluffy pancakes cooked on the hob and named for the way that the batter is dropped from a spoon into the pan to form each one. Squash gives them a little sweetness and a lovely pale orange colour. Choose a starchy squash, such as butternut, acorn, kabocha or harlequin, avoiding pumpkin, which is too wet. I've also made them with pea purée in place of squash for a slightly ghoulish green at Halloween.

¼ squash, peeled and deseeded (150g prepared weight)
100g gluten free white flour (or a mix of 50g rice flour and 50g tapioca flour)
40g buckwheat flour
1 tsp gluten free baking powder
1 tsp ground psyllium husk

40g butter, cut into small pieces, plus extra for cooking and to serve
2 eggs, separated
130ml whole milk
1 tsp light muscovado sugar
Sea salt

Cut the squash into dice and cook in a steamer for about 10 minutes until soft. Drain and mash well, then set aside to cool.

Put the flours, baking powder, psyllium and a good pinch of salt into a large bowl and whisk to combine. Rub in the butter roughly with your fingertips, leaving quite a few small lumps. Now stir in the egg yolks, mashed squash and milk, using a wooden spoon.

Beat the egg whites in a scrupulously clean bowl to soft peaks, using a balloon whisk or electric whisk. Add the sugar and continue to beat until stiff peaks form. Fold gently into the squash mixture, just until no white is showing. Use the batter straight away.

Heat a heavy-based frying pan over a low heat. Brush lightly with butter, using a heatproof brush or a folded wad of kitchen paper. The pan is hot enough when a little of the batter dropped in sizzles lightly (keep the heat fairly low).

Place tablespoonfuls of batter evenly around the pan, leaving room in between to turn them. Cook for a few minutes until set on the bottom and just starting to set around the edge. Carefully flip the drop scones over, using a palette knife and your fingers, and cook on the other side for 30 seconds to 1 minute, until just set underneath. Check to see if they are ready by tapping with your fingertips – they should not be squidgy.

Keep the drop scones warm in a low oven while you cook the rest. Serve with butter.

variation: raisin drop scones
For sweeter teatime drop scones, follow the method above, adding 2 tbsp caster sugar to the egg whites, 1 tsp ground cinnamon to the flour, and a handful of raisins when you fold in the whites.

hazelnut pan bread serves 4

I first made this on a camping trip. Cooking it in a heavy-based pan gave it a lovely crust that I wanted to replicate at home. Flavoured with hazelnuts, coffee, maple syrup and dates, it makes for a grown up slice of something that sits between cake and cornbread, with a slightly chewy, dark crust. It is best made in a small, deep cast-iron pan, suitable for use under the grill (or in the oven), and served with thick yoghurt and fruit.

1 very ripe banana
90g ground hazelnuts
2 eggs
1 tbsp maple syrup or molasses
2 tbsp hazelnut or almond butter
A pinch of sea salt
60g dried dates, pitted and finely chopped
½ tsp bicarbonate of soda

½ tsp ground coffee (optional)
A handful of chopped walnuts (optional)
A large knob of unsalted butter (or duck fat or lard) for cooking
Juice of ½ lemon

equipment
Ovenproof heavy-based pan, 15cm in diameter and 5cm deep

Place the small, deep ovenproof pan over a low heat, to heat up.

Mash the banana in a large bowl, using a fork. Add all the other ingredients except the butter and lemon juice, and beat with a wooden spoon until the mixture is smooth.

Add the butter or other fat to the pan and allow it to melt and foam (but don't let it burn). Swirl it around the pan to coat the sides. Beat the lemon juice into the bread batter and scrape it all gently into the pan. Place a lid on the pan and cook over the lowest possible heat for 10 minutes, until the batter is risen and puffy looking, but still wet and uncooked.

Meanwhile, preheat the grill to medium low, or the oven to 170°C/Gas 3 (top and bottom heat, not fan) if your pan doesn't fit under the grill.

Take the lid off the pan and gently ease the pan under the grill (not too close to the heat source), or into the preheated oven. Let the bread cook for about 10–15 minutes until the top is golden brown and firm to the touch.

Slide a knife around the edge of the bread, place an upturned plate on top and invert, using oven gloves to protect your hands. Slice the bread and eat warm.

english sourdough muffins makes 8

These simple breakfast muffins are tender and full of holes with a mild malty flavour from the sorghum and brown sugar. Sometimes they look like crumpets and at other times they are more akin to breakfast muffins (a cruffin or a mumpet, anyone?). You will need metal rings to shape the muffins. They are best eaten straight from the pan, with a generous curl of salty butter or as part of a cooked breakfast.

for the sponge
55g sorghum flour
40g buckwheat flour (white teff flour works too)
40g rice flour
25g potato starch
80g brown rice sourdough starter (see page 74)
240ml warm water
2 tsp ground linseed or 1 tsp ground psyllium husk

for the muffins
½ tsp bicarbonate of soda
20g muscovado sugar (optional)
2 tsp lemon juice
½ tsp sea salt
20g butter (or duck fat or lard) for greasing and cooking

equipment
4 crumpet rings (or other metal rings 8–9cm in diameter)

First make the sponge. Mix all the ingredients together in a large bowl and leave in a warm place for 6 hours or in a cooler place for up to 12 hours, until risen and mousse-like in texture. Do this before bed if you want the muffins for breakfast.

When you are ready to make your muffins, add all the muffin ingredients except the butter to the sponge. Whisk everything together in a jug until completely smooth. The mixture needs to be cooked straight away.

Heat a large heavy-based frying pan over a medium heat. (If you have enough crumpet rings, you can use two pans to cook them all at once.) Generously smear the inside of your crumpet rings with butter, duck fat or lard and place them in the pan(s) to heat. Add a knob of your chosen fat to the middle of each crumpet ring and allow it to melt and sizzle a little.

Pour the mixture evenly into the rings until they are about three quarters full. Turn the heat down to medium low and let the muffins cook until most of the top is starting to set, leaving an uncooked patch about 2cm across in the middle.

Using tongs or a folded wad of kitchen paper, carefully pick up the hot rings and lift them off the muffins in the pan. Use a palette knife to turn the muffins over gently without burning your fingers. Cook for 1–2 minutes and then transfer the muffins to a wire rack to cool a little. Repeat with the remaining mixture.

Eat the muffins while they are still warm with butter and jam or marmalade if you like, or freeze and toast them from frozen, sprinkling them with a little water first.

variation: **yeasty muffins**

If you do not have a rice starter, you can make the muffins with yeast and yoghurt. Just make up the sponge with the following ingredients: 70g rice flour, 55g sorghum flour, 40g buckwheat flour, 25g potato starch, 260ml warm water, 20g full fat Greek yoghurt, 5g fresh yeast and 2 tsp ground linseed or 1 tsp ground psyllium husk. Mix everything together and leave the sponge to ferment for 3–4 hours, or overnight in the fridge. To make the muffins, follow the same method as the main recipe.

french toast serves 1

It is worth making an extra loaf of brioche, so you have some left over for French toast the next morning. Sliced thickly, the egg soaks almost through to the centre of the bread, making the middle moist and the outside more like a buttery pancake. I like mine just as it is, with a sprinkling of cinnamon and a drizzle of honey, but you may like to top it with fruit compote, crème fraîche and a dusting of icing sugar. It's good made with any bread, but the heavier sourdoughs make a heartier and more savoury version.

1 egg

A splosh of cream or milk

A pinch of salt

1 tsp sugar (if you want the toast sweet)

2 thick slices of gluten free brioche (see page 99)

A large knob of unsalted butter for frying

Beat the egg in a bowl with the cream or milk, salt and sugar if using, until frothy. Pour onto a lipped plate.

Lay the brioche slices on the egg and allow it to soak in for a minute or so. Turn over and soak the other side. Your bread may not absorb all the egg, but try to give it time to soak up most of it.

Gently heat a large knob of butter in a heavy frying pan, until it just starts to froth, but not brown.

Put your eggy bread into the pan and adjust the heat so that the egg cooks, but the butter doesn't burn. After a few minutes, check the underside and when it is tinged with golden brown, flip the French toast over and do the other side.

Serve immediately, with fruity/creamy/syrupy accompaniments of your choice. If you are making more than one batch, keep the first batch warm in a low oven while you cook the rest.

chestnut and apple muffins makes 12

These muffins remind me of a moist and nutty Dorset apple cake, but they are savoury enough to be appropriate for breakfast. If you like them a bit sweeter, just add a little extra sugar. Tins of unsweetened chestnut purée are available from most supermarkets, as well as delicatessens.

4 large eggs
100g light muscovado sugar (or 140g
    for a sweeter version)
200g tin or packet unsweetened
    chestnut purée
2 tsp vanilla extract
2 heaped tsp mild honey
1 scant tsp sea salt
60g tapioca starch or cornflour
2 tsp gluten free baking powder

2 tsp ground cinnamon
200g ground almonds (or hazelnuts)
4 heaped tsp linseed, ground
2 eating apples
60g raisins
Flaked almonds, to finish (optional)

equipment
12-hole muffin tray and 12 paper
    muffin cases

Preheat the oven to 180°C/Fan 160°C/Gas 4. Line the 12-hole muffin tray with the paper muffin cases.

Put the eggs, sugar, chestnut purée, vanilla, honey and salt into a large bowl and beat together, using a balloon whisk, until the mixture is frothy and slightly pale.

Sift in the tapioca starch or cornflour, baking powder and cinnamon, then tip in the ground almonds (or hazelnuts) and linseed. Whisk well until the mixture is smooth, paler and slightly thicker.

Peel, core and finely chop the apples. Fold into the batter, along with the raisins.

Spoon the mixture evenly into the muffin cases and sprinkle with flaked almonds, if you like. Bake for 30–35 minutes until the muffins are golden and well risen, and a skewer inserted into the centre of one comes out clean.

As soon as they are cool enough to handle, lift the muffins out of the tray onto a wire rack and leave to cool completely.

Freeze any muffins that are not eaten within 24 hours. Allow to defrost at room temperature for a couple of hours before eating, or slice in half and grill from frozen.

variation: pear and chocolate muffins
Use a couple of barely ripe pears in place of the apples, and swap in good quality dark chocolate, cut into chunks, for the raisins.

carrot and clementine muffins makes 12

These muffins are a real treat when summer fruit is merely a memory and clementines are at their height of loveliness. We like to eat them for breakfast at Christmas – freshly baked in a cinnamon scented kitchen. Using ground almonds or coconut flour in place of starchier grain flours (and the extra fibre from the carrots and linseed) makes them a surprisingly sustaining breakfast.

120g salted butter (or coconut oil plus
   a pinch of sea salt)
4 large eggs
185g maple syrup or date syrup
2 heaped tsp ground cinnamon
1½ tsp bicarbonate of soda
200g peeled carrots, finely grated
30g linseed, ground
Grated zest and juice of 2 clementines

350g ground almonds or coconut flour
A large handful of chopped walnuts and
   a few raisins or chopped dried apricots
   or dates (optional)

equipment
12-hole muffin tray and 12 paper
   muffin cases

Preheat the oven to 180°C/Fan 160°C/Gas 4. Line the 12-hole muffin tray with the paper muffin cases.

Melt the butter or coconut oil in a small saucepan and set aside to cool.

Put the eggs, maple or date syrup, cinnamon and bicarbonate of soda into a large bowl and beat together, using a balloon whisk, until frothy, then whisk in the melted butter or oil. Using a wooden spoon, beat in the grated carrots, linseed, clementine zest and juice, and the ground almonds or coconut flour. Add in the walnuts and dried fruit, if using.

(Alternatively, put everything except the clementine juice, grated carrots and optional walnuts and dried fruit in a food processor or stand mixer and blend until thick and creamy. Add the clementine juice and beat just until incorporated, then gently stir in the carrots, walnuts and dried fruit using a rubber spatula.)

Spoon the mixture evenly into the paper cases and bake for 30–35 minutes, until the muffins are golden brown, risen and firm, and a skewer inserted in the centre of one comes out fairly clean (the carrots will make the mixture a little stickier).

Leave in the tray for 5 minutes, then transfer the muffins to a wire rack and leave to cool completely.

Store in an airtight container and eat within 2 days, or freeze and then defrost for a couple of hours before eating.

bread

If you are used to bread recipes with a simple ingredients list of flour, yeast, water and salt, gluten free bread recipes might seem complicated at first, but the key to a successful gluten free loaf is combining neutral and flavour flours with some starch to get a balance of all the different qualities. Making bread with just one type of flour isn't really a viable option. Once you've got the hang of the basics, you can experiment with different combinations.

In most traditional bread recipes, gluten holds water in the dough, so gluten free flours can produce a dry, heavy loaf if they are not given enough hydration. The extra water in a gluten free dough needs to be bound up by something that creates a gel (psyllium husk, linseed or gum), or a very absorbent starch such as tapioca or potato starch, in order to hold the bubbles of carbon dioxide created by yeast.

Gluten also forms the web-like protein structure that gives a loaf its characteristic springy texture and helps to brown the crust. Without it, you need to use protein from other sources – like eggs, yoghurt and milk – to help soften the crumb and provide a little colour.

The three stage sourdough process that I have developed uses a rice sourdough starter to inoculate the dough with wild yeasts and lactic bacteria, which occur naturally on the outer part of all grains. The 'starter' is simply a runny paste made from brown rice flour and water, which matures to bubbly perfection over 4 to 5 days. Once made, this can be kept dormant in the fridge and woken up with a feed and some warmth when you want to bake. The second stage is to use some of the starter to make a 'sponge' by combining it with water and wholegrain flours (these need the longest ferment time of all the flours and contain extra wild yeasts). Finally, the dough is made by adding some starch, often an egg, some linseed or psyllium, salt and sometimes a little extra yeast to give the loaf a kick.

If you would like to use yeast in baking recipes, use a gluten free dried yeast or buy fresh yeast from a reliable supplier so that you know it is not contaminated with wheat – online suppliers are often good, and some supermarkets sell it. Don't buy yeast direct from a bakery unless you know that you are not sensitive to gluten contamination.

Because the recipes that follow use a combination of several different flours, precise weighing is the key to success. A set of decent digital scales will make weighing simple and exact. Water is given as a weight in these recipes because it is easier to judge that way – just pop your jug on the scales, then zero the scales and pour until you get the correct weight.

Most of my bread recipes use 2lb (1kg) loaf tins – my favourites are narrow and tall, for a good crust-to-crumb ratio, and it's worth investing in a few of these for batch baking bread. When your confidence grows, try your hand at baking with a baguette pan too.

Buy some psyllium husk, pectin and linseed, so that you always have the extra bits that make gluten free loaves chewy, moist and wholesome. When your loaves are baked, the best way to keep them fresh is to freeze them, as homemade gluten free bread goes stale and hard quickly, without the softening properties of gluten or preservatives. For convenience, freeze the bread ready sliced (see page 24), so you can take out slices as you need them.

brown rice sourdough starter

This recipe uses the yeasts inherent in brown rice flour to create a starter, which you can use for baking sourdough bread and pancakes. It will work with a mixed white and brown rice flour, such as Doves Farm's version, but not with a pure white rice flour. Don't be tempted to use tap water – the chlorine it contains will inhibit the fermenting process. It will take 4 to 5 days in a warm place to get the ferment bubbling. Adding a bunch of grapes will introduce more wild yeasts for a more vigorous starter. Then you just keep the starter in the fridge, 'feeding' it when you want to bake.

You can also make starters with teff flour, quinoa flour, sorghum flour, millet flour or buckwheat flour, but I find a rice starter the mildest flavoured and cheapest to maintain.

day 1
150g brown rice flour
200g tepid mineral or filtered water
A small bunch of unwashed organic grapes

Mix the flour and water together in a bowl and settle the grapes into the paste, still on their stalks. Cover with a polythene bag or plate and leave in a warm place for 24 hours.

day 2
45g brown rice flour
60g tepid mineral or filtered water

Lift out the grapes carefully and discard. Stir the mixture well and add the flour and water, then stir again. Re-cover and leave for another 24 hours.

day 3
45g brown rice flour
60g tepid mineral or filtered water

Stir the mixture, then add the flour and water, and stir again. By now the starter should be starting to bubble and smell a little yeasty. Re-cover and leave for another 24 hours.

day 4
90g brown rice flour
120g tepid mineral or filtered water

Stir, then add the flour and water, and stir again. Re-cover and leave for a final 24 hours.

(continued overleaf)

day 5

After leaving it to stand for the final 24 hours, you will have a starter ready to make bread and pancakes with. Transfer the starter to a plastic container with a cover for storing in the fridge. (You could also use a Kilner type jar without the rubber seal – don't use a glass container with a tight lid, in case gases build up and cause the glass to crack.)

If your starter doesn't look bubbly after 4 days, just feed it for another couple of days, as per Day 2, and keep it in a warmer place, or stand the container in a warm bath of water to encourage the yeast along.

Keep your starter in the fridge and refresh it with 90g brown rice flour and 120g tepid water the day you want to use it. Mix in the flour and water and then bring it up to room temperature by standing the container in some warm water for an hour or so, until the starter has risen up and looks moussey. This is the right amount of feed for one loaf, so if you're making more than one loaf, increase the quantity of flour according to how many loaves you are baking. You will be left with enough starter to maintain the culture between bakes. Your starter will be happy in the fridge for up to a couple of weeks between feeds.

If you need to keep it for longer without feeding, freeze and feed it when you defrost it again. It will be slower to get going though, so you might need to feed and give it a couple of days at room temperature to wake it up. Alternatively, just put it into a container with very little air space above the starter and it should be alright for a month or so. When you feed it again, let the starter rise up and look a little bubbly before you use it.

If your starter seems less vigorous than it should be, you can kickstart it by adding 1 tbsp live yoghurt, water kefir or milk kefir. Alternatively, dunk a few unwashed organic grapes on the stem or a handful of raisins tied in a muslin bag into the starter and leave at room temperature for 4 days. When the starter is back to full strength, keep it in the fridge and refresh in the usual way before baking.

sourdough with sunflower seeds makes 1 loaf

This loaf has a nice open structure because the dough is a little wetter and the flours are starchier than denser sourdoughs. The high proportion of rice flours make for a sweeter loaf with a pleasingly chewy crumb and crusty crust. If you do not have sweet rice flour then you can use one of the alternatives, but it won't rise quite as well. Sunflower seeds bring a nuttiness that really comes into its own when you toast a slice and slather it in butter. Sesame or pumpkin seeds are also delicious. Refresh your starter with 75g rice flour and 100g warm water about an hour before you make the loaf.

for the sponge

150g brown rice sourdough starter (see page 74 and above)

200g brown rice flour (plain rice flour will work too)

50g buckwheat flour

315g tepid water

for the sourdough

100g potato starch (or arrowroot or tapioca starch for a stickier crumb)

50g sweet rice flour (or maize or millet flour for a more cakey loaf)

2 tsp ground psyllium husk

50g sunflower seeds, plus extra for sprinkling

1 large egg

6g sea salt

1 tsp light muscovado sugar (optional)

Butter for greasing (optional)

equipment

1kg (2lb) loaf tin

First, mix the sponge ingredients together in a large bowl, cover and set aside in a warm place for 3–6 hours, or overnight in a cool place, until it has risen up a little.

When your sponge has fermented for long enough, beat in all the sourdough ingredients except the butter, using your hands or a wooden spoon until completely smooth – it will be more like cake batter than a standard dough texture.

Line the loaf tin with baking parchment, or butter the inside and coat with sunflower seeds. Scrape the mixture into the tin. Smooth the surface with a spoon and sprinkle with sunflower seeds.

Leave to rise, uncovered, in a warm place for 2–5 hours (the time will depend on your sourdough starter). The sourdough is ready to go in the oven when it has risen by about a third. The top will start to crack, look a little puffy and feel tender to light pressure from your finger. Don't let the dough over rise, or the loaf will collapse completely when you put it into the oven.

When the loaf is almost ready, preheat the oven to 230°C/Fan 210°C/Gas 8. At the same time, put a roasting tray on the bottom shelf and boil a kettle of water.

Carefully place the risen loaf in the oven – you need to do this gently because the dough is soft. Pour boiling water into the roasting tray to half fill it; this will create steam. Bake for 20 minutes, then carefully remove the tray of boiling water, turn the oven down to 200°C/Fan 180°C/Gas 6 and bake the loaf for a further 45–55 minutes.

To tell if your loaf is cooked, take it out of the tin, using a cloth, and squeeze the sides: it should feel firm, not wobbly. If it still seems uncooked, return to the oven without the tin at 160°C/Fan 140°C/Gas 3 for 15–20 minutes. You'll learn to judge when a loaf is ready once you've baked a few. If you find it's a little undercooked as you slice it, just toast it.

Transfer the loaf to a wire rack to cool. Leave until completely cold before slicing. Any bread that will not be eaten within 24 hours is best frozen in slices (see page 24).

oat and chestnut sandwich bread makes 1 loaf

If you are lucky enough to tolerate oats then you can use their stretchy quality to make a lovely soft brown bread that is perfect for sandwiches. You can easily make your own oat flour to order from porridge oats, using a food processor or dedicated gluten free electric coffee grinder (with blades). This loaf has a crisp but not crunchy crust, and the crumb has a delightful spring. You can use either a sourdough starter or yoghurt for the sponge – they are both great, but the yoghurt makes a slightly cakier loaf.

for the sponge
100g brown rice sourdough starter
   (see page 74), or 70g full fat Greek
   yoghurt and 35g rice flour
175g rice flour
100g chestnut flour
60g oat flour
15g ground linseed
450g tepid milk or water, or a mixture
   of both

for the sourdough
12g fresh yeast (or 4g quick dried)
100g potato starch
50g unsalted butter, melted and cooled,
   plus extra (optional) for greasing
2 egg whites
2 tsp psyllium husks
1 tsp liquid pectin (optional)
7g sea salt
A handful of rolled oats or ground linseed
   for sprinkling

equipment
1kg (2lb) loaf tin

First, mix the sponge ingredients together in a large bowl, cover and set aside at room temperature for 3–6 hours, or overnight in a cool place, until it has risen up a little. (The longer you leave it, the more sour tasting the loaf will be.)

When you are ready to start the loaf, if using fresh yeast, mash it in a small bowl with a little of the wet sponge mix until smooth. Add back to the sponge bowl, along with the rest of the sourdough ingredients except the oats or linseed. Beat well with a wooden spoon or your hands until the mixture is lump free. If using dried yeast, beat into the sponge mix and rest for 15 minutes, before adding the other sourdough ingredients.

Line the loaf tin with baking parchment, or butter the inside of the tin and coat with rolled oats or ground linseed. Scrape the mixture into the tin, level with a spoon and sprinkle with more oats or linseed.

Leave to rise, uncovered, in a warm place for about an hour, until the dough has risen by about a third and little cracks appear in the top. If your kitchen is cool, give it an extra 30 minutes, but don't let it over rise or you will have a big hole in your bread.

When the loaf is almost ready, preheat the oven to 230°C/Fan 210°C/Gas 8. At the same time, put a roasting tray on the bottom shelf and boil a kettle of water.

Very gently ease the loaf tin into the oven – if you tap or bang it at this stage it will collapse, as there is no gluten in the mixture to hold the bubbles in. Pour boiling water into the roasting tray to half fill it. This will create a nice steamy atmosphere that helps swell the loaf and create a thin, crisp crust.

Bake for 20 minutes, then turn the oven down to 200°C/Fan 180°C/Gas 6 and bake for another 45 minutes. When the loaf has been in the oven for 30 minutes, cover it loosely with foil to stop it burning, but note that the crust will be fairly dark anyway. Take the foil off 5–10 minutes before the end of baking to avoid a soggy crust.

The loaf is ready when it has shrunk away from the sides of the tin a little and sounds hollow when tapped on top. Leave it in the tin for 10 minutes, then lift out and press the side of the loaf with your fingers to see if it feels firm. If not, just put it back in the oven without the tin at 180°C/Fan 160°C/Gas 4 for another 10–15 minutes to dry out the crumb a little.

Transfer the loaf to a wire rack to cool. Leave until completely cold before slicing. Any bread that will not be eaten within 24 hours is best frozen in slices (see page 24).

buckwheat and squash bread makes 1 loaf

This sourdough acquires a lovely pale orange colour and sweetness from steamed squash. Because squash varies in starchiness and moisture, it is best added last; also be prepared to add a little more starch and flour if the dough is very sloppy. Use a dense, nutty squash such as acorn, kabocha, butternut or Turk's head. To make this 100 per cent sourdough, just leave out the yeast and allow the loaf to prove for an extra 2–3 hours. Refresh your starter with 75g rice flour and 100g warm water about an hour before you make the loaf.

for the sponge
200g brown rice sourdough starter
  (see page 74 and above)
100g buckwheat flour
100g millet flour
175g tepid water

for the sourdough
8g fresh yeast (or 3g quick dried)
50g tapioca or arrowroot starch
40g sweet rice flour or maize flour

40g ground linseed
60g egg white (2 medium egg whites)
6g sea salt
250g steamed or roasted squash
Butter for greasing (optional)
A handful of sesame seeds for sprinkling

equipment
1kg (2lb) loaf tin

First, mix the sponge ingredients together in a large bowl, cover and set aside at room temperature for 3–6 hours, or overnight in a cool place, until it has risen up a little.

When you are ready to start the loaf, if using fresh yeast, mash it in a small bowl with a little of the wet sponge mix until it is completely smooth. Add back to the sponge bowl, along with the starch, rice or maize flour, ground linseed, egg white and salt. Beat well with a wooden spoon or your hands until the mixture is completely lump free. If using dried yeast, beat into the sponge mix and set aside for 15 minutes, before adding the other sourdough ingredients.

Add two thirds of the squash to the mixture and squidge everything together with your hands until completely smooth. Decide whether your dough can take more squash – it should have the texture of a stiffish cake batter. If it looks very sloppy, add an extra 1 tbsp each of starch and rice or maize flour, to absorb the extra liquid.

Line the loaf tin with baking parchment, or butter the inside and coat with sesame seeds. Scrape the mixture into the tin. Smooth the surface and sprinkle with sesame seeds.

Leave to rise, uncovered, in a warm place for 1–2 hours until risen by about a third and cracks have appeared across the surface.

When the loaf is almost ready, preheat the oven to 230°C/Fan 210°C/Gas 8. At the same time, put a roasting tray on the bottom shelf and boil a kettle of water.

Carefully place the loaf in the oven. Pour boiling water into the roasting tray to half fill it; this will create steam. Bake for 15 minutes, then carefully remove the tray of hot water and turn the oven down to 200°C/Fan 180°C/Gas 6. Bake for a further 45–55 minutes, loosely covering the loaf with foil if the crust appears to be darkening too quickly.

To tell if your loaf is cooked, take it out of the tin carefully, using a cloth, and squeeze the sides: it should feel firmish and not wobbly. If it still seems uncooked, return to the oven without the tin at 160°C/Fan 140°C/Gas 3 for another 10–15 minutes to dry out the crumb a little.

Transfer the loaf to a wire rack to cool. Leave until completely cold before slicing. Any bread that will not be eaten within 24 hours is best frozen in slices (see page 24).

caraway black bread makes 1 loaf

Molasses and caraway seeds make this a dark, complex loaf with a moist chewy crumb somewhat reminiscent of pumpernickel. It is delicious spread with cream cheese and topped with gravadlax or smoked salmon, but also lovely with butter and a slice of good cheese. It makes great toast too, with a savoury rather than sweet topping. If you'd like to make it completely yeast free then just omit the yeast and prove the loaf for an extra 2–3 hours – it will be a little more sour and have a slightly denser texture.

for the sponge
150g brown rice sourdough starter
   (see page 74)
100g rice flour
75g brown teff flour (white teff flour
   will work too)
50g buckwheat flour
15g fine polenta
300g tepid water

for the sourdough
8g fresh yeast (or 3g quick dried)
75g sweet rice flour or yellow maize flour
50g tapioca starch

50–75g molasses (more for a sweeter,
   darker loaf)
60g ground linseed
1 large egg
7g sea salt
1 tsp liquid pectin
1–2 tsp whole caraway seeds
Butter for greasing (optional)
Polenta (optional) and caraway seeds
   for sprinkling

equipment
1kg (2lb) loaf tin

First, mix the sponge ingredients together in a large bowl, cover and set aside at room temperature for 3–6 hours, or overnight in a cool place, until it has risen up a little.

When you are ready to make the loaf, if using fresh yeast, mash it in a small bowl with a little of the wet sponge mix until it is completely smooth. Add back to the sponge bowl, along with the rest of the sourdough ingredients except the butter, polenta and caraway seeds. Beat well with a wooden spoon or your hands until the mixture is completely lump free. If using dried yeast, beat into the sponge mix and set aside for 15 minutes, before adding the remaining sourdough ingredients.

Line the loaf tin with baking parchment, or butter the inside and sprinkle with polenta and about 2 tsp caraway seeds for a crunchier crust. Scrape the mixture into the tin. Wet your hands and smooth the top of the loaf. Slash the top of the loaf with a sharp knife to make indentations and sprinkle generously with caraway seeds.

Leave to rise, uncovered, in a warm place for about 2 hours until the dough has risen by about a third. The top will look a little puffy and feel tender to light pressure from your finger. It is important to treat the loaf gently – any sharp knocks will cause it to collapse.

When the loaf is almost ready, preheat the oven to 220°C/Fan 200°C/Gas 7. At the same time, put a roasting tray on the bottom shelf and boil a kettle of water.

Very gently ease the loaf tin into the oven. Pour boiling water into the roasting tray to half fill it; this will create steam. Bake for 20 minutes, then carefully remove the tray of hot water and turn the oven down to 180°C/Fan 160°C/Gas 4. Cover the loaf loosely with foil and bake for a further 50 minutes, removing the foil for the last 5–10 minutes.

To tell if your loaf is cooked, take it out of the tin carefully, using a cloth, and squeeze the sides: it should feel firmish and not wobbly. If it still seems uncooked, return to the oven without the tin at 160°C/Fan 140°C/Gas 3 for another 15–20 minutes to dry out the crumb a little. If you find it's a little undercooked when you slice it, you can toast it.

Transfer the loaf to a wire rack to cool. Leave until completely cold before slicing. Any bread that will not be eaten within 24 hours is best frozen in slices (see page 24).

lighter sourdough loaf makes 1 loaf

This loaf is a gentle introduction to the wonders of sourdough, with a little more starch and some butter to moisten the crumb. Adding yeast will give a slightly lighter textured and milder flavoured loaf, but you can leave it out for a true sourdough – just allow the loaf to prove for an extra 1–1½ hours. Sugar softens any sourness from the starter, so add it only if you prefer a milder flavoured bread. Sliced thinly, it is a good loaf for sandwiches – freeze it sliced and you can make these straight from the freezer in the morning, for a packed lunch. Refresh your sourdough starter with 75g rice flour and 100g warm water at least an hour before you make the sponge.

for the sponge
200g brown rice sourdough starter
    (see page 74)
125g rice flour
25g buckwheat flour
25g sorghum flour
300g tepid water

for the sourdough
8g fresh yeast (or 3g quick dried)
100g potato starch
100g tapioca starch

25g maize flour (or millet flour)
25g ground linseed, plus extra (optional)
    for sprinkling
25g salted butter, softened,
    plus extra (optional) for greasing
1 large egg
15g muscovado sugar (optional)
7g fine sea salt
1 tsp cider vinegar

equipment
1kg (2lb) loaf tin

First, mix the sponge ingredients together in a large bowl, cover and set aside in a warm place for 2–4 hours, or overnight in a cool place, until it starts to bubble. The longer you leave it at this stage, the sourer your loaf will be.

When you are ready to start the loaf, if using fresh yeast, mash it in a small bowl with a little of the wet sponge mix until it is completely smooth. Add back to the sponge bowl, along with the rest of the sourdough ingredients. Beat well with a wooden spoon or your hands until the mixture is completely lump free. If you are using dried yeast, beat it into the sponge mix and leave to stand for 15 minutes, before adding the remaining sourdough ingredients.

Line the loaf tin with baking parchment or butter the inside and coat with ground linseed. Scrape the mixture into the tin and tap the tin to level the dough.

Leave to rise, uncovered, in a warm place for 1–1½ hours, until the dough has risen by about a third and little cracks appear in the surface. The top will look a little puffy and feel tender to light pressure from your finger. It is important to treat the loaf very gently – any sharp knocks will cause it to collapse.

Preheat the oven to 230°C/Fan 210°C/Gas 8. At the same time, put a roasting tray on the bottom shelf and boil a kettle of water.

Very gently ease the loaf tin into the oven – if you tap or bang it at this stage it will collapse, as there is no gluten in the mixture to hold the bubbles in. Pour boiling water into the roasting tray to half fill it. This will create a nice steamy atmosphere that helps swell the loaf and create a thin, crisp crust. Bake for 15 minutes, then turn the oven down to 200°C/Fan 180°C/Gas 6. Bake for a further 45 minutes, loosely covering the loaf with foil if the crust appears to be darkening too quickly.

To tell if your loaf is cooked, take it out of the tin carefully, using a cloth, and squeeze the sides: it should feel firmish and not wobbly. If you find it's a little undercooked when you slice it, you can toast it. (If I'm unsure whether my loaf is completely cooked, I often take it out of the tin and leave it in the cooling oven for half an hour to dry out the crumb a little.)

Transfer the loaf to a wire rack to cool. Leave until completely cold before slicing. Any bread that will not be eaten within 24 hours is best frozen in slices (see page 24).

chestnut and buckwheat cheaty sourdough makes 1 loaf

This loaf is made with yoghurt in place of a traditional sourdough starter. The lactic bacteria make the bread more digestible, while the yoghurt's proteins help to soften the crumb, and the tangy flavour lends a slight sourness that is reminiscent of sourdough. Although chestnuts themselves are pretty dense, the flour makes surprisingly tender bread. The flavour can vary from sweet and nutty to smoky, so no two loaves will be quite the same. You need to add yeast to this dough to make it rise.

for the sponge
90g chestnut flour (or teff flour)
220g buckwheat flour
40g brown rice flour
30g millet grain (or quinoa)
100g live yoghurt
300g tepid water

for the sourdough
12g fresh yeast (or 4g quick dried)
50g ground almonds (or ground
   sunflower seeds or coconut flour)

40g tapioca starch
50g ground linseed
1 large egg
1 tbsp maple syrup or date syrup
   (or ½ tbsp brown sugar)
6g sea salt
Butter for greasing (optional)
Sesame or sunflower seeds for sprinkling
   (optional)

equipment
1kg (2lb) loaf tin

First, mix the sponge ingredients together in a large bowl, cover and set aside at room temperature for 6–12 hours. The longer you leave it, the more sour your loaf will be.

When you are ready to start the loaf, if using fresh yeast, mash it in a small bowl with a little of the wet sponge mix until it is completely smooth. Add back to the sponge bowl, along with the rest of the sourdough ingredients except the butter and sesame or sunflower seeds. Beat well with a wooden spoon or your hands until the mixture is completely lump free. If using dried yeast, beat into the sponge mix and set aside for 15 minutes, before adding the remaining sourdough ingredients.

Line the loaf tin with baking parchment or butter the inside and coat with sesame or sunflower seeds. Scrape the mixture into the tin and tap the tin to level the dough. Sprinkle with more seeds, if you like.

Leave to rise, uncovered, in a warm place for 1½–2 hours, until the dough has risen by about a third and little cracks appear in the top.

When the loaf is almost ready, preheat the oven to 220°C/Fan 200°C/Gas 7. At the same time, put a roasting tray on the bottom shelf and boil a kettle of water.

Very gently ease the loaf tin into the oven. If you tap or bang it at this stage it will collapse, as there is no gluten in the mixture to stabilise it. Pour boiling water into the roasting tray to half fill it; this will create a nice steamy atmosphere.

Bake for 20 minutes, then turn the oven down to 200°C/Fan 180°C/Gas 6 and bake for another 45 minutes, covering loosely with foil after 30 minutes to stop the bread from burning. The crust will be fairly dark on this loaf, so don't be alarmed by the colour.

To tell if your loaf is cooked, check that it has shrunk away from the sides of the tin a little and sounds fairly hollow when tapped on top. Leave in the tin for 5 minutes, then lift out the loaf and tap it to see if it feels firm. If not, put it back in the oven without the tin at 180°C/Fan 160°C/Gas 4 for another 10–15 minutes.

Transfer the loaf to a wire rack to cool. Leave until completely cold before slicing. Any bread that will not be eaten within 24 hours is best frozen in slices (see page 24).

baguettes makes 2

These delightful crusty, soft crumbed loaves are a departure from wholefood for me. It's just not possible to produce something like this without some rocket fuel in the form of potato starch. On the rare occasions when only something white and crusty will do, bake these baguettes. To shape them, you will need to treat yourself to a proper baguette pan.

for the sponge
140g sorghum flour
20g fresh yeast (or 6g quick dried)
240g tepid water

for the dough
45g salted butter, plus extra for
  greasing
270g potato starch
80g tapioca starch

1 tsp ground psyllium husk
1 tsp xanthan gum
110g egg white (3 large egg whites)
6g sea salt
2 tsp light muscovado sugar
1 tsp cider vinegar
Sesame seeds or rice flour for sprinkling

equipment
Baguette pan

First, mix the sponge ingredients together in a large bowl until smooth. Cover and set aside for an hour to ferment.

When you are ready to make the dough, melt the butter and allow to cool until tepid.

Sift the potato starch, tapioca starch, psyllium and xanthan gum together into a large bowl, then add the sponge and all the remaining ingredients except the sesame seeds or rice flour. Beat with a wooden spoon or your hand, or using a stand mixer fitted with the paddle attachment, until the mixture is completely smooth and forms a stiff dough.

Grease the baguette pan with butter and sprinkle generously with sesame seeds or rice flour. Place scoops of the mixture along the two loaf moulds and gently form into baguette shapes, leaving 2–3cm clear for expansion at both ends. Leave to rise in a fairly warm place until almost doubled in size, about 1–1½ hours.

When the loaves are almost ready, preheat the oven to 230°C/Fan 210°C/Gas 8. At the same time, put a roasting tray on the bottom shelf and boil a kettle of water.

Gently place the baguette pan in the oven. Pour boiling water into the roasting tray to half fill it. Bake the loaves for 15 minutes, then turn the oven down to 200°C/Fan 180°C/Gas 6 and bake for a further 20–30 minutes until golden, covering loosely with foil if they appear to be over colouring. They should feel firm underneath if you squeeze them.

Transfer the baguettes to a wire rack and leave to cool completely before eating. Freeze any you won't eat that day as they will be rock hard the next morning.

focaccia makes 1

From holidays in Liguria, I have fond memories of buying freshly baked focaccia, split and filled with cheese or ripe tomatoes, or simply soaked with good olive oil. This is my version – a bit crustier, but still delicious. Chestnut flour lends a sweet smokiness that mingles nicely with the olive oil. Pectin keeps it moist, but you could leave it out.

for the sponge
100g gluten free white flour
80g tapioca starch
40g maize or millet flour
40g chestnut flour
2 tsp ground psyllium husk
20g fresh yeast (or 7g quick dried)
280g tepid water

for the focaccia
150g potato starch
30ml olive oil, plus extra for drizzling
1 large egg
5g sea salt
2 tsp liquid pectin
1 tsp light muscovado sugar
Flaky sea salt for sprinkling

equipment
25cm square or round deep baking tin

First, mix the sponge ingredients together in a large bowl until smooth, cover and leave in a warm place for an hour to ferment.

When you are ready to make the dough, sift the potato starch into the sponge mixture and then add the rest of the ingredients except the flaky salt. Either squidge the mixture with your hands to remove all lumps or put the mixture into a stand mixer fitted with the paddle attachment and beat until smooth. It should be like a cake batter; add a little water if it seems too stiff.

Line the bottom of the baking tin with baking parchment and drizzle a little olive oil over the surface. Scoop the mixture into the tin and smooth gently. Set aside in a draught free place to rise until it has doubled in size, about 30–45 minutes. When the dough is almost ready, preheat the oven to 230°C/Fan 210°C/Gas 8. At the same time, put a roasting tray on the bottom shelf and boil a kettle of water.

Using a well oiled finger, press holes in the dough, all the way to the bottom randomly across the loaf. Re-oil your finger if it starts to stick. Drizzle olive oil over the surface of the dough, filling the holes with oil, then sprinkle generously with flaky sea salt.

Transfer the focaccia to the oven. Pour boiling water into the roasting tin to half fill it. Bake for 25 minutes, then lower the oven setting to 200°C/Fan 180°C/Gas 6 and bake for a further 20–25 minutes. Transfer the focaccia from the tin to a wire rack and leave to cool completely, before slicing or tearing. Slice and freeze any you won't eat that day.

almond flatbread makes 1

More closely resembling naan than a true flatbread, this has a pillowy, soft texture, thanks to the beaten egg white and baking powder. It's great for mopping up juices from curries and stews. Let your imagination run free with the flavourings – stirring chopped chives, coriander, parsley, garlic or caramelised onion into the mix – or serve them simply adorned with black nigella (or other) seeds.

Butter for greasing (optional)
Sesame seeds or poppy seeds for
   sprinkling on the baking sheet
   (optional)
4 large eggs, separated
20g ground linseed
100g potato starch

150g ground almonds, coconut flour
   or ground cashews
250g full fat Greek yoghurt
2 tsp gluten free baking powder
1 tsp sea salt
Nigella, poppy, cumin, fennel or
   sesame seeds for sprinkling

Preheat the oven to 200°C/Fan 180°C/Gas 6. At the same time, put a roasting tray on the bottom shelf and boil a kettle of water. Generously butter a baking sheet and sprinkle liberally with sesame or poppy seeds, or line with a sheet of baking parchment.

Put the egg yolks, linseed, potato starch, ground nuts or coconut flour, yoghurt and baking powder into a large bowl and beat with a balloon whisk or electric whisk until the mixture is smooth, pale and creamy.

In a large, clean bowl, whisk the egg whites with the salt, using a balloon whisk, electric whisk or stand mixer, until stiff peaks form.

Stir a spoonful of the beaten egg white into the almond mixture to loosen it, then carefully fold in the rest using a spatula, without knocking out too much air.

Spoon the mixture onto the baking sheet and gently spread into an oval or teardrop shape, about 2cm thick. Sprinkle with your chosen seeds.

Put the baking sheet into the oven and pour boiling water into the roasting tin to half fill it. Bake the flatbread for about 12–15 minutes, depending on thickness, until risen, golden and springy to the touch. This flatbread is best eaten within a few hours of baking.

teff pitta breads makes about 15

Pecan and teff make a warm, malty, moreish pair in these dark, chewy pittas. Pecan meal is rich and nubbly, giving the crumb a wonderful tenderness – if you can't buy any, just make your own in a food processor by blitzing nuts to a coarse meal consistency. Teff is a natural partner for most nuts, so try substituting Brazils for a creamy flavour or coconut for toasty sweetness.

for the sponge
20g fresh yeast (or 7g quick dried)
175g tepid water
115g white teff flour
60g millet flour
25g ground linseed

for the pittas
115g pecan meal (or other ground
  nuts, or oat flour)
60g tapioca starch
2 tbsp olive oil or melted coconut
  oil or melted butter

2 tbsp date syrup or honey
1 large egg
7g sea salt
½–1 tsp ground psyllium husk (if needed)
Butter or olive oil for greasing
Teff flour for sprinkling and/or shaping
Milk or water for brushing
Sesame seeds for sprinkling (optional)

equipment
4 large baking trays (2 will do at a push)

First, make the sponge. If using fresh yeast, cream it with a little of the water in a large bowl and then mix in the teff and millet flours, the linseed and the rest of the water. If using dried yeast, just add it along with the flours. Cover and leave to rest in a warm place for an hour to let the yeast develop and flours hydrate.

When you are ready to bake, add the pecan meal, tapioca starch, oil or butter, date syrup or honey, egg and salt to the bowl and squidge together with your hands or beat with a wooden spoon until completely smooth. Leave to stand for 10 minutes, to allow the starch and nut meal to absorb some of the water in the dough.

Your dough should still be soft but not unmanageable. If it is too wet to handle, add ½ tsp psyllium and rest again for a few minutes. If it still seems a little sticky, repeat with another ½ tsp psyllium. Your pittas will be tender if you work with a wetter dough, but you still need to be able to pick up a lump of it with floured hands.

Generously butter or oil the baking trays and sprinkle with sesame seeds or teff flour.

Make a pile of teff flour on your work surface. Scoop a large egg sized lump of dough out of the bowl with a spoon and plop it into the flour. Flour both hands well and gently place the floury ball into your floured palm. Pat to flatten a little, flouring your fingers if necessary, and then transfer gently to one of the baking trays. Pat the dough out to an oval, about 6–7mm thick, making sure the depth is even. Repeat with the rest of the dough, placing 3 or 4 ovals on each tray. The pittas won't expand hugely, so space them about 3cm apart. If you only have a couple of large baking sheets you can shape and bake the pittas in two batches.

Brush with milk or water and sprinkle with sesame seeds, if using. Put each tray into a large, roomy plastic bag, or cover lightly with oiled cling film. Leave in a draught free place to prove for about 1½–2 hours until the pittas start to look puffy.

When the pittas are ready, preheat the oven to 240°C/Fan 220°C/Gas 9. At the same time, put a roasting tray on the bottom shelf and boil a kettle of water.

Just before the pittas are due to go in, sprinkle them and the baking trays with water; this will help to form a nice thin crust.

Put the pittas into the oven. Pour boiling water into the roasting tin to half fill it; this will create a nice steamy atmosphere. Bake for 8–12 minutes, until the crust is just starting to turn golden brown around the edges. Don't over bake or you will have crackers. The pittas may well puff up in the oven, but don't be dismayed if this doesn't happen – there will still be a pocket for you to slide a knife into and spoon in a scrumptious filling.

Transfer to a rack to cool. These pittas are delicious warm, with a slick of creamy butter and a trickle of local honey. Freeze any that won't be eaten on the day and warm in the oven from frozen.

brioche makes 1 loaf

With a soft cakey texture and buttery goodness plumping every moist crumb, this is the bread to bake for birthdays and celebrations. If you have a yearning for French toast, want to make a legendary bread and butter pudding or just need some breadcrumbs for fish fingers, this is the one – nothing else comes close. Lactic butter really works best here, as it keeps its fresh, buttery flavour longer. Brioche is particularly delicious spread with yet more butter and some really good fruity preserve.

70g sorghum flour
60g rice flour
140g potato starch, plus extra
    for dusting
60g tapioca starch
4 eggs
10g fresh yeast (or 3g quick
    dried)
80g tepid water
30g light muscovado sugar
4 tsp psyllium husks
2 tsp liquid pectin

8g sea salt
150g unsalted butter (ideally lactic butter,
    see page 36), softened, plus extra for
    greasing

for the glaze and topping
1 egg, beaten
Pearl sugar for sprinkling (optional)

equipment
1kg (2lb) loaf tin (ideally tall and narrow)

Put all the ingredients except the salt and butter into a large bowl and beat thoroughly until completely smooth. Cover and set aside to rise at room temperature for 2 hours.

When the dough is ready, beat the mixture with a wooden spoon to loosen the structure and sprinkle in the salt. Now add the butter, a couple of teaspoonfuls at a time, beating well between each addition to make sure it is fully incorporated before adding the next. Alternatively, use a stand mixer fitted with the paddle attachment.

Put the dough into a clean bowl, cover with cling film and place in the fridge to prove slowly for 12–20 hours. This will also firm up the butter so that you can shape your loaf.

Once the dough has proved, generously butter the loaf tin.

Knead the crumbly dough briefly and then roll it out (between two pieces of cling film dusted with potato starch) to a rectangle, making the short side the same length as your loaf tin.

Roll the dough from a short side, using the cling film to help, forming an even sausage shape. Lift the dough with both hands and ease gently into the prepared tin. Leave to prove slowly at room temperature for about 2½–3 hours, until the dough looks puffy.

(continued overleaf)

When the brioche is almost ready, preheat the oven to 220°C/Fan 200°C/Gas 7. At the same time, put a roasting tray on the bottom shelf and boil a kettle of water.

Gently brush the surface of the loaf with beaten egg and sprinkle with pearl sugar, if you like. Pour boiling water into the roasting tray to half fill it. This will create a nice steamy atmosphere that helps swell the loaf and create a thin, crisp crust. Bake for about 40 minutes until the crust is golden brown and the brioche feels fairly firm at the sides.

Leave in the tin for 10 minutes, then turn out and place on a wire rack. Allow to cool completely before slicing. Any brioche that won't be eaten on the day is best frozen in slices (see page 24). Toast from frozen or use to make French toast (see page 68).

variation: **chocolate swirl brioche**

Prepare the dough and roll out as for the main recipe. Spread generously with chocolate hazelnut spread (about 250g), or sprinkle with 150g finely chopped chocolate and 75g finely chopped toasted hazelnuts and dot with 25g soft salted butter. Roll up, put into the tin, prove for the final time and brush with beaten egg as for plain brioche; if you like, you can slash the top of the loaf before proving to reveal the chocolate inside. Bake as above, but for just 30 minutes at 220°C/Fan 200°C/Gas 7, then turn the oven setting down to 200°C/Fan 180°C/Gas 6 for another 20 minutes.

breadcrumbs

Gluten free breadcrumbs are a great thing to stash in the freezer, ready to top gratins, add to meatballs, crumb fishcakes, or use in steamed puddings, including the marmalade pudding on page 219 and Christmas pudding on page 220. These are all good options:

sourdough breadcrumbs

You can make breadcrumbs from any of the sourdough loaves in this book. Either use fresh bread, or save crusts and offcuts in a labelled bag in the freezer for turning into breadcrumbs later.

If you want soft crumbs, cut off any crusts and don't toast the bread first; for heartier crumbs, leave the crusts on unless they are particularly tough. Lightly toast the bread to dry it out (this can be done from frozen), then cut into chunks and blitz to fine crumbs in a food processor. Store in a labelled bag in the freezer for up to a couple of months.

brioche, focaccia, baguette or scone breadcrumbs

These all make lighter crumbs that are softer and more absorbent than sourdough. Brioche crumbs are particularly good for fish fingers, although the others work well too. There is no need to cut the crusts off scones. Prepare as for soughdough crumbs (above).

commercial gluten free breadcrumbs

You can make your own breadcrumbs using shop bought gluten free bread. They are likely to be softer and gummier than crumbs made from your own bread, with less flavour, but they are OK at a pinch!

gluten free oatcake crumbs

Oatcakes make very fine and tasty crumbs that are super absorbent. Simply crush them in a strong plastic bag using a rolling pin, until the crumbs are fine enough. These work well for coating fishcakes or making cheesecake bases, but not in pudding recipes or gratins where liquid is involved.

oats

Gluten free oats are great for coating things like fish fillets, fishcakes and croquettes. These are best dipped into seasoned rice flour, then beaten egg and finally coated with oats for a wholesome crust.

ground almonds

You can use ground almonds in the same way as oats (above), but bear in mind that they will burn at a lower temperature than oats. Ground almonds are also great for extending meatballs, producing a softer texture and absorbing liquid.

pastry

Gluten free pastry has a reputation as a difficult beast – fragile to work with and crumbly in the mouth. It's true that my pastries do require a little more care than stretchy gluten filled pastry, but you can also roll and re-roll to your heart's content without worrying about toughening the dough, as there is no gluten network to develop. You may need to add a little more liquid than you are used to, and to rest the pastry for longer before you roll – to allow the flours to hydrate (overnight is ideal).

You will definitely benefit from rolling your pastry between two sheets of cling film or baking parchment dusted with a little tapioca starch. I use cling film for puff and for other pastries if I am lining a flan tin, but you can use either. If making a rich buttery pastry, you might not need to roll it at all, using your fingers instead to smooth the delicate pastry into a flan tin, or form a little pie in your hand.

I like to make pastry by hand so that my fingers can test the texture of the crumb, check for the right amount of water, and feel the character of the dough forming beneath them. Do, however, feel free to make pastry in a food processor or stand mixer if you like – just be careful not to process the butter too much. Precision is important with pastry, especially puff and choux. Using digital scales to measure your flours and liquids will ensure that you get the best results every time. To measure liquids, just put the jug onto the scales, zero the scales, and pour the liquid into the jug. In some recipes I give a weight measurement for egg. To measure whole egg or egg white, simply crack into a jug and whisk until lightly frothy, which will make it easier to pour just a little bit at a time when you weigh the egg.

The tarts and pastries that follow use one of five gluten free recipes: shortcrust pastry, chestnut pastry, almond pastry, choux pastry or buttery puff; you'll find these at the end of the chapter. I hope you will treat them as launchpads for your own floury journey. Why not swap shortcrust for chestnut pastry in a sweet tart, or make your pasties with puff? Forget what you know about standard wheat pastry and dive in.

You can buy gluten free puff and shortcrust pastries if you are too short of time to make your own. They won't have the same flavour and buttery freshness as your homemade version, but should work just the same. The advantage of making your own pastry is that you can choose the very best ingredients and avoid the gums and emulsifiers that are usually found in commercial products.

If time is often an issue for you, try doubling or tripling a recipe, and freeze the pastry in 2–3cm thick discs. Wrap each piece in parchment and seal in a freezer bag with the date on it. Most pastry will keep well like this for a couple of months, although puff starts to lose its flakiness after a month. Defrost your pastry in its wrapping in the fridge overnight and leave it at room temperature for 10 minutes before you roll it out.

puff pastry straws makes about 24

Layers of buttery pastry, topped with something punchy, these savoury straws are pretty much irresistible. You can choose your own flavour combination from the list of suggestions here: fennel seeds and caster sugar is my favourite, but thyme leaves and sesame seeds (illustrated opposite) comes a close second.

½ quantity puff pastry (see page 132), chilled
Tapioca or potato starch for dusting
1 egg, beaten (optional)

savoury flavours
Parmesan
Smoked paprika and sea salt
Turkish dried chilli flakes or nigella seeds and sea salt

Thyme leaves and sesame seeds
Caramelised onion

sweet flavours
Vanilla extract and caster sugar
Runny honey and sesame seeds
Fennel seeds and caster sugar
Ground cinnamon and caster sugar
Orange zest and caster sugar

Preheat the oven to 230°C/Fan 210°C/Gas 8. Line a baking sheet with baking parchment.

Roll out the puff pastry between two sheets of cling film dusted with tapioca or potato starch to about a 7mm thickness. Remove the cling film. Using a sharp knife or pastry cutter, cut into straws, about 15cm long and 2.5cm wide. Place them on the prepared baking sheet, spacing them at least 1cm apart.

If using vanilla extract, paint this over the straws and then brush with egg and sprinkle generously with caster sugar. Don't let the egg run over the sides, or they will stick together and won't rise into flaky layers.

If using honey, brush this over the straws, leaving a margin around the edge so it doesn't drip down and seal everything together. Sprinkle generously with sesame seeds.

For all other flavours, brush only the top of the pastry with beaten egg, taking care not to drip over the edges. Sprinkle with your chosen topping.

If your kitchen is warm, chill your straws in the fridge or freezer before baking.

Bake for 10–15 minutes until the straws are puffed up and starting to turn golden. Then reduce the heat to 200°C/Fan 180°C/Gas 6 and bake for another 10–15 minutes to cook through. The straws should be deeply golden.

Transfer to a wire rack and leave to cool. Eat within 24 hours, or crisp up again in the oven at 200°C/Fan 180°C/Gas 6.

devon pasties makes 4

Scrumptious served straight from the oven with a salad or two for supper, or eaten cold for a picnic or packed lunch, these pasties are the ideal way to use up leftovers. You can freeze the pasties uncooked – cook from frozen, allowing an extra 10 minutes or so.

1 quantity shortcrust pastry (see
   page 128), chilled
Tapioca or potato starch for dusting
1 egg, beaten, for glazing

for the lamb and pea filling
300g lamb mince (or cooked lamb)
1 bunch of spring onions, chopped
100g frozen peas

Grated zest and juice of ½ unwaxed lemon
100g Cheddar, grated, or feta, crumbled
A handful of flat leaf parsley, chopped
1 large egg yolk
Sea salt (optional) and black pepper

equipment
17cm plate, for cutting around

While the pastry is chilling, make the filling. Place a large frying pan over a high heat and add the lamb mince with a good few grinds of pepper. Cook, moving the mince around to break up any clumps, until it takes on some colour. Take off the heat and add the spring onions, frozen peas and lemon juice. (If using cooked lamb, shred, including some of the fat, and mix everything together; there's no need to defrost the peas.) Stir in the cheese, parsley and lemon zest. Taste for seasoning and add salt and more pepper if needed. Add the egg yolk and just enough water to give a moist filling. Leave to cool.

Preheat the oven to 200°C/Fan 180°C/Gas 6. Line a baking tray with baking parchment.

Divide the pastry in two. Roll out one half between two sheets of baking parchment dusted with tapioca or potato starch to a thickness of 5–6mm. Lift off the top sheet and cut the pastry into two circles, using a side plate as a guide, and a sharp knife. Peel away the excess, leaving the pastry circles on the parchment.

Make a little half moon shape of filling on one side of each pastry circle, leaving a 1.5cm margin around the edge. Don't be tempted to pile on too much filling. Dampen the edge with water. Put your hand under the paper and lift the empty side of the pastry up over the filling to bring the edges together. Press down gently, using the paper to help you. Crimp the pasty edges with a fork to seal. Repeat with the rest of the pastry and filling.

Lift the pasties onto the baking tray and make a few slashes in the top of each one. Brush with beaten egg and bake for about 30 minutes until the pastry is crisp underneath and nut brown around the edges; it should feel firm over the plumpest part of the pasty.

Serve the pasties as soon as they are cool enough to handle, or transfer to a wire rack once the pastry has firmed up a bit and leave to cool before serving.

sausage rolls makes 12

Sausage rolls are a great picnic treat. Keep some puff pastry on hand in the freezer and you can conjure up a batch at short notice. They work well with shortcrust, but puff has the edge in terms of flaky decadence. The sausagemeat filling is easy to make, but you can use gluten free sausages, removed from their casings instead – you will need 450g. The sausage rolls can be frozen uncooked; defrost them in the fridge before baking.

½ quantity puff pastry (see page 132)
   or 1 quantity shortcrust pastry
   (see page 128), chilled
Tapioca or potato starch, for dusting
1 egg, beaten, for glazing

for the sausagemeat filling
1 tsp lard or duck fat
1 onion, finely chopped
350g organic pork mince
75g breadcrumbs (ideally sourdough)
Ground allspice, grated nutmeg and/or
   ground cinnamon (optional)
Sea salt and black pepper

While the pastry is chilling, make the filling. Heat the fat in a frying pan. Add the onion with a pinch of salt and cook gently for 10 minutes until translucent, then leave to cool.

Mix the onion with the pork mince, breadcrumbs, ½ tsp salt, ¼ tsp pepper and a generous pinch of allspice, nutmeg and/or cinnamon, if using, until well combined. To check the seasoning, fry a morsel, then taste and adjust the main mixture accordingly – adding more salt, pepper and/or spices. Chill while you roll out the pastry.

Cut the pastry in two; wrap one piece and return to the fridge. Roll out the other piece between two sheets of cling film dusted with tapioca or potato starch to a 22–24cm square. Cut in half, using a sharp knife or pastry cutter, so you have two long rectangles.

Spoon a quarter of the sausagemeat down one long side of one pastry rectangle, about 2cm in from the edge. Dampen the opposite edge of the pastry with a little water and use the cling film to help you lift that side of the pastry up and over the filling, bringing the edges together; pinch them to seal. Roll up tightly in the cling film and place in the fridge to chill, while you make another three rolls in the same way.

Preheat the oven to 230°C/Fan 210°C/Gas 8. Line a baking tray with baking parchment. Unwrap the rolls, slice off the ends to neaten, then slice each into three and place seam side down on the baking tray. Brush with beaten egg. Make several diagonal slashes across the top of each sausage roll, almost through the pastry.

Bake for 15 minutes, then lower the oven setting to 200°C/Fan 180°C/Gas 6 and bake for a further 20–25 minutes. If in doubt, slightly over bake, so you don't get a soggy interior. Eat hot or cold; the sausage rolls will keep for a couple of days in the fridge.

garlic and mushroom choux buns makes 8

Once you have mastered choux, the world of retro dinner party food is your oyster. Savoury choux buns were popular in the 1970s and are due for a revival in my opinion. Meaty portobello mushrooms, chives and garlicky crème fraîche make a delicious filling. They are ideal to serve if you're entertaining vegetarians. For convenience, the choux buns can be baked ahead and frozen; defrost and crisp up in the oven for 5–10 minutes at 200°C/Fan 180°C/Gas 6 before filling.

1 quantity choux paste (see page 131)

for the filling
60g salted butter
4 garlic cloves, finely chopped
4 large portobello mushrooms, roughly
  chopped

300g full fat crème fraîche
A handful of chives or flat leaf parsley
  leaves, chopped
Sea salt and black pepper

equipment
Piping bag and a large plain nozzle

Preheat the oven to 240°C/Fan 220°C/Gas 9. Line a large baking sheet with baking parchment and dab a little choux paste under the corners to hold the paper in place.

Using a large piping bag fitted with a large plain nozzle, pipe the choux paste into 8 large buns on the baking sheet, spacing them well apart. Bake for 15 minutes, then lower the oven setting to 200°C/Fan 180°C/Gas 6 and bake for a further 15–20 minutes, until the buns are firm and crisp. Turn off the oven at this point.

Puncture the bottom of the buns with a skewer and return the upturned buns to the cooling oven for another 20 minutes or so to dry out.

Make the filling while the buns are in the oven. Melt the butter in a large frying pan, add the garlic and mushrooms and sweat gently until the mushrooms have softened; don't let the garlic take on any colour.

Transfer the garlicky mushrooms to a bowl and leave to cool slightly for a few minutes, then mix in the crème fraîche and herbs. Season with salt and pepper to taste.

Cut the choux buns almost in half, using a serrated knife. Spoon the mushroom mixture onto the bottom halves, dividing it evenly, and squidge the tops back on.

The choux buns are best served straight away. If they are not eaten within an hour of assembling, they will start to go soggy.

roasted tomato
pissaladière makes 4 large or 12 small slices

Topped with caramelised onions, anchovies and olives, pissaladière is a salty sweet, pastry based relative of the pizza. My version includes cherry tomatoes; it's also good with strips of roast pepper in place of the tomato and some thin slices of spicy saucisson. You could also add slices of mozzarella or grated Parmesan or Cheddar, if you like.

1 quantity shortcrust pastry (see page 128) or savoury almond pastry (see page 130), chilled
Tapioca or potato starch for dusting

for the topping
350g cherry tomatoes
75ml olive oil
Thyme or oregano leaves (optional)

A little butter or duck fat
2 red onions, sliced into rings
Roasted red pepper strips (optional)
Good quality tinned anchovies (optional)
Black olives, pitted and halved (optional)
Sea salt and black pepper
Basil leaves, to finish

Preheat the oven to 180°C/Fan 160°C/Gas 4. For the topping, lay the cherry tomatoes on a baking tray. Drizzle with the olive oil, sprinkle with thyme or oregano leaves, if you have any to hand, and season with salt and pepper. Roast for about an hour until the skins have burst. Set aside to cool a little. Turn the oven up to 200°C/Fan 180°C/Gas 6 if using shortcrust pastry; leave the oven setting at 180°C/Fan 160°C/Gas 4 if using almond pastry.

While the tomatoes are in the oven, heat the butter or duck fat in a frying pan over a low heat. Add the onions and sauté very slowly until soft and sweet. Set aside to cool a little.

Roll out the pastry between two sheets of baking parchment dusted with tapioca or potato starch until about 4–5 mm thick. Peel off the top sheet of parchment and lift the pastry onto a baking sheet, still on the parchment; there is no need to neaten the edges. Prick all over with a fork and bake for 10–15 minutes until pale golden.

Remove from the oven, but leave the pastry on the parchment. Spread the caramelised onions evenly over the pastry base, right to the edges. Spoon the tomatoes evenly over the onions and squash with your fingers or a fork. Add any optional extras: make a lattice with pepper strips or anchovies and dot with olives, if using.

Bake for another 15–20 minutes or until the topping is bubbling and the base is golden brown – err on the side of overcooking to make sure that the pastry is crisp all the way through. Cut into slices and serve hot or at room temperature, topped with basil leaves.

leek and bacon quiche serves 4

This quiche makes a great addition to a picnic or lunchbox and can be baked a couple of days in advance. Take the time to slowly cook the leeks so they become meltingly sweet – a wonderful partner for salty bacon and cream. Make sure your pastry case is well cooked before you add the filling – the bottom should be as crisp as the edges.

½ quantity shortcrust pastry (see page 128) or savoury almond pastry (see page 130), chilled
Tapioca or potato starch for dusting
1 egg, beaten, for brushing

for the filling
1 tsp duck fat or lard
6 rashers of unsmoked back bacon, derinded

50g butter
2 large leeks (white and pale green parts), well washed and chopped
5 eggs
200ml double cream
180ml whole milk
Black pepper (optional)

equipment
24cm loose-bottomed flan tin

Preheat the oven to 200°C/Fan 180°C/Gas 6 if using shortcrust, or 180°C/Fan 160°C/Gas 4 for almond pastry. Line the base of the flan tin with a disc of baking parchment.

Roll out the pastry between two sheets of cling film dusted with tapioca or potato starch to about the thickness of a £1 coin. Peel off the top sheet and invert the pastry over the flan tin, easing it onto the base and sides. Peel off the cling film and patch any holes in the pastry. Using a rolling pin or sharp knife, remove the excess pastry overhanging the rim. Prick the pastry all over with a fork.

Line the pastry case with baking parchment, to come above the edge of the case. Fill with baking beans or dried beans and bake 'blind' for 10 minutes. Lift out the baking beans and parchment. Brush the pastry case with beaten egg and return to the oven for 5–10 minutes until the base is cooked through. It should feel firm and the pastry should be golden. Lower the oven setting, if necessary, to 180°C/Fan 160°C/Gas 4.

Meanwhile, make the filling. Heat the duck fat or lard in a frying pan and fry the bacon rashers until they have taken some colour; remove and set aside. Add the butter to the pan. Once it has melted, add the leeks and cook until soft and sweet smelling, about 15–20 minutes. Set aside to cool a little. Cut the cooked bacon into strips.

In a bowl, beat the eggs, cream and milk until well combined. Stir in the leeks, bacon and some pepper if you like (the bacon will provide enough salt). Pour into the pastry case. Bake for 35–40 minutes, until slightly risen and light golden brown on top. It should still have a little wobble in the middle, but not too much or it won't set. Allow to cool slightly and serve just warm. This quiche will keep in the fridge for 2–3 days.

chocolate éclairs makes 8

Although a stack of profiteroles is impressive, I prefer the generosity of a gooey cream éclair, filled with temptation and lavishly topped with glossy chocolate. It is important to use a chocolate with a slightly lower cocoa solids content than usual, to avoid the icing splitting. Once you've mastered choux you can experiment with the fillings, just don't mess with the formula – something delicately luscious in the middle and a flavoursome slick of icing on the top.

1 quantity choux paste (see page 131)

for the filling
400ml whipping cream
2–4 tsp caster or light muscovado
  sugar

for the icing
125ml double cream
125g milk or dark chocolate (50–60%
  cocoa solids), chopped into small pieces

for the topping
Chopped pistachios and/or freeze-dried
  raspberries

equipment
Piping bag, a large plain nozzle and
  a small longer nozzle

Preheat the oven to 240°C/Fan 220°C/Gas 9. Line a baking sheet with baking parchment and dab a little choux pastry under the corners to hold the paper in place.

Using a large piping bag fitted with a large plain nozzle, pipe the choux paste into eight 13cm lengths on the baking sheet, spacing them at least 4cm apart and flicking your wrist a little at the end of each piped line to break off the dough. Dab a wet finger on the pointed end of each éclair so that it will be rounded once baked.

Bake for 15 minutes until the éclairs are puffed and just starting to colour, then lower the oven setting to 200°C/Fan 180°C/Gas 6 and bake for a further 10–15 minutes, until the choux is firm and crisp.

Pierce the side of each éclair a couple of times with a skewer to release the steam. Return to the oven for another 5 minutes and then turn the oven off, leaving the éclairs inside for another 10 minutes or so to dry. Transfer to a wire rack to cool completely.

While the éclairs are in the oven, make the icing. In a small pan over a medium heat, bring the cream almost to the boil. Take off the heat, add the chocolate and leave to melt for a couple of minutes, then stir. The consistency should be like thick double cream; if it seems a little thick, add 2–3 tsp boiling water and stir until the icing is glossy again. Set aside to cool a little, until thick enough to coat the éclairs without running off.

(continued overleaf)

Meanwhile, make the filling. Pour the cream into a bowl, stir in the sugar until it dissolves and then whip until softly thick. Put into a piping bag fitted with a small nozzle, or use a teaspoon to fill the éclairs.

When you are ready to assemble, cut each of the éclairs in half lengthways, using a sharp knife, and remove any soft pastry from the middle. Spoon or pipe the cream into the base of the éclairs. Dip the tops into the icing and gently press onto the cream filled bases. Sprinkle with chopped pistachios and/or freeze-dried raspberries.

Eat straight away, or allow the chocolate to set in a cool place, but don't leave it more than an hour before eating or the buns will go soggy.

variation: **dairy free éclairs**

For the filling, use 400ml chilled almond, hazelnut or coconut crème pâtissière (see page 137). For the icing, replace the cream with 80ml hazelnut or almond milk and 80g coconut oil. Make the icing as for the main recipe, but warm the milk and coconut oil together with a pinch of sea salt until the coconut oil is melted. There shouldn't be any need for boiling water. Note that dairy free icing will take longer to set. Fill and ice the éclairs as above.

chocolate and coconut tarts makes 6

A chewy coconut crust is a delightful foil for rich, smooth ganache. The crust for these little tarts will soften after a few hours if you make it with honey, but with maple syrup it will remain crisper. The dark ganache benefits from being chilled; if you can find carob molasses, it will lend a malty, salt-caramel gooeyness, but honey is good too. You could also fill the cases with fresh fruit and softly whipped cream. For convenience, the tart cases can be made ahead and frozen, then filled after thawing.

for the coconut crust
Butter or lard for greasing
150g desiccated coconut
1 egg white
100g honey or maple syrup
A pinch of sea salt

for the ganache
240ml double cream, or 150g coconut
   milk and 50g coconut oil
1 tbsp honey or 50ml carob molasses and
   1 tsp honey
180g dark chocolate (60–70% cocoa
   solids)

equipment
6 mini tart tins

Preheat the oven to 170°C/Fan 150°C/Gas 3. Generously grease the tart tins and put a disc of baking parchment in the base of each.

For the coconut crust, put all the ingredients into a large bowl and beat together with a wooden spoon until the mixture holds together. Spoon into the tart tins and smooth the mixture neatly over the bottom and up the sides, using the back of a teaspoon, to ensure you have an even layer all the way around.

Bake for 10–12 minutes or until the top edges are just turning light golden brown and the base of the tart cases feels set, but still a little soft. Let cool in the tins for a few minutes.

Once the crust is set, run a sharp knife around the edge of each tart to loosen the cases, then transfer them to a wire rack to cool completely. (The tart cases can now be frozen on a parchment lined tray, then packed into a plastic box and returned to the freezer.)

While the tart cases are cooling, make the ganache. Gently heat all the ingredients except the chocolate in a small pan over a low heat until the mixture is smooth and just steaming. In the meantime, finely chop the chocolate.

Remove the pan from the heat before the cream mixture starts to bubble. Immediately add the chocolate and stir until smooth. Pour the ganache into the coconut cases and leave to cool, then chill for an hour or so before serving. Eat within 48 hours of making.

date pastries makes 24 small pastries

These pastries, known as *kleicha*, are the national sweet treat of Iraq. When my brother-in-law married a gorgeous Iraqi woman, the table was piled high with fresh dates and pastries. Each pastry had been filled with spiced fruit paste and pressed into a beautiful mould so that it looked like a sea urchin, or lotus flower. My version is much less sweet than the real thing, but best enjoyed in the same way, with a small cup of strong coffee.

for the pastry
1 quantity chestnut pastry
  (see page 129), chilled
Chestnut flour or rice flour
  for dusting
Caster sugar for coating (optional)

for the date and cardamom filling
215g dried stoned dates
125ml water
75g salted butter
2–4 tbsp rosewater (strength varies)
15 green cardamom pods, seeds extracted
A pinch of sea salt

While the pastry is chilling, make the filling. Place the dates in a small pan with the water and butter. Bring to a simmer and cook, stirring, until the dates have broken down and absorbed the water. Add the rosewater a spoonful at a time, tasting as you go.

Grind the cardamom seeds with the salt to a powder, using a pestle and mortar. Stir into the date paste and check the consistency – it should be like clotted cream. Cook for a little longer if it seems too soft. Set aside to cool completely.

Preheat the oven to 180°C/Fan 160°C/Gas 4. Line a baking tray with baking parchment. Have ready a little bowl of chestnut or rice flour and another of caster sugar.

For apricot sized pastries, pinch off about a large teaspoonful of the pastry and roll gently into a ball, then roll lightly in the flour. Place the ball in your palm, poke your finger into it and start to pinch it with your finger and thumb into a little pinch pot. Work quickly, or the pastry will become oily. Flour your fingers and hand if anything starts sticking.

Put a scant teaspoonful of filling into the pastry and gently bring up the sides around it; use your fingers to stroke the pastry up over the top and pinch the edges together gently to close. Roll gently into a ball shape, then roll in sugar to coat if you wish. Place seam side down on the parchment lined baking tray. Continue until all the mixture is used up.

To decorate the pastries, take a skewer or cocktail stick and press it onto the surface to mark a star pattern. Bake for about 20 minutes, until they are golden brown and crisp, watching carefully to make sure they don't burn, as the sugars will caramelise easily. If in doubt, turn your oven down by 10°C. Transfer to a wire rack to cool.

The pastries will keep in an airtight container in a cool place for at least a week.

frangipane mince pies makes 12

A cut above your regular mince pie, these are deliciously succulent. If it's not the festive season, try replacing the mincemeat with some berries. Don't be tempted to make the pies in a smaller bun tray, as they need a generous amount of frangipane on top.

Butter for greasing
1 quantity sweet shortcrust pastry
   (see page 128) or sweet almond
   pastry (see page 130), chilled
Tapioca or potato starch for dusting
400g gluten free mincemeat

for the frangipane
100g ground almonds
40g potato starch
1 tsp gluten free baking powder

100g salted butter, softened
100g light muscovado sugar
1 tsp vanilla extract
2 eggs

to finish (optional)
Icing sugar for dusting

equipment
12-hole muffin tray

Preheat the oven to 200°C/Fan 180°C/Gas 6 if using shortcrust, or 180°C/Fan 160°C/ Gas 4 for almond pastry. Butter the muffin tray moulds and line the bottom of each with a disc of baking parchment.

Roll out the chilled pastry between two sheets of baking parchment dusted with tapioca or potato starch, dusting the pastry with more starch if it seems sticky. Lift off the top sheet. Using a 10cm cutter, cut out 12 circles. Lift the pastry circles from the paper with a palette knife and use to line the muffin tray moulds, pressing the pastry up the sides a little; it should just come to the top. Patch any holes and prick the bases with a fork. If the pastry is too soft to shape, chill it in the fridge first, for 10–15 minutes.

Bake the pastry cases for 12–15 minutes until starting to turn golden at the edge, then remove and set aside. Turn the oven down, if necessary, to 180°C/Fan 160°C/Gas 4.

To make the frangipane topping, sift the ground almonds, potato starch and baking powder into a bowl. Add the butter, sugar, vanilla extract and eggs, and beat well with a balloon whisk or electric hand whisk until light, smooth and fluffy.

Place a couple of teaspoonfuls of mincemeat in each pastry case. Spoon the frangipane over the mincemeat and bake for about 30 minutes until the frangipane is risen and firm to the touch. A skewer inserted into the frangipane should come out clean.

Leave in the tins for 10 minutes, then carefully run a thin, sharp knife around each tart to loosen it from the tin. Let cool for another 10–20 minutes to firm up before transferring to a wire rack. Serve warm or at room temperature, dusted with icing sugar if you like.

peach and almond turnovers makes 4

Make these turnovers when fresh peaches are at their best. During baking, the butter oozes out of the filling, turning the pastry base into a crisp and decadent foil for the juicy peach. They also work well with apples and blackberries, ripe pears and fresh figs.

1 quantity shortcrust pastry (see
   page 128), chilled
1 egg, beaten, for glazing
Caster sugar for sprinkling (optional)

for the peach and almond filling
4 ripe peaches
100g salted butter, chilled and diced

50g ground almonds
75g light muscovado or rapadura sugar
2 tsp vanilla extract

equipment
17cm plate, for cutting around

While the pastry is chilling, make the filling. Peel and chop the peaches into small dice; set aside. Put the butter cubes into a large bowl and add the ground almonds, sugar and vanilla extract. Turn gently with a spoon to coat the butter lumps with the almonds and sugar, separating them as you go. Add the diced peaches and turn to combine evenly.

Preheat the oven to 200°C/Fan 180°C/Gas 6. Line a baking tray with baking parchment.

Cut the pastry in two; wrap one piece and return to the fridge. Roll out the other piece between two sheets of baking parchment to a 5–6mm thickness. Lift off the top sheet of parchment and cut the pastry into two circles, using a side plate as a guide, and a sharp knife. Peel away the excess, leaving the pastry circles on the parchment.

Make a little half moon shape of filling on one side of each circle, leaving a 1.5cm margin around the edge. Don't be tempted to pile on too much filling. Dampen the edge of each circle with fingers dipped into water. Put your hand under the paper and bring the empty side of the pastry up over the filling to bring the edges together. Press down gently, using the paper to help you. Crimp the edges of the pasty with a fork to seal. Repeat with the rest of the pastry and filling.

Lift the turnovers onto the prepared baking tray and make a couple of slashes in the top of each one. Brush with beaten egg and sprinkle with a little caster sugar, if you like. Bake for 25–30 minutes, or until the pastry is crisp underneath and golden brown around the edges.

Serve the turnovers as soon as they are cool enough to handle, or transfer to a wire rack once the pastry has firmed up a bit and leave to cool before serving.

lemon and honey tart serves 6

I prefer the simplicity of pastry and lemon curd to a custardy lemon tart, where the cream rather takes over. The clean, sharp tang of lemon is soothed a little by the clover honey and butter into a delicate, floral lemon curd. If you use lactic butter it's even better, as it has an extra butteriness that really makes the lemon sing.

Butter for greasing
½ quantity sweet shortcrust pastry
   (see page 128) or sweet almond
   pastry (see page 130), chilled
Tapioca or potato starch for dusting
1 egg, beaten, for brushing

for the lemon curd
8 large egg yolks
A pinch of sea salt

150g clover honey (or other mild
   flavoured honey)
Finely grated zest of 1 unwaxed lemon
125ml lemon juice
50g caster sugar (optional)
225g cold unsalted butter, diced

equipment
20cm loose-bottomed flan tin

Preheat the oven to 200°C/Fan 180°C/Gas 6 if using shortcrust, or 180°C/Fan 160°C/ Gas 4 for almond pastry. Butter the sides of the flan tin; line the base with parchment.

Roll out the pastry between two sheets of cling film dusted with tapioca or potato starch. Peel off the top layer of cling film and drape over a rolling pin, cling film uppermost. Ease the pastry into the flan tin and then peel off the cling film. Gently press the pastry into the case and patch any holes.

Prick the base with a fork and trim off excess pastry with a knife. Line the pastry case with baking parchment and baking beans. Bake 'blind' for 10 minutes, then take out the parchment and beans. Brush the pastry case generously with beaten egg and bake for another 15–20 minutes until golden and cooked through. Set aside to cool.

For the lemon curd, in a bain marie or heatproof bowl over a pan of gently simmering water, stir together the egg yolks, salt, honey, lemon zest and juice. For a sweeter curd (this is quite tart), add the sugar. Whisk until it feels hot to the touch. Add a couple of chunks of butter, whisking constantly until melted. Continue adding the butter in this way, until it is all incorporated and the mixture is glossy and thicker.

Continue to cook, whisking constantly, for another 5–10 minutes or so until the curd is thickened; it will thicken further on cooling.

Pour the lemon curd evenly into the pastry case and leave to cool for at least 2 hours to firm up. You can refrigerate the tart, but the curd will have little beads of condensation on the top. Serve with crème fraîche or whipped cream.

blackberry bakewell tart serves 6

Cooking blackberries takes me back to my childhood and foraging along the hedgerows. Here, a jammy blackberry compote complements frangipane beautifully. For a summer version, use raspberries to fill, and replace the vanilla in the frangipane with lemon zest.

Butter for greasing
½ quantity sweet shortcrust pastry (see page 128) or sweet almond pastry (see page 130), chilled
Tapioca or potato starch for dusting
1 egg, beaten, for brushing

for the fruit filling
250g blackberries
Grated zest of 1 unwaxed lemon
40g light muscovado sugar, to taste
2 tsp cornflour, blended to a paste with 1 tbsp water

for the frangipane
100g ground almonds
40g potato starch (or an extra 25g ground almonds)
1 tsp gluten free baking powder
100g salted butter, softened
100g light muscovado sugar
1 tsp vanilla extract
2 large eggs

for the topping
20g flaked almonds

equipment
23cm loose-bottomed flan tin

Preheat the oven to 200°C/Fan 180°C/Gas 6 if using shortcrust, or 180°C/Fan 160°C/Gas 4 for almond pastry. Butter the sides of the flan tin; line the base with parchment.

To make the fruit filling, put the blackberries, lemon zest and sugar into a small pan and cook until the juices have run and started to reduce a little, 10 minutes or so. Add the cornflour paste and cook, stirring, until thickened. Set aside to cool.

Roll out the pastry between two sheets of cling film dusted with tapioca or potato starch and use to line the flan tin (as for the tart on page 122). Prick the base with a fork. Trim off the excess pastry. Line the pastry case with parchment and baking beans. Bake 'blind' for 10 minutes, then take out the parchment and beans. Brush the pastry case generously with beaten egg and bake for a further 5 minutes until golden and cooked through. Let cool. Lower the oven setting to 180°C/Fan 160°C/Gas 4, if necessary.

To make the frangipane, sift the ground almonds, potato starch, if using, and baking powder into a bowl. Add the remaining ingredients and beat well until smooth and fluffy.

Spoon the fruit filling into the pastry case, spoon the frangipane on top and level the surface. Sprinkle with flaked almonds and bake for 50 minutes, or until the frangipane is cooked. To test, insert a skewer into the frangipane layer: if it comes out with no wet crumbs clinging, it's done. Serve warm or at room temperature, with cream if you like.

pear tarte tatin serves 4–5

To make a tarte tatin with wheat based puff pastry, you can just drape it over the pears and chuck it in the oven. This method is different because the gluten free flours in the pastry are sensitive to moisture and don't crisp the same way when baked over steamy fruit. The secret is to bake the pastry and pears separately, assembling them afterwards. I like the pear halves all higgledy piggledy, with a few blackberries nestled amongst them if I have some. You may favour a neater approach with pear slices arranged just so.

- ½ quantity puff pastry (see page 132), chilled
- Tapioca or potato starch for dusting

for the pear topping
- 800g semi-ripe pears (about 4)
- 50g butter, plus extra for greasing

- 75g dark muscovado sugar
- 1 tsp vanilla extract
- A handful of blackberries (optional)

equipment
- 20cm round or square ovenproof dish

Roll out the pastry between two sheets of cling film dusted with tapioca or potato starch to about a 7mm thickness. With a sharp knife, cut a circle or square just 2mm smaller than your baking dish. Put the pastry on a baking tray lined with baking parchment and chill in the fridge while you prepare the fruit.

Peel, halve and core the pears. Melt the butter with the sugar and vanilla extract in a wide, lidded pan (ideally one that can fit all the pear halves in roughly one layer) over a low heat. Add the pears to the pan and put the lid on. Bring to a simmer and then turn the heat down low. Cook until the pears are just soft to the point of a knife, about 20–30 minutes, turning them over so they get an even soaking in the caramel.

Preheat the oven to 240°C/Fan 220°C/Gas 9. Arrange the pears cut side down in your baking dish. If you want to slice them, do so now and arrange neatly in concentric circles. If you have blackberries, pop them in any gaps between the pears.

Reduce the caramel a little if you need to – it should lightly coat the back of a spoon. Pour the caramel over the pears and cover with a buttered piece of baking parchment.

Bake the pastry for 15 minutes, then lower the oven setting to 200°C/Fan 180°C/Gas 6 and put the dish of pears into the oven too. Bake for another 20–30 minutes until the pastry is deep golden brown and crisp throughout. Take both the pears and pastry out of the oven and leave to cool until just warm.

Remove the buttered parchment from the pears, then place the pastry on top of them. Place an upturned plate over the tin and invert the tarte tatin onto it. Scrape any caramel left in the tin over the pears. Serve with cream, if you like.

shortcrust pastry makes 450g (1 quantity)

The secret to great pastry is to keep everything cold and use only your fingers – not palms, when rubbing in fat. There is no need to worry about overdeveloping gluten here, but you don't want to melt the fat into the flour and end up with a greasy lump. It might seem like a lot of ingredients, but the finished pastry is short, nutty and buttery.

You can pre-make a pastry flour mix by multiplying the dry ingredient quantities below, whisking everything together in a large bowl or bucket, then weighing out bags of 295g. Each of these bags will make up one quantity of this pastry – enough for two tarts or four pasties. Alternatively, make a few batches of pastry and freeze (see page 103).

80g rice flour
90g sorghum flour, buckwheat flour,
    chestnut flour or white teff flour
50g tapioca starch
70g ground almonds
2–3 pinches of sea salt

3 tsp ground linseed
1 tsp ground psyllium husk
100g salted butter, chilled and diced
1 large egg, beaten
3–4 tbsp cold water

Mix the flours, tapioca starch, ground almonds, salt, linseed and psyllium together in a large bowl. Rub in the butter with your fingertips, until the mixture resembles rough breadcrumbs – don't go so far that it looks like sand. Stir in the beaten egg with a fork.

Sprinkle in some water and toss the crumbs with your fingers. Continue to add water in small amounts until the crumbs start to form clumps as you toss them. Avoid kneading the dough or squishing it together too much, just turn the crumbs with your fingers to encourage them to absorb the water. You will need to make the dough wetter than for a standard wheat dough, as the flours and linseed will take up slightly more water. The texture you're after is a soft putty rather than a firm dough; it should be almost sticky.

Knead briefly and gently to bring together into a ball. Flatten between two sheets of baking parchment to about a 5cm thickness and chill for at least an hour – overnight is ideal, so that the flour can soak up the water and produce a much more pliable pastry.

If it seems at all crumbly when you come back to it after an hour, simply crumble it into lumps and add 2–3 tsp water before re-kneading. You'll get the hang of how much water to add after you've made a couple of batches. Err on the side of too wet rather than too dry and your pastry will hold together better.

The pastry freezes well for up to 2 months. Defrost overnight in the fridge and use chilled.

variation: sweet shortcrust pastry
Add 50g light muscovado sugar with the flours.

chestnut pastry makes 600g (1 quantity)

Chestnut has a melt in the mouth quality that you don't often get with such a deeply flavoursome flour. In pastry it can become a crisp tart crust, or when used to make the date pastries on page 118, it has a satisfying fudgy texture, a crisp exterior and a lovely taste, reminiscent of brown bread. You can make it savoury or sweet, but chestnut really does come into its own once you pair it with muscovado. The pastry will turn nut brown when it is cooked.

100g chestnut flour
60g rice flour
80g tapioca starch
100g light muscovado sugar
2 tsp ground psyllium husk

1½ tsp gluten free baking powder
4 pinches of sea salt
180g unsalted butter, softened
80g full fat Greek yoghurt

Using a balloon whisk, combine the flours, tapioca starch, sugar, psyllium, baking powder and salt in a bowl. Rub in the butter roughly with your fingertips, leaving a bit of texture.

Stir in most of the yoghurt with a fork and mash to a soft dough, adding the rest of the yoghurt if needed.

Wrap the pastry in cling film, squash into a thick disc and chill for at least 2–3 hours, or preferably overnight. (However, if you are lining a tart case, it is better to chill it after you have lined the flan tin, rather than before – simply spread the unchilled pastry in the tart case with the back of a teaspoon, rather than try to roll it first, then chill.)

If you need to roll out the chilled pastry, then do so between two sheets of cling film dusted with potato or tapioca starch, working quickly as the pastry will become sticky when it warms up.

The pastry freezes well for up to 2 months. Defrost overnight in the fridge and use chilled.

almond pastry makes 450g (1 quantity)

Almonds are wonderful in pastry, lending the centre a satisfying chew and crisping the outside much like a toasted nut. Coconut flour gives a chewier crust – I prefer mine made with desiccated coconut (see page 31). The pastry is easier to roll out between two sheets of baking parchment or cling film, dusted with tapioca or potato starch. If the pastry becomes sticky as you roll it, chill again once rolled flat and then line your tart, or squidge it into the case with your fingers. This pastry will work as an alternative to shortcrust in any of the tart recipes, but it is too delicate for pasties and turnovers.

for savoury pastry

270g ground almonds or coconut flour
40g arrowroot or tapioca starch
20g ground linseed
1 tsp ground psyllium husk
2 large pinches of sea salt
45g cold unsalted butter, lard or
  coconut oil
1 medium egg
2–2½ tbsp water

Sift the ground almonds or coconut flour, arrowroot or tapioca starch, linseed, psyllium and salt into a bowl and rub in the fat with your fingertips. Beat the egg in a separate bowl until frothy, then add just enough to the pastry mix with 2 tbsp water to bind and form a dough. Bring together using your fingertips or a fork to avoid warming the fat and knead the dough lightly. Add up to another ½ tbsp water if it is crumbly.

Chill the pastry for several hours before rolling out.

The pastry freezes well for up to 2 months. Defrost overnight in the fridge and use chilled.

for sweet pastry

250g ground almonds or coconut flour
50g light muscovado sugar
30g arrowroot or tapioca starch
20g ground linseed
1 tsp ground psyllium husk
A large pinch of sea salt
45g cold unsalted butter, lard or
  coconut oil
1 medium egg
1–1½ tbsp water

Sift the ground almonds or coconut flour, sugar, arrowroot or tapioca starch, linseed, psyllium and salt into a bowl and rub in the fat with your fingertips. Beat the egg in a separate bowl until frothy, then add just enough to the pastry mix with 1 tbsp water to bind. Bring the dough together using your fingertips or a fork to avoid warming the fat and knead the dough lightly. Add up to another ½ tbsp water if it is crumbly.

Chill the pastry for several hours before rolling out.

The pastry freezes well for up to 2 months. Defrost overnight in the fridge and use chilled.

choux paste makes 450g (1 quantity)

A simple white gluten free flour mix gives good results here. If you have some sweet rice flour, try using this as part of the flour mix – the high amylopectin content makes for the biggest puff. When you bake choux buns, make sure they are dry inside, as they may seem cooked and firm, yet still be full of doughy strands. If you squeeze a cooked bun and there is any squidge, put them back into a low oven to dry out. If in doubt, choose a sacrificial bun and check.

70g salted butter
130ml water
A large pinch of sea salt
A large pinch of sugar
110g gluten free white flour

1 tsp liquid pectin
140g beaten egg (about 3 eggs)

equipment
Piping bag and a large plain nozzle

Melt the butter in a medium saucepan over a low heat. Add the water, salt and sugar and bring to a gentle boil. Sift the flour onto a sheet of baking parchment. Take the pan off the heat and immediately tip in the flour all in one go, stirring vigorously as you do so. Beat until the mixture is fairly smooth.

Immediately return to a medium heat and beat until the mixture forms a sticky lump, leaving the sides of the pan more or less clean. You need to cook it for a minute or two at this stage to get the starch to gelatinise.

Transfer to a stand mixer fitted with the dough attachment, or a mixing bowl if using an electric hand whisk. Allow it to cool just a little until you can bear to touch it, but no more or it won't take enough egg to puff. Add the pectin, but don't stir it in just yet.

Beat the eggs again with a fork until lightly frothy, then add to the dough mix a little at a time, beating well between each addition until the mixture is smooth again. You may not need all the egg, so go carefully at the end, because a teaspoonful too much can make the difference between floppy choux and one that puffs. You are looking for a mixture that just drops off the spoon if you shake it – just a little stiffer than a cake batter.

Continue beating until the mixture is cold. (If you are making this dairy free, it helps to chill the mixture and give it another beat to firm up the fat.) You should end up with a choux paste that is smooth, elastic and pipeable, which has a very slight sheen. It needs to be used straight away.

variation: **dairy free choux paste**
Replace the butter with 60g coconut oil, lard or duck fat, plus a pinch of salt.

puff pastry makes 900g (1 quantity)

Puff pastry is a long process, so make it when you have a day at home and can return to it every couple of hours. The feeling of triumph when your misshapen dough packet starts to look like pastry makes it all worthwhile. The result is pastry that shatters under your fork into crisp buttery layers – not quite as soft and flaky as wheat puff, but very good nonetheless. Lactic butter works best here, as it doesn't melt so quickly. Puff pastry freezes well, so it's a good idea to make enough for a couple of recipes (as here) and freeze half for another time. You can use ground psyllium husk instead of xanthan gum, but you won't get such distinct layers and the dough will be crumblier to work with.

60g sorghum flour
60g sweet rice flour
50g rice flour, plus extra for
    dusting
90g cornflour
90g potato starch

40g tapioca starch, plus extra for
    dusting
¾ tsp xanthan gum
6g sea salt
330g cold unsalted butter (ideally
    lactic butter, see page 36)
170–190ml ice cold water

Make the dough first. Using a balloon whisk, combine the flours, starches, xanthan gum and salt in a large bowl. Cut 110g of the butter into dice and rub into the flour mixture, using just your fingertips, until the mixture looks like breadcrumbs.

Add most of the water, stirring with a fork, then use your hands to knead everything into a smooth, firm dough. Add more water only if it seems a little crumbly. If you add a little too much, just flour your surface with a little rice flour and knead the dough a little to firm it up. Squash the dough into a square about 3cm thick, wrap in cling film and put into the fridge for 15 minutes to chill.

Meanwhile, make the butter packet that will be encased in the dough. Lay out a sheet of baking parchment on the work surface and slice the butter into three or four pieces. Lay the butter in the centre of the parchment, sprinkle with 1½ tbsp rice flour and cover with another sheet of parchment. Bash firmly with a rolling pin until it is flattened. Lift off the parchment and fold the butter in half and in half again. Repeat the bashing a couple of times, sprinkling in any flour that escapes. Stop if the butter looks sticky or shiny.

Form the butter into a 15cm square and wrap in cling film. Return to the fridge for no longer than 10 minutes to firm up a little. You want butter that is soft enough to take the impression of your finger, but not spreadable.

To roll out your dough, lay a long piece of cling film on the work surface and dust with tapioca starch. Put the square of dough on top and cover with another layer of cling film.

(continued overleaf)

Roll the four corners of your square to form four flaps and flatten a square in the centre, about the size of your butter packet. The dough should now look like a flower with four petals, with a double thickness square in the centre. Your flaps (or petals) need to be long enough to wrap over the butter packet. Remove (and keep) the top layer of cling film.

Place the unwrapped butter packet in the centre of the dough and firmly fold each flap over, using the cling film to help you get a good tight fit. Repair the dough so that no butter is visible, by pressing and smoothing. Press the top of the parcel a couple of times with a rolling pin to stabilise it and then dust with tapioca starch.

Turn the parcel over, dust with tapioca starch, replace the top sheet of cling film and roll it gently into a rectangle roughly three times longer than it is wide. Start gently and keep dusting with tapioca as you go. Avoid pressing hard on any one area, so that you spread the butter inside the pastry rather than making a dent in the dough. As you roll, the pastry may crack along the edges, but pinch it together only if you see large bits of butter emerging. Work quickly to avoid the butter melting. Remove the top layer of cling film and brush off any excess tapioca starch with a dry pastry brush.

Now for your first turn. Fold the bottom third of the rectangle up to the middle using the cling film to help. Fold the top third over this. Press your little finger into the bottom right hand corner of the dough to mark one turn. If any butter is showing, chill your dough for half an hour or so before continuing, otherwise you should be OK to continue.

Turn the parcel 90° clockwise, so that the finger mark is on the bottom left. Roll and fold exactly as before to make the second turn. Make two little finger marks in the bottom right hand corner as a reminder. Wrap and return to the fridge for a couple of hours.

Take the pastry out of the fridge 10 minutes or so before you start rolling again. When ready, gently tap your rolling pin along the length of the packet a few times to help soften the butter before you start rolling. Continue rolling, folding and chilling, as above, until you have completed 6 turns. You should be able to do turns 3 and 4 together, but chill between 5 and 6, as the butter warms up quickly when it gets that thin. After the 6th turn, roll out the pastry until it is about 2.5cm thick, wrap in cling film and chill for at least a couple of hours before use.

When you use your pastry, take it out of the fridge 15–20 minutes before you roll it, so that it becomes pliable. Roll out to about a 5–6mm thickness. Cut with a sharp knife or pizza wheel; don't scrunch and re-roll the pastry. If your kitchen is warm, chill the cut pastry before you bake. Bake as suggested in the individual recipes, making sure that the pastry is cooked right through and a deep golden colour before you take it out of the oven, especially if it has moist ingredients on top.

Puff pastry freezes well for up to 2 months. Allow it to defrost overnight in the fridge and use chilled.

dairy free butter makes 390g (1 quantity)

Dairy butter is an emulsion of water in oil, meaning that tiny particles of liquid are suspended in the fat. When trying to substitute non-dairy fats, the problem is that natural fats still tend to be 100 per cent fat, with no water suspended in them. In puff pastry, you rely on the water in the butter to make steam, so pure coconut oil, lard or dripping won't give the right effect. This butter substitute has a similar fat profile to butter and includes some liquid suspended in the fat, emulsified with egg yolk. It melts more quickly than butter, so when you use it, keep everything well chilled and chill puff pastry between each turn, rather than every two turns. You can use this butter in other dairy free recipes, but coconut oil, lard or duck fat is often a more convenient substitute.

120g virgin coconut oil
270g lard or beef dripping
36g (about 3) egg yolks,
   lightly beaten

39g almond, rice or coconut milk
   (see method, second step)

Allow the fats to come to room temperature, or melt very slightly and cool until just set. The fats must not be liquid when you blend them with the milk and egg, or you won't get a good emulsion.

Make up the beaten egg yolks to 75g with the almond, rice or coconut milk, on your scales. In a food processor, blend the fats until creamy. Add half of the egg yolk and milk mixture to the fats and blend until incorporated. Scrape down the sides of the bowl. Add the rest of the egg yolk mix and blend until whipped and creamy looking.

Scrape the mixture into a small tub and chill until set.

crème pâtissière makes 550ml

Crème pâtissière is simply a very thick, eggy custard stabilised with some flour. Although milk is the classic base, it works well with tinned coconut milk for a dairy free version. You can flavour it with all sorts of things, but bear in mind that whatever you add to it must be the same texture as the crème pâtissière, or you'll make it runny. Add any flavourings after you've taken it off the heat. Once cooled, pipe the crème pâtissière into choux buns or sandwich it between layers of puff pastry or sponge. It's also great with the same amount of whipped cream folded through, for a rich custardy mousse filling.

400ml whole milk (or coconut
   almond or hazelnut milk)
4 egg yolks

50g caster sugar
1 tsp vanilla extract
45g cornflour

Heat the milk gently in a small pan until it starts to steam.

Meanwhile, beat the egg yolks, sugar and vanilla extract together in a bowl until well mixed. Add the cornflour and stir vigorously with the balloon whisk until the mixture forms a thick, pale orange paste.

Stand the bowl on a folded tea towel, so it won't spin around when you add the milk. Pour the hot milk slowly into the mixture, beating all the time with the whisk. Return to the pan and whisk constantly over a medium to low heat until the mixture thickens.

Scrape into a bowl and whisk again to make sure it is completely smooth. Lay a piece of cling film or buttered paper on the surface of the crème pâtissière to stop a skin forming as it cools.

snacks, salads and soups

Vegetables bring life to any meal, whether you roast them slowly until meltingly soft and sweet, whiz them into a dip to savour with some crunchy crackers or curate a paintbox salad. We thrive on variety in all things, but with vegetables this is especially true, as the more colour you can get on your plate the better you will feel. Our bodies long to follow the seasons, with light, crisp greens in the summer and sweet rooty veg in the winter. The more you follow nature in what goes on your plate, the stronger your innate sense of what feels good to eat, when, and how much.

Many gluten free grains are slow release, keeping you fuller for longer, and these are a great addition to your lunchbox. Wholegrain basmati, red Camargue, black Venus and wild rice are good alternatives to plain white rice. Buckwheat groats, red and pearl quinoa, millet and amaranth are even slower release and make great bases for salads – soak, cook and store flat in the freezer for instant access (see page 23).

Gluten sensitivity can go hand in hand with a need to go easy on grain based food such as bread and pasta – even the gluten free kind – especially when first diagnosed. Think about adding another portion of vegetables to your plate rather than cutting a slice of bread or adding rice. There are many ways to make vegetables interesting; for example, leftovers from the night before can be marinated in vinaigrette for an instant pickle to add to your lunch. Root mash of any kind makes a great accompaniment to a meal when formed into a patty and fried in a little butter.

For an instant increase in veg intake, try serving salads in the perfect cup of a chicory leaf or gem lettuce. Swap your sandwiches for quinoa salad or a hearty veg soup. In place of crisps and olives on your dinner party table, have some garlicky dips and irresistibly crisp crackers. Make too much of everything in this chapter – for hungry moments and busy weeks – and fill the freezer with vibrant soups that make an almost instant meal.

sea salt crackers makes about 40

These crunchy crispbreads are perfect for dipping into yoghurt or hummus. Fermenting the teff flour gives them a savoury wheatiness and they are irresistible with a sprinkling of sea salt, chilli flakes and/or seeds: sesame, cumin, caraway and nigella are all good. You can use gluten free white flour instead of the rice and tapioca combination, if you wish.

for the sponge
140g brown rice sourdough starter
  (see page 74), or 60g rice flour and
    80g live yoghurt
60g teff flour
90ml warm water
2 tbsp ground linseed (18g)

for the crackers
50ml olive oil
80g rice flour
60g tapioca starch, plus extra for dusting
15g muscovado sugar (optional)
6g sea salt
2 tsp ground psyllium husk
1 egg, beaten, for glazing
Flaky sea salt, Turkish dried chilli flakes
  and/or seeds for sprinkling

For the sponge, mix the ingredients together in a large bowl, using a wooden spoon, until smoothly combined, then cover and set aside at room temperature for 3–6 hours.

To make the crackers, add the olive oil, rice flour, tapioca starch, sugar if using, salt and psyllium to the sponge and mix well. Knead to a firm dough, adding a little water to bring it together if it is crumbly. Leave to rest for half an hour.

Preheat the oven to 200°C/Fan 180°C/Gas 6 and have a couple of baking sheets ready.

Break the dough into 3 or 4 pieces. Place one portion on a sheet of baking parchment dusted with tapioca starch and dust the dough with a little more starch. Cover with a sheet of cling film and roll out thinly, until the thickness of a 1p coin and almost as big as your baking sheet. Leave the edges irregular. Repeat with a second portion of dough.

Remove the cling film and lift the dough, still on the parchment, onto the baking sheets. Mark the dough into long fingers with a pizza wheel (or leave whole and break into shards after baking). Brush with beaten egg, then sprinkle with sea salt flakes and/or seeds.

Bake for 10–15 minutes until the crackers are crisp and golden brown, checking after 8 minutes. If they appear to be turning too dark at any point, but are still soft, turn the oven down slightly. They shouldn't be pliable at this stage, but they will crisp up more on cooling. If you rolled them a little thicker and they are still chewy, return to the oven at 180°C/Fan 160°C/Gas 4 to dry out for another 10–15 minutes.

Leave to cool on the baking sheets. Roll out and bake the remaining dough in the same way. Store the crackers in an airtight container and eat within a week or two.

courgette and macadamia nut hummus serves 4

Hummus simply means 'chickpea' in Arabic, and the dish we think of is more correctly known as *hummus-bi-tahina*. During a period when I gave up pulses to help heal my gut, I developed an insatiable longing for some garlicky hummus. I found this combination of courgette and macadamia nuts provided just the right fresh, clean, savoury flavour to satisfy that craving. Even if you can eat chickpeas happily, this is worth a try, as it's quick to make and delicious.

1 whole garlic bulb
6 tbsp olive oil, plus extra for drizzling
2 large courgettes
200g macadamia nuts (or cashews
  or Brazil nuts)

125g light tahini
2 tbsp lemon juice
1 tsp sea salt
Toasted cumin seeds, paprika or chopped
  parsley, to finish

Preheat the oven to 180°C/Fan 160°C/Gas 4. Cut the garlic bulb in half horizontally and place both halves, cut side up, on a baking tray. Drizzle with a little olive oil and bake for about 45 minutes until the cloves are soft. Leave until cool enough to handle.

Peel the courgettes if you would like a pale coloured dip like hummus, then grate; you should have about 200g grated courgette.

Put the nuts into a food processor and pulse until roughly chopped; do not over-process. Add the grated courgettes to the blender. Squeeze the soft garlic cloves out of their skins and add these too, along with the tahini, lemon juice and salt. Pulse briefly to combine, then with the motor running, add the olive oil through the funnel and blend until creamy. Taste for seasoning.

Scrape the hummus into a serving dish, drizzle with olive oil and sprinkle with toasted cumin seeds, paprika or parsley. Serve with sea salt crackers (see page 140), flatbreads (see page 94), pitta breads (see page 96) or raw vegetable sticks to scoop up the dip.

variations

pistachio hummus (*Illustrated on previous page.*) For a bright green version, use pistachios instead of macadamia nuts. Soak 200g pistachio nuts in water to cover for a couple of hours, then drain. Make the hummus as above, leaving the skin on the courgettes and adding a handful of flat leaf parsley leaves.

red pepper hummus For a sweet red hummus, replace half the courgette with 180g roasted and skinned red peppers – or the ones that you can buy ready prepared in a jar. This is lovely with toasted cumin seeds scattered over.

roast carrot dip serves 4

This bright orange, garlicky purée has the unctuous texture of hummus, yet it doesn't contain any pulses. Use it as a dip for vegetable sticks and breads, or spread on toast, stir into soup or spoon onto steamed vegetables. The rooty sweetness is also a perfect foil for spiced lamb meatballs (such as the Persian meatballs on page 190). The dip will keep in the fridge for a few days – if you can resist it that long. (Illustrated on page 141.)

5 large carrots
A glug of olive oil, plus extra for drizzling
A large pinch of sea salt
2–3 garlic cloves, roughly chopped
1 tsp cumin seeds or ½ tsp ground
   cinnamon

Grated zest of 1 unwaxed lemon
Juice of ¼ lemon, plus extra to taste
1 tbsp light tahini
½ tsp Turkish dried chilli flakes or
   a large pinch of hot paprika

Preheat the oven to 180°C/Fan 160°C/Gas 4.

Peel or scrub the carrots and cut them into rough chunks. Scatter on a baking tray, drizzle generously with olive oil and use your hands to turn and coat the carrots in the oil. Sprinkle with the sea salt, chopped garlic, cumin or cinnamon, and the lemon zest. Roast for 45–60 minutes until soft and starting to colour a little.

Let the carrots cool a little, then tip them into a food processor. Add the lemon juice, tahini, a glug of olive oil and the chilli flakes. Whiz until evenly combined and the mixture starts to become smoother. If the dip is too thick, add more olive oil and a little water. Taste and decide if you need more lemon juice, salt, chilli flakes, cumin or cinnamon, then purée until the mixture is as smooth as you like it.

Scrape the dip into a bowl and drizzle with olive oil to serve.

parmesan crisps makes about 24

These delicate, lacy wafers are like the best bits of cheese on toast – the bubbly, crispy bits. They partner a wintry squash soup wonderfully, and are great broken over a green salad. Of course, you can also enjoy them on their own as a snack.

160g Parmesan
80g breadcrumbs (see page 101)
   or oatcake crumbs

Turkish dried chilli flakes or black pepper
   (optional)

Preheat the oven to 190°C/Fan 170°C/Gas 5. Line two large baking trays with baking parchment. If you would like regular crisps, draw 12 circles, 8cm in diameter, on each sheet of parchment, then turn the paper over on the trays. (If the trays are not large enough to take all the wafers, you can bake them in batches.)

Grate the cheese using a fairly fine grater, but not one of those ultra fine Parmesan graters – you want a bit of texture. Mix the Parmesan and breadcrumbs together. If you like a bit of heat, add a few pinches of chilli flakes or black pepper.

Make flat piles of the mixture on the baking sheets inside the circles, or freeform if you prefer rustic anarchy. Make sure there are no gaps in the crumb mixture otherwise the wafers won't stick together.

Bake for 10–12 minutes, until the cheese has melted and started to turn golden; don't let it become brown. Leave the wafers on the trays for a few minutes to firm up and then transfer to a wire rack to cool. If they aren't crisp, pop them back in the oven for 5 minutes, but don't overcook or they will taste burnt.

For maximum crispness, the wafers are best eaten on the day they are made, but you can store them in an airtight container for a day or so.

quinoa salad serves 1

Quinoa salad is, for me, a lunchbox staple that changes with the seasons and whatever is in the fridge. This is less of a recipe and more a guide to quantities and method. Quinoa can be soaked, cooked and then frozen, or kept in the fridge for a day or two, so that you always have the base for a quick supper or packed lunch. Cook more veg than you can eat for supper to give you some to include in your lunch the next day. Keep feta, seeds, chorizo and veg preserved in oil to hand – to add flavour and variety to your salads.

for the quinoa
150g cooked quinoa
or
60g dry quinoa, soaked overnight in
    plenty of water
60ml water
A dash of vinegar or lemon juice
Sea salt and black pepper

for the protein
A handful of any of the following:
    cooked chicken, roast beef or roast
    lamb, ham, tuna, sardines, anchovies,
    chickpeas, Puy lentils, butter beans,
    chorizo, hard-boiled eggs or feta

for the veg
2 handfuls of any of the following:
raw cucumber, peppers, tomatoes,
    celery, baby spinach, watercress,
    rocket, radishes, grated carrot and
    beetroot, onion, garlic, cauliflower
    florets, mushrooms, bean sprouts,
    micro greens

roast carrots, parsnip, beetroot,
    courgette, aubergine, pepper, cherry
    tomatoes, squash
steamed peas, green beans, runner beans,
    broad beans, broccoli, sweetcorn, sweet
    potato, squash
pickled radishes, garlic, beetroot, onions,
    sauerkraut, cornichons, capers, olives,
    gherkins
preserved in oil artichoke hearts, peppers,
    mushrooms, tomatoes

for the herbs
Rocket, basil, parsley, dill, coriander,
    chives, mint, thyme leaves and flowers,
    oregano, leaves and flowers, marigold
    flowers, borage flowers, nasturtium
    leaves and flowers, fennel tops and
    flowers

for the dressing
Olive oil
Lemon juice or cider vinegar

If using soaked, dry quinoa, then drain and wash well in a sieve under cold running water until no froth appears. Tip into a saucepan and add the water and vinegar or lemon juice. Bring to the boil, cover tightly and turn the heat down. Cook for 10–15 minutes, until all the water is absorbed and the grain is soft. Leave covered for 5–10 minutes, then fluff up with a fork. If using frozen quinoa for a lunchbox, just add it frozen – no need to thaw.

(continued overleaf)

Next decide on your protein source – a handful should be about right. Use something that you had the night before shredded, flaked or chopped, and/or crumble in some feta or add a few chunks of chorizo. Puy lentils, beans or a couple of chopped hard-boiled eggs are good options too.

Now choose your veg, ideally something in season – just over two large handfuls will be about right. Roast veg are a deliciously sweet and soft option. Fresh herbs will add both interest and nutrients.

Chop or slice your veg and protein and combine with the quinoa in a bowl. Season with salt and pepper, bearing in mind whether you've added feta, anchovies, olives or other salty things. Liberally dress with olive oil and either lemon juice or vinegar, or shake up a vinaigrette in a little jar. If you are using leaves and flowers, you might want to leave these separate until the last minute.

If your quinoa salad is destined for a lunchbox, pack it into a tightly sealing container, to avoid oil leaking out. Otherwise, arrange the salad on individual plates or a large platter.

note

If you have leftover steamed veg one day, you can make instant pickles for tomorrow's lunchbox by shaking together 1 part vinegar and 2 parts olive oil, pouring this over them and refrigerating for up to 3 days. A little chopped raw onion, a sliver of garlic or a few chives also provide a nice bit of flavour.

russian salad serves 4

I make this colourful salad all year round in various guises, depending on what is in season: asparagus and watercress in spring; young broad beans, marigold petals, mint and cucumber in the summer; roast squash and sweetcorn in the autumn. Vary the herbs as you like and choose whatever allium is in season: red onion, spring onion, chives or wild garlic. I like to spoon the salad into chicory leaves to serve as a canapé or starter.

450g waxy salad potatoes
150g frozen peas (a large mugful)
¼ red onion or 3–4 spring onions,
   finely chopped
A small handful of dill leaves, finely
   chopped, plus extra sprigs to garnish
3–4 tbsp mayonnaise, crème fraîche
   or full fat Greek yoghurt

A squeeze of lemon juice
150g cooked beetroot, roughly sliced
   or diced
100g radishes, halved or quartered
Sea salt and black pepper
16–20 crisp chicory leaves, to serve
   (optional)

Bring a pan of water to the boil and add the potatoes. Cook until tender to the point of a knife, about 15 minutes. Drain and allow to cool completely.

Bring a small pan of water to the boil, add the peas and bring back to the boil as quickly as possible. Drain and refresh in cold water to keep the colour. Drain and put into a bowl.

Add the chopped onion(s) and dill to the peas. Cut the cold potatoes into smallish dice and add these too. Stir in the mayonnaise, crème fraîche or yoghurt and a squeeze of lemon juice. Taste for seasoning and add salt and pepper if you like.

Add the beetroot and radishes to the bowl and turn gently, just enough to incorporate, but not enough to turn the whole thing candy floss pink.

Spoon the salad into chicory leaves to serve, if you like. Arrange on a large plate, sprinkle with pepper and garnish with dill sprigs.

winter slaw serves 4

The vibrant colours, fresh crunch and sharp barberries in this salad make it highly appealing. Packed with vitamin C and healthy antioxidants, it is just the thing to counter any overindulgence during the party season. I sometimes add a couple of spoonfuls of kimchi or pickled vegetables to mine for a piquant kick.

½ small red cabbage
¼ red onion, finely chopped
2 carrots
½ pomegranate
A handful of flat leaf parsley, leaves
   picked
50g currants
15g dried barberries (or unsweetened
   dried cranberries or dried cherries)

for the dressing
3 tbsp extra virgin olive oil
1 tbsp lemon juice
Sea salt and black pepper

Slice the cabbage into very fine, long slivers with a sharp knife and put into a bowl with the chopped onion. Peel the carrots, then use the peeler to pare long thin ribbons of carrot and add these to the bowl. (You may not be able to make the whole thing into ribbons – just eat the bit left at the end.)

Loosen the skin of the pomegranate a little by pulling it apart with your fingers. Then hold it, cut side down, over a separate bowl and bash with a wooden spoon until all the seeds fall out. Discard any bitter pith.

Add half of the pomegranate seeds to the bowl of cabbage and carrot, along with the parsley, currants and dried berries or cherries.

Put the olive oil and lemon juice into a small screw-topped jar. Add a pinch of salt and a few grinds of pepper, then put the lid on and shake well until the dressing emulsifies. Taste and add more lemon juice or seasoning, if required.

Just before serving, pour the dressing over the salad and toss gently to coat, then sprinkle with the remaining pomegranate seeds.

green tabouleh serves 4–6

It's so simple to replace bulgur wheat with quinoa in this traditional Middle Eastern herb salad, which makes a flavoursome addition to a mezze style meal. It's also a lovely foil for rich meats like lamb. Tabouleh can be made purely with parsley, so if you don't have all the other herbs, make it anyway. The main thing is to use only a little quinoa, to ensure the salad is vibrantly green, which is its defining characteristic. If you have a pomegranate to hand, sprinkle the ruby seeds over the salad for a burst of tart flavour.

120g quinoa
120ml water
A squeeze of lemon or a dash of vinegar
20cm piece of cucumber
4 spring onions, finely sliced
20g mint leaves
30g coriander leaves
30g parsley leaves
40g watercress

for the dressing
Juice of 2 limes
100ml olive oil
4 pinches of sea salt

to finish (optional)
1 pomegranate

Soak the quinoa overnight in water to cover generously. When you are ready to cook it, wash the quinoa in a sieve under cold running water until no froth appears.

Put the quinoa and water into a small pan with a tight fitting lid. Add a squeeze of lemon or a dash of vinegar, bring to the boil and then reduce the heat to a simmer. Cook for 10–15 minutes until the water is absorbed and then take off the heat. Leave the quinoa in the covered pan to steam for a further 10 minutes. Tip out onto a plate and fluff with a fork. Set aside to cool completely.

Halve the cucumber lengthways, scoop out the seeds with a teaspoon and dice the flesh. Place in a large bowl with the spring onions. Roughly chop the herbs and add to the bowl.

For the dressing, shake the ingredients in a screw-topped jar or whisk together in a bowl to emulsify.

Add the cooled quinoa to the other ingredients with the dressing and turn with your hands or a large spoon, until everything is combined.

If you have a pomegranate, cut it in half, extract the seeds (as described on page 150) and sprinkle these over the tabouleh. Serve straight away.

creamy squash soup serves 4

A good chicken stock turns the dense flesh of winter squash into a wonderful velvety soup. Bay leaves are often thrown into stock without a second thought, but they do impart a deliciously subtle flavour all of their own. I like to crumble some salty feta into the soup at the table and sprinkle on a spoonful of cumin, sesame or fennel seeds, toasted in a dry pan. A swirl of Greek yoghurt, some crispy bacon or even a handful of grated Cheddar are all delicious additions.

2 heaped tsp butter, coconut oil or
   duck fat
1 large onion, roughly chopped
4 carrots, diced
400g peeled and deseeded squash
   (about ½ medium acorn, kabocha or
   butternut)

2–3 bay leaves
1.5 litres chicken stock (see page 161)
Sea salt and black pepper

to finish (optional)
A chunk of feta
Toasted cumin, sesame or fennel seeds

Melt the fat in a medium saucepan over a low heat. Add the onion and cook gently, stirring occasionally, for a couple of minutes. Add the carrots to the pan with a pinch of salt. Cook gently, stirring from time to time, until the onions have started to turn a deep golden colour. This could take up to 20 minutes, but it's worth it.

In the meantime, roughly chop the squash into cubes. Add to the pan with the bay leaves, then pour in the stock and bring to the boil. Put the lid on and simmer gently until the squash and carrots are tender, about 15 minutes.

Take out the bay leaves and allow the soup to cool a little, if using a freestanding blender. Tip the soup into your blender (or use a stick blender in the pan), and blitz until velvety smooth. You might want to keep back some of the stock, in case the soup is a little too thin, or add a little boiling water after blending if it seems too thick. Taste for seasoning and add some salt and/or pepper if you think it needs it.

Pour the soup into warmed bowls. Crumble in some feta and sprinkle with toasted cumin, sesame or fennel seeds if you like, before serving.

spring soup serves 4

The period from March to early May is often called the hungry gap. When we had to rely only on what could be grown locally, this was the time of year when you longed for the first shoots of spring to blossom into something edible. Sprouting broccoli and a handful of frozen peas transform this from a winter broth into something fresh and invigorating. If you have any fresh herbs to add, all the better. Make sure you sweat the roots until they are caramel sweet, and keep the green veg as *al dente* as possible.

¾ medium celeriac
3 medium potatoes
4 carrots
2 celery sticks
4 tsp salted butter or olive oil
1 leek (white part only) or ½ onion, finely chopped
1 bay leaf

1 litre chicken or beef stock (see page 161) or ready made stock
350g shredded cooked meat (chicken, turkey, beef, lamb, pork, ham, rabbit, venison)
125g purple sprouting broccoli tops
A mugful of frozen peas
Sea salt and black pepper

Peel and chop the celeriac, potatoes and carrots into 1cm dice. Cut the celery sticks into 1cm pieces.

Heat the butter or olive oil in a large saucepan and add the celeriac, potatoes, carrots, celery, leek or onion and the bay leaf. Sweat gently, stirring occasionally, for about 10 minutes until the celery is translucent and the vegetables smell sweet.

Pour in the stock and bring to the boil. Lower the heat and cook until the vegetables are tender. Add the shredded meat and bring back to the boil, then the add sprouting broccoli and peas. Return to a simmer and cook just until the broccoli stems are *al dente*.

Season with salt and pepper to taste (you won't need any salt if your stock is salted). Add more stock if you think it needs it.

Serve the soup straight away in warmed bowls, while the peas and sprouting broccoli are still bright green.

variation: **vegetarian spring soup**
Make a vegetable stock with carrot and potato peelings, roots of onions, tops of leeks, dried mushrooms and some herbs – this only needs to be simmered for an hour or so. Instead of the shredded meat, add butter beans, flageolet beans or tempeh, and float a poached egg on each portion when you serve the soup.

easy pea soup serves 4

If you have fresh peas in your garden, use them to make this vibrant green soup. Shop bought peas in a pod, on the other hand, tend to be a disappointment, as their sugars turn to starch soon after picking and they lack flavour. Frozen peas are the answer – choose a good brand and they will be sweeter and more tender. You could substitute mint for the basil and dress up the bowl as much as you like – with crumbled feta (as shown), Greek yoghurt and/or extra virgin olive oil.

2 courgettes
4 tsp salted butter or olive oil
Grated zest of 1 unwaxed lemon
2 garlic cloves, roughly chopped
560ml boiling water
600g frozen peas
A few ice cubes
A squeeze of lemon juice

A big handful of fresh basil leaves,
    plus extra to finish
Sea salt and black pepper

to finish (optional)
Feta, Greek yoghurt and/or extra virgin
    olive oil

Finely chop the courgettes. Heat the butter or olive oil in a saucepan, add the courgettes with the lemon zest and sauté gently until transparent. Add the garlic to the pan and cook, stirring, for a few minutes until it starts to soften.

Pour in the boiling water and bring back to the boil. Add the frozen peas and let them come back to the boil, then remove from the heat almost immediately –when the peas are just tender and still bright green.

Throw in a few ice cubes to cool the soup down a bit and sit the pan in a bowl of cold water to stop the cooking process. Leave for 10 minutes or so to cool a little. Don't let the soup go completely cold, or you may overcook the peas when you heat it up again.

Tip the soup into a blender and add the lemon juice, basil leaves and a pinch of salt. Process until velvety smooth. Taste and decide whether it needs more basil, lemon and/ or salt. If it's too thick, then add a little boiling water.

When the flavour and consistency are just right, pour the soup back into the pan and bring very gently back up to serving temperature again. Divide between warmed bowls. Add some crumbled feta, a swirl of yoghurt and/or a drizzle of extra virgin olive oil if you wish. Finish with basil leaves and a generous grinding of pepper.

chestnut and chorizo soup serves 4

The chestnut season lets you know that autumn is in full swing. Roast chestnuts have the starchy quality of a baked potato, with a smoky sweetness that is fantastic with chorizo. You can also use pre-prepared chestnuts here, for something that is almost as good. If you need more protein, a poached or fried egg is a great addition.

400g fresh chestnuts (in shells)
125g chorizo or spicy salami, skinned
1 tsp butter or duck fat
A pinch of fennel seeds (optional)
4 carrots, roughly diced
1 large onion, roughly diced
1 celery stick, roughly diced
150g Swiss chard or rainbow chard

3 garlic cloves, finely chopped
2 sprigs of thyme, leaves picked
1 tbsp tomato purée
A large pinch of saffron threads

To finish (optional)
Greek yoghurt
Turkish dried chilli flakes

Preheat the oven to 220°C/Fan 200°C/Gas 7.

Make a cut in the top of each chestnut and roast in the oven for 15–20 minutes until tender. Leave until cool enough to handle, then peel, halve or quarter and set aside. (It's a lot quicker to use pre-prepared chestnuts, but you won't get the same smoky flavour.)

Cut the chorizo or salami into small chunks. Heat a saucepan over a low heat and add the chorizo chunks with the butter or duck fat and fennel seeds, if using. Cook gently for a few minutes until the chorizo oil starts to run. Add the diced veg and sauté gently for at least 20 minutes until they have taken on a deeper colour and smell sweet.

While the vegetables soften, slice the white stalk from the chard leaves and cut it into chunks; set aside. Shred the leaves finely and set these aside too.

Add the garlic to the pan with the thyme leaves and tomato purée and cook for a couple of minutes until the tomato smell rises from the pan. Add the chopped chestnuts, chard stalks, saffron threads and enough boiling water to cover everything by 2–3cm.

Bring to a simmer, put the lid on and lower the heat. Simmer gently for about 15 minutes until everything is soft. Taste for seasoning. Either leave the soup chunky or mash it a bit, leaving some texture – you're not aiming for a smooth result. If it's too thick, add a little water; if too thin, uncover, turn the heat up a bit and let bubble to reduce slightly.

Finally, add the chard leaves to the soup and bring back to the boil; this will be enough to cook them through.

Serve each portion topped with a spoonful of Greek yoghurt, if you like. If the chorizo is mild you may want to put some chilli flakes on the table.

oxtail soup serves 4

Oxtail needs to be cooked for a long time to break down all those delicious connective tissues into a velvety soup. This is a classic winter warmer, hearty enough to serve as a supper, with some buttery sourdough toast on the side. Risotto rice does the job of pearl barley here, adding a little pleasant texture and creaminess to an already succulent feast.

2 heaped tsp duck fat
850g–1kg oxtail pieces
2 heaped tsp butter or duck fat
3 medium carrots, diced
2 celery sticks, diced
2 leeks (white and pale green parts
   only), diced
A pinch of ground cinnamon
2 sprigs of rosemary

A few sprigs of thyme
2 bay leaves
700g jar passata
150ml red wine
750ml chicken stock (see right) or water
30g risotto or paella rice
Sea salt and black pepper
Chopped parsley, to finish

Heat the duck fat in a large saucepan and brown the oxtail pieces, in batches, on all sides. Remove and set aside.

Add the butter or duck fat to the pan. Once it has melted, add all the vegetables with the cinnamon and sauté gently until the leeks are translucent and everything is softened and coloured, about 10 minutes.

Add the herbs, oxtail, passata, wine, stock or water and a generous grinding of pepper. Bring to the boil, cover and simmer for 2–3 hours, until the meat is tender.

Add the rice and some salt. Cover and cook gently for another 45 minutes or so, until the rice is very soft.

Take out the oxtail and, when cool enough to handle, pick all the meat off the bones. Return the meat to the soup and heat through.

Ladle the soup into warmed bowls and sprinkle with a little chopped parsley to serve.

real stock makes about 1.5 litres

Use this nourishing stock to make your soups and they will taste deeply savoury, and have a velvet quality that comes from a slowly simmered bone broth. A cup of stock with an added pinch of sea salt is a much better nightcap than a tot of whisky, as the stock contains magnesium which helps to relax tense muscles and send you off to sleep. You don't have to include all of the vegetables listed here, but add at least a few of them.

Meat bones, either raw or leftover:
1–2 chicken carcasses, or 4–5 beef or lamb bones (plus any giblets, cartilage and skin)
2 bay leaves (or rosemary or thyme for lamb stock)
About 2 litres water
A capful of cider vinegar or white wine vinegar
Black pepper

for the vegetables
1 celery stick
1 carrot
½ onion
1 leek (green part)
Any soft root vegetables

If your carcasses or bones are raw, preheat the oven to 200°C/Fan 180°C/Gas 6 and put the bones into a large roasting tray. Roast them for 30–40 minutes, or until they start to take on a lovely golden colour and smell delicious. Bones from a roast dinner can just go straight in the saucepan (any germs will be killed during the long boil).

Put the bones, any giblets, cartilage, skin and bay leaves into a pan large enough to take everything and leave at least 5–7cm clear at the top. Roughly chop the vegetables and add to the pan. Pour in enough cold water to just cover everything. Add the vinegar and a good few twists of black pepper and bring to the boil.

Reduce the heat to a trembling simmer, cover with a tight fitting lid and simmer for at least 6 hours. I tend to make my stock after the evening meal, allow it to simmer all evening, turn it off and leave it to cool slowly overnight and then give it a few hours the next morning. If you can't boil it again until the next evening, put it into the fridge for the day and complete the stock in the evening. Always re-boil the stock if you have left it to cool in this way to ensure that it is bacteria free. Don't undercook it or the gelatine and minerals from the bones won't leach out.

When it is ready, strain the stock through a sieve into a large bowl and discard the bones and vegetables. Pour the stock into glass jars, put the lids on and refrigerate when cool. Alternatively, allow the stock to cool and then pour into freezer bags or ice cube trays for freezing. The stock keeps for up to 5 days in the fridge, or 3 months in the freezer.

simple meals

In our family, everyone eats gluten free. My son Finn and I both have coeliac disease and, although my husband could happily chomp through a loaf of bread if he wanted to, he doesn't feel the need to eat differently.

I mostly like to eat simple food. Some well chosen meat or fish and a plate full of tasty vegetables is my idea of heaven. However, there are times when you want something a little different – some fish fingers to dip into ketchup or a pizza for Friday night. Rather than offer you a bunch of inherently gluten free meals, I've provided some novel ways for you to get your carby fix in this chapter.

A meal is not a meal unless it comes with a pile of vegetables – or at least contains them. Most of the recipes in this chapter will benefit from a few portions of veg alongside. I like to butter mine, or drizzle them with olive oil. Sometimes I'll toss them with pesto or crème fraîche, or shave Parmesan over the top. You might like to douse yours in gravy or roast them gently in the oven with olive oil and anchovies.

Raw vegetables, meanwhile, can come to life with a zingy dressing or some toasted seeds. There are many ways to make vegetables the centrepiece of a meal...

squash risotto serves 4

This golden risotto is the kind of gentle carb fest you need after a hard day on your feet. I like it equally made with chicken stock or creamy almond milk. A little bay and nutmeg bring out the nutty flavour of squash, while the lemon zest counteracts the richness. For an Italian-style supper, start with prosciutto accompanied by steamed purple sprouting broccoli drizzled with some good olive oil, follow with squash risotto and finish with a serving of crisp chicory salad.

100g unsalted butter
1 onion, finely chopped
1 celery stick, finely chopped
450g peeled and deseeded squash
    (about ½ harlequin, acorn, crown
    prince or butternut)
850–900ml chicken stock (see
    page 161) or almond milk
1 bay leaf

175g arborio or other risotto rice
Finely grated zest of ½ unwaxed lemon
A pinch of freshly grated nutmeg
Sea salt and black pepper

to serve
Fried sage leaves (optional)
Parmesan
Olive oil for drizzling

Melt 60g of the butter in a wide saucepan, add the onion and celery and sauté gently until translucent, about 10 minutes. In the meantime, cut the squash into 1cm dice. Add to the pan and sauté gently until the squash starts to soften a little, about 10 minutes.

Heat the stock or almond milk in a separate pan with the bay leaf to just below a simmer; don't let it boil. Lower the heat to maintain it at this temperature.

Add the rice to the vegetables and turn to coat well in the buttery juices. Add a ladleful of stock or milk to the pan and gently stir until it is almost all absorbed by the rice. Add the bay leaf, too. Keep adding ladlefuls of liquid to the pan, stirring as you do so and waiting for each addition to be absorbed before adding the next.

Continue until the rice is cooked but still has the tiniest bit of bite, about 20 minutes; you might not need quite all of the liquid. The rice grains should be coated in a creamy sauce; don't let the liquid evaporate so much that the risotto thickens to the texture of oat porridge.

Stir in the lemon zest, nutmeg, remaining butter, a few pinches of sea salt and a generous grinding of black pepper. Put the lid on the pan and let rest for a few minutes.

Serve the risotto scattered with fried sage leaves if you like. Finish with a generous grating of Parmesan, an extra grinding of pepper and a drizzle of olive oil.

arancini makes about 18

These crisp, crumb coated balls of rice are supposedly just a way of using up leftover risotto, but it's definitely worth starting from scratch and cooking up some risotto if you don't have any leftovers. Feel free to improvise your own fillings, but choose something strongly flavoured and include a piece of cheese to get the classic oozing centre. My favourite crumbs for coating are brioche, but any gluten free breadcrumbs will do. Serve the arancini with salads and cured meats as a meal to feed 6 people.

for the risotto
1 litre chicken stock (see page 161)
A small pinch of saffron threads
  (optional)
250g arborio or other risotto rice
100g grated Parmesan
Sea salt
or
750g leftover risotto, chilled

for the filling
6–7 tsp basil pesto
50g mozzarella

for the coating and frying
100g rice flour
2 eggs, beaten
140g fine gluten free breadcrumbs
  (see page 101)
Lard, dripping or groundnut oil for
  deep-frying

If you're making your risotto from scratch, first bring the stock to the boil in a saucepan. Add the saffron, if using, followed by the rice. Bring back to the boil, then turn down the heat to a simmer and simmer gently until the rice is cooked and all the stock is absorbed. Stir in the Parmesan and season with salt to taste. Spread the rice out on a plate and put into the fridge to chill thoroughly. Alternatively, just use chilled leftover risotto.

To make the arancini, pinch up a small apricot sized piece of chilled rice and roll it into a ball. Poke your finger into the ball and, using a finger and thumb, make the ball into a little pinch pot with sides of an even thickness. Don't make it too thin or your pot will crack when you fill it.

Spoon in about ⅓ tsp pesto and a thumbnail sized piece of mozzarella to fill the cavity. Pinch off another small piece of rice, flatten it and use this to patch the top of the pot and make the ball round again. Roll very gently and pop on a plate while you shape the rest of the arancini in the same way.

Get three deep (soup size) bowls ready for coating the arancini. Put the rice flour into the first bowl, have the beaten eggs ready in the second and the gluten free breadcrumbs in the third.

Dip each rice ball into the flour first to coat all over, and then quickly into the egg to coat completely. Finally, drop the ball into the breadcrumbs and use a teaspoon to sprinkle the crumbs all over it. Pick the ball up when it is covered and roll it in your hands to fix the crumbs in place. Set aside and repeat to coat the rest of the rice balls.

The arancini can now be chilled for up to 24 hours before you fry them. Don't leave them any longer though because they contain cooked rice, which can be a source of food poisoning if it is not stored properly and consumed within 48 hours of cooking.

To deep-fry, heat your fat or oil in a deep, heavy saucepan to 170°C, or until a cube of gluten free bread dropped into the pan turns golden brown in a minute. Deep-fry the arancini in batches, for 3–4 minutes, turning them to ensure they colour evenly if the fat or oil doesn't cover them. They are ready when the crumbs are evenly golden brown.

Drain on kitchen paper and keep warm while you cook the rest, then serve.

vegetable tempura serves 3–4

Japanese tempura batter is thin and crisp. You can use it to coat anything, but seafood and vegetables are traditional. The veg listed below work particularly well; avoid any that contain a lot of water as they will turn soggy on frying. The sauce has that moreish combination of salty, sweet, sour, hot and umami, so you may find yourself searching for something else to dip into it when all the tempura is finished.

for the tempura
300g selection of vegetables: carrots, green beans, fine purple sprouting broccoli spears, thin asparagus spears, spring onions
75g cornflour
75g rice flour, plus extra for coating
1 tsp gluten free baking powder
150ml cold fizzy water
Groundnut oil or lard, for deep-frying

for the dipping sauce
2 tbsp tamari
2 tbsp toasted sesame oil
20 dashes of Tabasco
2 tsp muscovado sugar
1 tsp fish sauce
Juice of 1–2 limes

If using carrots or green beans, they need to be lightly cooked first: halve small carrots lengthways; cut larger ones into finger length sticks. Steam the veg until just *al dente*, then plunge into ice cold water to refresh. Drain well and dry on kitchen paper, then refrigerate until you are ready to cook. All other veg can be used raw; chill them before making your tempura.

For the dipping sauce, simply mix all the ingredients together. Taste and add more tamari, Tabasco and/or lime juice if needed. Pour into a small serving bowl.

To make your batter, mix the cornflour, rice flour and baking powder with a little of the water to make a paste, then whisk in the rest of the water to make a thin batter.

Heat a 5–7cm depth of oil or fat in a deep, heavy saucepan to 170°C; the pan should be no more than a third full. To check whether it is hot enough, drop in a cube of gluten free bread: it should turn golden brown in a minute.

Put a handful of rice flour into a small bowl. Take the veg out of the fridge. You will need to fry them in small batches. First dip the veg into the rice flour to coat and then into the batter. Now, using forks or tongs, lower each piece gently into the hot oil or fat. Deep-fry for a couple of minutes until crisp, then remove and drain on kitchen paper.

For a crisper coating, dip the tempura back into the batter and fry again. You may need more batter if you double dip, so be prepared to mix up some more if needed.

Serve the tempura with the dipping sauce (and provide finger bowls).

buckwheat pasta serves 2–3

Gluten free pasta had always been a disappointment to me until I started to experiment with making my own. This buckwheat pasta is flavoursome enough to cut into tagliatelle and enjoy simply with garlicky butter and Parmesan or a favourite pasta sauce; it also works well in the lasagne on page 194. The tagliatelle won't be as *al dente* as wheat pasta – it has its own identity.

70g buckwheat flour
50g brown rice sourdough starter
   (see page 74), or 20g rice flour
   and 40g full fat Greek yoghurt
3 tsp ground psyllium husk

50g tapioca starch, plus extra for
   sprinkling if needed
1 egg, beaten
1 tsp olive oil
2 pinches of sea salt

In a large bowl, mix the buckwheat flour with the brown rice starter, or rice flour and yoghurt. Set aside at room temperature for 6–12 hours, or for 24 hours in the fridge. This both hydrates the flour and develops the flavour of the finished pasta.

Mix in all the remaining ingredients and knead to a slightly tacky dough. You may need to add 1–2 tsp water to get it to come together, but try kneading it first for a while, as the dough can sometimes take a while to form.

Wrap the dough tightly in cling film and leave to rest in the fridge for at least an hour, or up to 24 hours, before rolling out and cutting.

When you're ready to roll out the dough, take it out of the fridge and check that it is firm but pliable. If it's still tacky, you will need a little extra tapioca starch. Break the dough into three pieces and roll out each one between two sheets of cling film dusted with tapioca starch until very thin (ideally 2mm thick). If it's sticking, take off the top sheet and dust the dough lightly with tapioca starch. Replace the cling film, flip the dough over and repeat with the other side, then continue to roll.

Using a pizza cutter, cut the pasta dough into long tagliatelle strips (or into sheets for lasagne) while still on the cling film. To keep the first tagliatelle strips out of the way, slide a palette knife underneath and drape them over a rolling pin suspended over a bowl. Keep putting the strips aside until all of the rolled pasta has been cut.

Bring a very large pan of water to a boil with a little olive oil added. When the water is boiling, drop in the tagliatelle, a few strips at a time. The pasta will cook quickly – in just a few minutes. Taste a bit to see if you are happy with it – remember, it won't be *al dente*. Drain the tagliatelle and serve straight away.

margherita pizza serves 3–4

I like a thin-based pizza, sparingly spread with a simple tomato sauce and baked as hot as the oven can go, until the base is invitingly crisp and the cheese is melted and bubbling. You are welcome to put pineapple and ham on your own creations, but I think that the holy trinity of bread, tomato and cheese is unbeatable.

for the pizza base
70g sorghum flour
10g fresh yeast (or 3g quick dried)
120g tepid water
140g potato starch
40g tapioca starch
25ml olive oil
1 large egg
1 scant tsp sea salt
1 tsp light muscovado sugar
1 tsp xanthan gum or 2 tsp ground
   psyllium husk
1 tsp cider vinegar
Fine polenta or rice flour for sprinkling

for the topping
400g tin plum tomatoes
2–3 fat garlic cloves, finely chopped
50ml olive oil, plus extra for drizzling
A pinch of sugar
A few drops of wine vinegar (optional)
2–3 mozzarella balls, each about 125g
Thyme or oregano leaves for sprinkling
   (optional)
Sea salt and black pepper

to finish
A handful of rocket leaves
Parmesan shavings (optional)

To make the pizza base, mix the sorghum flour, yeast and water together in a large bowl until smooth, then cover and set aside at room temperature for an hour to ferment.

In the meantime, make the tomato sauce for the topping. Chop the plum tomatoes and put them into a pan with the juice from the tin. Add the garlic and cook, covered, over a medium heat, for about 10 minutes. Stir in the olive oil, a couple of pinches of salt, a few good grinds of pepper, the sugar and a little vinegar if you think the flavour needs lifting. The olive oil will take a bit of stirring during cooking to get it to emulsify with the tomato. The sauce shouldn't be too thick, but if it's very thin, cook uncovered for a few minutes to drive off the excess water. Set the sauce aside to cool once you have made it.

When you are ready to make the dough, beat the remaining pizza base ingredients except the polenta or rice flour into the sorghum mixture, using a stand mixer fitted with a paddle attachment if you have one. If you do not have a mixer, use your hands to squidge out all the lumps and beat the mixture until smooth.

Sprinkle some flat baking sheets with fine polenta or rice flour. Sprinkle the work surface with fine polenta or rice flour and scoop up a quarter of the dough with floured fingers.

(continued overleaf)

Roll into a ball and then roll out on your floured surface into a thin circle. Keep moving it to check it hasn't stuck and lightly flour the surface to make sure the rolling pin doesn't stick either.

When the circle is about 5mm thick, pick up an edge gently and slide the rolling pin underneath it. Use the rolling pin to help you transfer the delicate dough to a prepared baking sheet. Repeat with the rest of the dough. Make smaller pizzas if you're struggling to handle the dough.

Divide the tomato sauce between the pizzas and gently spread it out using the back of a spoon. Slice the mozzarella balls and lay them on top. Sprinkle with thyme or oregano leaves, if you have some, and drizzle any exposed dough with a little olive oil.

Leave to rise at room temperature for about an hour (or 30–45 minutes if your kitchen is very warm) until the dough looks a little puffy.

Preheat the oven to 250°C/Fan 230°C/Gas 10, or as high as it will go.

Bake the pizzas on their trays for 6–8 minutes, or until the cheese is bubbling and the base is cooked underneath. Scatter with rocket leaves and Parmesan shavings, if you like, and serve straight away.

root vegetable gratin serves 4–6

A gratin is a hearty vegetable dish with a crisp, oven-bronzed breadcrumb topping. I like to use gluten free sourdough crumbs for their savouriness, but of course, you can use shop bought gluten free bread. Vary the root vegetables according to what you have to hand, but if you include celeriac, swede or turnip, only use a small amount, as these are too watery to work well here in any quantity.

Butter for greasing
250g waxy potatoes, such as Charlotte (unpeeled)
3 medium parsnips
¼ medium squash, such as acorn, kabocha or butternut
1 leek (white part only), roughly diced
225ml double cream

100ml whole milk
75g gluten free breadcrumbs (see page 101)
100g Cheddar, grated
Sea salt and black pepper

equipment
23cm square deep baking dish

Preheat the oven to 220°C/Fan 200°C/Gas 7. Butter the baking dish.

Cut the potatoes across into 1.5cm thick slices. Peel and cut the parsnips and squash into thick slices, roughly the same size as the potatoes.

Scatter a third of the leek over the bottom of the prepared dish, then cover with a third of the potatoes, parsnips and squash. Season with a pinch of salt and lots of black pepper. Repeat these layers to use all of the vegetables.

Pour over the cream and milk and cover the dish with foil. Bake for 45–60 minutes, until the veg are completely tender. If the gratin looks dry at this point, you can pour in a little more cream and milk. Turn the oven down to 200°C/Fan 180°C/Gas 6.

Mix the breadcrumbs and cheese together and grind in some black pepper. Sprinkle this mixture evenly over the top of the veg and return the gratin to the oven, uncovered, for another 20–30 minutes, until everything is bubbling, crisp and golden.

parsnip rösti makes 4

I actually prefer these parsnip rösti to the traditional potato version, as they are softer textured, with a crisp exterior and slightly sweet flavour that works particularly well with gamey flavours. They taste best when you cook them reasonably slowly and let the outside catch ever so slightly – like the crispy bits in the corner of a tray of roast veg. If you do not have any metal rings to hand for shaping, the rösti can be made freeform.

400g parsnips (about 2 large ones)
1 large egg, beaten
2 tbsp cornflour or arrowroot
Duck fat, lard or coconut oil, for frying
Sea salt
Butter or crème fraîche, to serve
(optional)

equipment
4 x 10–12cm crumpet rings or other
metal rings for shaping (optional)

Peel and coarsely grate the parsnips and put into a large bowl. Add the egg, cornflour or arrowroot and a couple of good pinches of salt. Mix well to combine.

Heat a heavy-based frying pan over a medium heat and grease the four crumpet rings, or other metal rings. Add 2 tsp fat to the pan and let it melt.

Pop the metal rings into the pan and fill with the parsnip mixture, packing it down a little: it should be no more than 2cm thick, or they won't cook through. If you don't have any rings, simply make little piles of the mixture in the pan and squash them down a bit.

Allow the rösti to cook for a few minutes and then check the underside by lifting it up with a palette knife. If the underneath is deep golden brown, lift off the rings using tongs or a tea towel and turn the rösti over to cook the other side. If you struggle to get the rings off, just run a butter knife around the inside of each one.

Serve the rösti straight away, topped with a knob of butter or a dollop of crème fraîche, or just as they are as a side dish; they are also a good addition to the burgers on page 192.

variation: squash, sweet potato or celeriac rösti
You can also make the rösti with squash, sweet potato or celeriac. Because these veg hold more moisture than parsnips, the method is slightly different. Add the salt to the grated veg, cover and set aside for 30 minutes. Squeeze the grated veg between your hands to remove as much liquid as possible. Tip into a bowl, add the egg and cornflour and mix well, then shape and cook the rösti as above.

omelette 'noodles' serves 1

These omelette noodles can be eaten just like pasta, with a generous scoop of pesto; they also make a brilliant addition to stir-fries and soups. Once you've got the hang of swirling the egg around the pan to make a very thin omelette, the world is your noodle.

Butter or duck fat, for frying
3 eggs
A splash of milk (or dairy free
    alternative)
A pinch of salt

Heat a well seasoned frying pan, add a generous knob of butter or duck fat and allow it to melt gently over a medium low heat.

Meanwhile, in a bowl, beat the eggs with the milk and a pinch of salt.

Wipe the pan lightly with a wad of folded kitchen paper, so that you have a thin film of melted fat over the whole surface.

Pour in about a quarter of the egg – enough to just coat the whole pan thinly. Swirl it around in an even layer before it gets a chance to set. If the pan is too hot, the egg will stick and bubble – just turn the heat down if this happens.

Allow the egg to cook for a minute or so, until the edges of the omelette start to curl up a little. Grab the edge of the omelette and carefully peel it up and away from the pan – or tip it out of the pan onto a board.

Grease the pan with a little more fat and repeat with the rest of the egg until all your omelettes are made.

Roll up each omelette and cut across to make the noodles. Put back into the frying pan to heat through and then toss with your sauce. They are more delicate than pasta, so go easy on the mixing.

variation: egg rolls

These thin omelettes can also be used in place of flour tortillas to make wraps for lunch, or a quick supper from leftovers. Just place your filling to one side of the omelette, fold up the bottom and roll it up like a cigar.

courgette tortilla serves 3–4

This is one of those very useful recipes that can be adapted to accommodate whatever ingredients you have to hand – leftover cold potatoes and/or courgettes, or other cooked veg can be used, and cheese is a welcome addition. As a main meal, the tortilla will feed three with some salad or buttered greens on the side, or you can serve it in small wedges as part of a mezze style spread, or to take on a picnic. It's also delicious cold, so you can eat it hot for supper and then take it to work for lunch the next day.

- Duck fat, chicken fat, groundnut oil or butter, for cooking
- 1 medium onion, finely chopped
- 2 large courgettes, chopped
- 5 new potatoes (unpeeled)
- 6 large eggs
- A big handful of spinach, roughly shredded
- 1 tsp salted capers, rinsed, drained and chopped (optional)
- Sea salt and black pepper

Heat 2 tsp fat or oil in a frying pan. Add the onion and courgettes and sauté gently until the onion is soft and the courgette has started to take on some colour, about 10 minutes.

Meanwhile, bring a pan of water to the boil and add the potatoes. Cook them in their skins until tender to the point of a knife, about 15 minutes. Drain and leave until cool enough to handle, then dice.

In a large bowl, beat the eggs well, then add the onion, courgettes, potatoes, spinach and capers, along with a couple of large pinches of salt and a good grinding of pepper. Mix well.

Heat another 1 tsp fat or oil in the frying pan (if using butter, don't let it burn). Pour the egg mixture into the hot pan and cook undisturbed for a few minutes, then turn the heat down a little. Pull the sides of the tortilla towards the middle slightly, using a fork, to allow some of the runny mixture to flow out to the edges. After about 10 minutes the tortilla should have only a bit of runny egg left on the top.

You can now pop the tortilla under a hot grill for a few minutes to finish cooking, or apply the following traditional method.

Protecting your hands with oven gloves, upturn a large plate on top of the pan. Holding the pan and plate firmly together, flip them over to unmould the tortilla onto the plate. Lift the pan off the tortilla – don't be alarmed by any runny egg oozing out. Heat the pan again and add another 1 tsp fat. When hot, slide the tortilla back in. Tuck any loose edges under for a seamless golden crust all around. Cook for 1–2 minutes to set any runny egg.

Invert the tortilla, as before, onto a clean plate and serve cut into wedges.

celeriac fishcakes serves 3-4

Even the most determined fish avoider can be brought round with a fishcake. Celeriac pairs brilliantly with fish and makes for a lighter fishcake than the traditional potato. Lemon zest transforms and freshens tinned salmon, but fresh fish of any kind works here. I like to fry my fishcakes in a little duck fat rather than bake them, as they form a delicious crust on the outside.

30g unsalted butter, duck fat or
    coconut oil
1 large celery stick (or onion), finely
    diced
½ celeriac, peeled and cut into chunks
1 large egg

½ tsp grated lemon zest
A squeeze of lemon juice
85g ground almonds
2 x 215g tins wild red salmon, drained, or
    400g cooked sustainable fish, flaked
Sea salt and black pepper

Melt a third of the butter or other fat in a small saucepan and sauté the diced celery (or onion) for 10 minutes, until translucent. Remove and set aside to cool. Meanwhile, steam (rather than boil) the celeriac until tender. Set aside to cool until tepid.

Put the celeriac into a food processor with the egg, a couple of pinches of salt, the lemon zest and juice, and a good few twists of black pepper. Process until fairly smooth. (Alternatively, mash well by hand.) Scrape the mixture into a bowl.

Add the sautéed celery, ground almonds and flaked fish. Mash with a fork to combine. If the mixture seems too wet, add some more ground almonds. It should just hold together enough for you to shape into patties. If you leave it to sit for half an hour it will be easier to work with, as the almonds will have absorbed more of the moisture.

Scoop small satsuma sized lumps out of the bowl, press into a ball in your cupped hands and flatten slightly. Place on a tray while you shape the rest. You can refrigerate these for up to 24 hours now, or freeze for later (defrost before frying, or bake from frozen).

When you're ready to eat, heat the rest of the fat in a heavy-based frying pan. Fry the patties over a medium heat for 2–3 minutes on each side, or until a deep golden brown crust forms, turning them very carefully with a palette knife. (Or place on a parchment lined tray, melt the remaining butter or other fat and brush over the fishcakes, then bake at 220°C/Fan 200°C/Gas 7 for 12–15 minutes.) Drain on kitchen paper.

Serve at once, with homemade tartare sauce or yoghurt, and lots of buttery vegetables.

variation: crunchy fishcakes
For an extra crunchy crust, before frying, dip each fishcake into rice flour or other gluten free flour or breadcrumbs to coat all over, then dip into a bowl of beaten egg, then back into the flour. Repeat the egg and flour dipping once more. Fry as above.

fish fingers serves 4

Fish fingers are so easy to make, it's a wonder we ever buy them. I really like these with a brioche crumb coating, because it gives them an authentic golden colour and ensures they crisp up beautifully, but sourdough breadcrumbs are a slower energy release option. You can make these with any sustainable white fish you like, including frozen fish fillets – just defrost in the fridge before coating.

400g sustainable fish fillets, such as
  cod, hake, pollock, haddock or whiting
150g gluten free white flour, or rice
  flour or cornflour
1 heaped tsp sea salt
2 eggs

175g gluten free breadcrumbs, ideally
  brioche, sourdough or baguette
  (see page 101)
Lard, dripping or groundnut oil for
  shallow frying
Black pepper

Check your fish for any pinbones, removing any you find with kitchen tweezers. Slice the fish into roughly 12 fingers and pat dry with kitchen paper.

Get three deep plates or wide bowls ready for coating the fish fingers. Put the flour into the first bowl and season with the salt and a good grinding of pepper. In the second bowl, beat the eggs well with a fork. Put the breadcrumbs into the third bowl.

Take one piece of fish and press it into the flour. Turn and repeat to coat both sides, then tap off any excess. Pop it into the egg and turn it over quickly with a fork or your fingers, to coat completely. Drop the fish into the crumbs and use a spoon to cover it with crumbs. Using your other hand, turn the fish over to make sure it is fully coated, then set aside on a clean plate. Repeat with the rest of the fish.

Heat a 1cm depth of fat in a deep, heavy-based frying pan. When it is hot, fry the fish fingers, in batches if necessary, for a few minutes each side until the crumb coating is golden. Unless your fish pieces are very thick, this should be enough to cook them right through. If in doubt, break one open and check that the fish inside is hot and opaque.

Drain the fish fingers on kitchen paper and serve straight away, with a leafy salad, or peas or green beans.

fish pie serves 5–6

Simple to make and as soothing as a plump eiderdown, fish pie relies on good produce. A little smoked fish adds depth and contrast to the creamy béchamel, and celeriac brings a touch of aniseed to the mash. I also like some flat leaf parsley in my sauce, for the fresh grassy notes it provides. The pie will be just as good reheated the next day.

600g sustainable fish fillets, such as
    cod, hake, pollock, haddock or whiting,
    ideally including some smoked fish
800g floury potatoes
300g celeriac
500ml whole milk
1 bay leaf
125g unsalted butter
1 small onion, finely diced

35g cornflour or tapioca starch, blended
    to a paste with 2 tbsp cold milk
A handful of flat leaf parsley, leaves
    picked and chopped
Sea salt and black pepper

equipment
20cm diameter pie dish

Check your fish for any pinbones, removing any you find with kitchen tweezers.

Peel the potatoes and cut in half if large. Place in a saucepan, add water to cover and boil for 15–20 minutes, until tender. Peel and chop the celeriac into large chunks, then add to the potato pan for the last 10–15 minutes of cooking. Both the potatoes and celeriac should be tender to the point of a knife.

Meanwhile, preheat the oven to 220°C/Fan 200°C/Gas 7.

In a large saucepan or frying pan, heat the milk with the bay leaf until it starts to steam. Add the fish fillets and poach gently for a few minutes until barely cooked; don't let the milk boil. Take the fish out, break into large chunks and place in the pie dish. Pour the milk into a jug and reserve for the sauce. Wash and dry the pan.

Melt 50g of the butter in the pan and add the onion. Sauté gently until golden and translucent. Pour in the milk and bring to the boil. Now add the cornflour or tapioca paste, stirring constantly; the sauce should thicken instantly as it comes to the boil.

Stir in the chopped parsley and taste for seasoning, adding a grinding of pepper (salt probably won't be needed, as the smoked fish is likely to provide enough). Pour the sauce over the fish and mix gently to combine.

Drain the cooked potatoes and celeriac and mash with the remaining 75g butter and a couple of pinches of salt until smooth and creamy. Taste for seasoning, adding pepper and more salt if needed. Pile on top of the fish, push right to the edges and fluff up the surface with a fork. Bake for 25–30 minutes until the mash is tinged with gold.

lamb and potato cakes makes 4

This recipe takes unassuming lamb mince and humble potatoes and turns them into something that is far more than the sum of its parts. A little dexterity is required to get perfectly uniform patties, but even the most rustic effort will boast a delicious golden crust and lemony, cardamom scented interior. Don't be put off by the lengthy method; the patties are really quite simple to make and you can prepare them in advance if you like, keeping them in the fridge until you are ready to cook.

for the potato dough
650g floury potatoes
1 heaped tbsp gluten free white flour
   (or sorghum flour or cornflour)
Sea salt

for the lamb filling
30g salted butter or duck fat
1 medium red onion, finely chopped
200g lamb mince
Grated zest of 1 unwaxed lemon
40g pine nuts

6 cardamom pods, seeds extracted
1 tsp ground cinnamon
¼ tsp black pepper
Juice of ¼–½ lemon
A very large handful of flat leaf parsley,
   leaves picked and finely chopped

for frying
Lard, dripping or coconut oil

For the potato dough, peel the potatoes and cut in half if large. Place in a saucepan, add water to cover and boil until tender to the point of knife, about 15–20 minutes. Drain and leave until cool enough to handle.

Meanwhile, for the filling, melt the butter or duck fat in a frying pan, add the onion and sauté gently until translucent. Add the lamb mince and lemon zest and cook on a medium heat, stirring occasionally, until the lamb releases its fat and takes on a little colour.

In the meantime, toast the pine nuts in a dry frying pan, shaking the pan regularly, until they are tinged with gold. Tip onto a plate and set aside.

Grind the cardamom seeds with a pinch of salt, using a pestle and mortar.

Pour off all but 1 tbsp fat from the frying pan and reserve. Add the ground cardamom, cinnamon and black pepper to the pan with a pinch of sea salt and stir for 30 seconds.

Stir in the juice of ¼ lemon and 1 tbsp water, scraping the bottom of the pan with a wooden spoon to deglaze. Stir in the pine nuts and chopped parsley, taste for seasoning and sharpness and add more salt, pepper or lemon juice if you think it needs it. Set aside while you make the potato dough.

(continued overleaf)

Mash the potatoes well with a couple of pinches of sea salt. Stir in the flour and knead to form a smooth dough. Add a little more flour if it seems sticky.

Divide the potato dough into quarters and flour your hands well. Roll one of the dough portions into a ball in your hands and flatten to a patty, about 1cm thick. Allow it to take on the cupped shape of your palm, so that you have a hollow for the lamb mixture.

Put a quarter of the lamb mixture into the hollow. Close your palm a bit and bring the sides of the potato up over the lamb to enclose it completely. Pinch and smooth as you go, flouring your hands if the patty start to stick.

Roll the potato cake around between your palms to smooth the shape and squash it a little until it looks like a slightly flattened jam doughnut, about 10cm in diameter and 2.5–3cm thick. Repeat to make the other 3 potato cakes. Alternatively, you can make mini potato cakes by dividing the mixture into eight and shaping the patties about 4cm in diameter and 2cm thick. (At this stage, you can refrigerate them for up to 24 hours before cooking.)

When you are ready to cook, heat a generous knob of lard (or dripping or coconut oil) and the reserved lamb fat in a frying pan until hot, but not smoking. You need about a 3mm depth of fat in the pan.

Lower the potato cakes into the pan using a fish slice and leave them to cook for a few minutes, until they have formed a deep golden crust underneath. Don't let them cook too quickly, or the inside won't be hot enough. Turn and cook the other side in the same way and then drain on kitchen paper.

Serve the potato cakes as soon as they are cooked, with Greek yoghurt and a leafy salad on the side if you like.

flatbreads topped with lamb

makes 8 small flatbreads

These flatbreads are a kind of Turkish pizza – the sort of street food that you fold up and pop in your mouth as you wander around a market. Although the lamb topping is rich, the gentle heat of Turkish chilli flakes and zing of the lemon cuts through it beautifully. I'm always thrilled to scatter anything with vibrant pomegranate seeds, but they do also provide a sweet, tangy kick that complements the lamb. A great dinner party starter, as you can make everything in advance and bake the flatbreads when you're ready to eat.

for the dough
70g sorghum flour
10g fresh yeast (or 4g quick dried)
80g lukewarm water
140g potato starch
40g tapioca starch, plus extra for
   dusting
1 scant tsp sea salt
1 tsp light muscovado sugar
1 tsp xanthan gum or 2 tsp ground
   psyllium husk
50g full fat Greek yoghurt
25ml olive oil
1 large egg
1 tsp cider vinegar
Fine polenta or rice flour for dusting
Extra virgin olive oil for drizzling

for the topping
250g lamb mince
½ red onion, finely chopped
1 tsp Turkish dried chilli flakes, to taste
1 tsp sweet paprika
½ tsp ground cumin
1 heaped tsp tomato purée or red pepper
   paste
2–3 ripe tomatoes, chopped
2–3 tsp lemon juice (optional)
Sea salt

to serve
½ pomegranate
A few handfuls of flat leaf parsley, leaves
   picked
Lemon slices
Turkish dried chilli flakes
Greek yoghurt

In a large bowl, mix the sorghum flour, yeast and water together with a wooden spoon until smooth. Set aside at room temperature for an hour to ferment.

In the meantime, make the topping. Put the lamb mince into a large frying pan and cook over a moderate heat for a few minutes until the fat starts to melt and coat the bottom of the pan. Add the chopped onion and fry gently until it smells sweet and the lamb has taken on a little colour, about 15 minutes.

Add the chilli flakes, paprika and cumin. Cook, stirring, for a minute, until the spices are fragrant, then add the tomato or pepper paste, chopped tomatoes and 2–3 tbsp water. Cook for about 2 minutes, until the water has evaporated but the lamb is still moist.

Season with salt and brighten the flavour with lemon juice if you think it needs it. If you like your lamb spicier, add more chilli flakes. Set aside to cool.

To make the dough, beat the rest of the ingredients except the polenta or rice flour and extra virgin olive oil into the fermented sorghum mixture in the bowl, or using a stand mixer fitted with the paddle attachment. If you do not have a mixer, use your hands to squidge out all the lumps and beat the mixture until smooth. Set aside for a few minutes for the dough to firm up a little.

Sprinkle three baking trays with fine polenta or rice flour. Dust the work surface with tapioca starch. Scoop up an eighth of the dough with floured fingers and roll into a ball in your hands, then roll out on your dusted surface to a thin round. Keep moving the dough to ensure it hasn't stuck and lightly flour the surface to make sure the rolling pin doesn't stick either.

When the circle is about 5mm thick, pick up an edge gently and slide the rolling pin underneath it. Use the rolling pin to help you transfer the delicate dough to the floured baking tray. Repeat with the rest of the dough. (You can roll the dough between two sheets of cling film if you find it difficult to work with.)

Divide the lamb topping between the dough bases and gently spread it out using the back of a spoon. Drizzle any exposed dough with a little olive oil.

Leave the lamb-topped bases uncovered to prove for about an hour (or 30–45 minutes if your kitchen is very warm) until the dough looks a little puffy.

Preheat the oven to 250°C/Fan 230°C/Gas 10, or as high as it will go.

Meanwhile, to extract the pomegranate seeds, loosen the skin of the fruit a little by pulling it apart with your fingers. Then hold it, cut side down, over a bowl and bash with a wooden spoon until all the seeds fall out. Discard any bitter pith.

Bake the flatbreads for 6–8 minutes, or until the base is cooked underneath. Serve each one scattered with parsley leaves, pomegranate seeds and a couple of thin slices of lemon. Hand round extra chilli flakes for those who like it hot and Greek yoghurt for those who would like a little soothing.

persian meatballs *serves 4*

Long, gentle simmering and restrained spicing transform lamb mince and root veg into a deeply flavoured dish. The trick here is not to stir anything. Persian food makes a virtue of slow cooking, so be patient with the onions and they will become wonderfully sweet. By using just enough liquid, the juices from the meat and sweetness of the veg create a rich and delicious sauce – just enjoy the alchemy that happens when you allow time to do the work. This dish is best made in a wide, heavy pan, which must have a close-fitting lid.

for the meatballs
500g lamb mince
1 small onion, grated
1½ tsp ground cinnamon
2 pinches of freshly grated nutmeg
1 clove, ground to a powder with a pinch
   of salt
Sea salt and black pepper

for the vegetables
2 tsp butter, duck fat or coconut oil
2 onions, finely chopped
3 celery sticks, finely chopped
1 tsp ground turmeric or a big pinch of
   saffron threads

200ml boiling water
4 bay leaves
2 pinches of Turkish dried chilli flakes
6 large carrots, peeled and cut into 1cm
   slices on the diagonal
2 x 400g tins plum tomatoes
6 scrubbed new potatoes or 1 small
   celeriac, peeled and cut into cubes

to serve
Coriander leaves
Sliced spring onions
Lemon wedges
Greek yoghurt
Turkish dried chilli flakes

To make the meatballs, put the lamb mince into a large bowl and add the grated onion, cinnamon, nutmeg, ground clove and a couple of pinches of black pepper. Use your fingers to work the mixture until everything is well combined. Roll the mixture into walnut sized balls and set aside.

Heat the butter, fat or oil in a wide, heavy-based pan with a close-fitting lid. Add the chopped onions and sauté gently until they are translucent. Add the chopped celery and continue to fry over a low heat, stirring occasionally, until the onions are golden and sweet smelling.

Sprinkle the turmeric into the pan and stir for a minute or so to fry off the bitter taste. Or simply add the saffron threads (no need to cook these out).

Pour in the boiling water, add the bay leaves and chilli flakes and bring back to the boil. Lower the heat to a simmer and gently place the meatballs in the pan. Spread out the sliced carrots on top. Add a little more water if needed – to come about halfway up the meatballs. Put the lid on the pan and simmer gently for an hour, without stirring.

Spoon off some of the fat if there seems to be too much – it's fine to leave a bit to make the sauce unctuous. Drain and chop the tinned tomatoes, reserving the juice. Tip the tomatoes over the meatballs, and add some of the reserved juice if it looks like the liquid level has fallen to below halfway up the meatballs. Keep the remaining tomato juice, in case it is needed later on.

Add the chopped potatoes or celeriac and season with salt and pepper. Put the lid back on and simmer over a very low heat, without stirring, for another hour until the sauce has reduced a little. If the sauce gets too thick before the hour is up, add some more tomato juice. If it still looks a bit too thin after an hour, take the lid off and simmer for another half an hour until the sauce is thick and velvety (about the thickness of ketchup). Taste for seasoning at this point; it should have a nice balance between savoury and tart.

Serve in bowls, scattered with some coriander leaves and sliced spring onions. Put lemon wedges, Greek yoghurt and extra chilli flakes on the table for people to add to their plate. A crisp green salad is a good accompaniment.

beef burgers with portobello mushrooms serves 4

The main thing to consider with a burger is the provenance of your meat. Your burger will only be as good as the mince you buy, so get some organic beef mince for these. You don't need breadcrumbs or eggs to bind your burgers, but a handful of fresh herbs will bring out the savouriness of the meat. Grilled portobello mushrooms, oozing garlicky butter, take the place of the more traditional bun. They make it more of a knife and fork meal, but an amazingly succulent one.

for the burgers
500g organic beef mince
½ red onion, very finely chopped
A handful of oregano leaves, or coriander or parsley, finely chopped
Duck fat, beef dripping or lard, for cooking
Sea salt and black pepper

for the mushrooms
4 large portobello mushrooms, stalks removed
1 garlic clove, finely chopped
4 tsp salted butter or duck fat, softened

First make your burgers. In a large bowl, mix the beef mince with the onion and season with 3 good pinches of salt and plenty of pepper. Add the chopped herbs and mix well. Squidge everything together with your hands and then divide into 4 portions and shape into round flat patties. Set aside.

Preheat the grill to medium. Place the mushrooms open side up on the grill tray. Mix the garlic with a pinch of salt and crush to a purée with the back of a knife. Work this into the softened butter or duck fat and then dot over the brown mushroom gills. Grill the mushrooms until they have softened a little – the butter or duck fat should be sizzling, but don't let the garlic catch.

While the mushrooms are under the grill, cook your burgers. Heat 2 tsp fat in a large frying pan over a medium high heat. Add the burgers and cook for 2 or 3 minutes each side, keeping the heat in the pan reasonably high, but not smoking. To check the burgers, press them with your fingers; the firmer they feel, the more well done they are. Cut one open to check that they are cooked to your liking and piping hot through to the middle.

To serve, place a mushroom on each plate, top with a burger and sprinkle with a little salt and pepper. Serve with a leafy salad on the side, and new potatoes if you wish.

lasagne serves 6

Although lasagne can seem quite a production process, if you prepare the elements at a leisurely pace, fitting them around your day, the whole thing can be assembled and ready to go with a minimum of fuss. I like to use my buckwheat pasta, as the darker nutty flavour goes well with beef, but shop bought pasta will do. Buy good quality meat from a butcher – it will make all the difference. Also consider doubling up the quantity, to bake and freeze the extra lasagne in portions for healthy ready meals.

for the meat sauce
2 tsp butter
4 rashers of back bacon, snipped into
    pieces
2 medium carrots, diced
½ celery stick, diced
2 garlic cloves, finely chopped
400g beef mince
200g pork mince
A pinch of ground cinnamon
2 x 400g tins plum tomatoes
About 400ml red wine (optional)
A small handful of oregano or few sprigs
    of thyme
Sea salt and black pepper

for the béchamel sauce
60g salted butter
800ml whole milk
1 bay leaf
50g cornflour or tapioca starch
Freshly grated nutmeg
120g Parmesan or Grana Padano, grated

for the pasta
1 quantity buckwheat pasta (see page 170)
    or shop bought gluten free lasagne
    sheets

equipment
23cm square deep roasting tin

To make the meat sauce, melt the butter in a large saucepan, then add the bacon and cook gently for a few minutes. Tip in the carrots, celery and garlic and sweat for a few minutes more.

Now add the beef and pork mince to the pan, along with a pinch of cinnamon, and turn up the heat a little. Allow the meat to take on a little colour, stirring occasionally; do not allow the garlic to catch and go brown.

Add the tomatoes to the pan with their juice. Half fill one of the tomato tins with wine (or water if you prefer) and tip this into the pan too. Add the herbs, then cover and leave to simmer very gently for 2–3 hours.

Once the sauce is cooked, check that it is the right consistency by scraping a spoon across the bottom of the pan. If the sauce is thick enough, the spoon will leave a clear channel. If it fills in immediately, there is too much liquid, so take the lid off and turn up the heat to drive off the excess moisture. Season the sauce with salt and pepper to taste. Set aside to cool.

To make the béchamel sauce, melt the butter in a medium saucepan and add 700ml of the milk, along with the bay leaf. Heat until just below boiling, then take out the bay leaf.

Mix the remaining milk with the cornflour or tapioca starch to a loose paste. Add to the pan in a thin trickle, stirring as you do so. Continue to stir until the sauce thickens. Take off the heat and season with salt and a little grated nutmeg. Set aside until you are ready to assemble the lasagne.

Preheat the oven to 220°C/Fan 200°C/Gas 7.

To roll out the buckwheat pasta, break the dough into three pieces and roll out each one between two sheets of cling film dusted with tapioca starch until very thin (ideally 2mm thick). If it's sticking, take off the top sheet and dust the dough lightly with tapioca starch. Replace the cling film, flip the dough over and repeat with the other side, then continue to roll.

Cut each of the 3 pasta sheets into 4 rectangles; keep them covered with cling film so they don't dry out.

To assemble the lasagne, spread a third of the meat sauce in the bottom of the roasting tin and spoon a quarter of the béchamel sauce evenly on top. Sprinkle with a quarter of the Parmesan and top with a layer of pasta rectangles. Repeat these layers twice and then top with the remaining béchamel. Sprinkle with the rest of the Parmesan.

Bake for 30–40 minutes until the top is bubbling and golden tinged. Serve with a crisp salad. If you have any left over, it will be even better the next day – reheated in the oven at the same temperature, covered loosely with foil, until piping hot.

scotch eggs makes 4

These are perfect picnic fare, or even food to take on a walk – being portable and high in protein. I also find making them deeply satisfying. Sourdough crumbs give a delicious savoury edge, but you can use whatever gluten free bread you have.

4 eggs
400g pork mince, or 450g gluten free
  sausages
A small handful of herbs, such as sage,
  parsley and thyme, leaves picked and
  finely chopped
40g gluten free soft breadcrumbs
  (see page 101), optional
1 egg yolk, beaten (optional)
Sea salt and black pepper

for coating and frying
A large handful of rice flour
1 egg, beaten
100g gluten free breadcrumbs
  (see page 101)
Lard, beef fat or groundnut oil for
  deep-frying

First, boil your eggs. Put them into a small saucepan and cover with cold water. Bring to the boil and boil for 3–4 minutes: 3 minutes will give you a very soft yolk, but makes the process a little trickier; 4 minutes gives a fudgy yolk. Drain and cool quickly in iced water. Peel once cool and remove any membrane.

For the crumb coating, set up three bowls. Put the rice flour into one bowl, the beaten egg into another and the breadcrumbs in the third.

If using pork mince, put it into a large bowl and add the herbs, soft breadcrumbs, beaten egg yolk, 1 scant tsp salt and lots of black pepper. Mix thoroughly, squidging the mixture with your hands to combine evenly. If you are using sausages, just snip and remove the casings, then mix the meat with the herbs; there is no need for breadcrumbs or egg yolk.

Place a piece of cling film on the work surface and place a quarter of the pork mince on it. Pat out with your fingers into a circle, about 14cm in diameter.

Roll a peeled egg in the flour and place in the middle of the mince circle. Lift the corners of the cling film and bring the mince around the egg. Squeeze gently through the cling film until the egg is almost enclosed and then pop the ball into your hand and squeeze gently to completely seal the egg inside. Repeat with the rest of the eggs.

To coat the balls, using one hand, roll one of the scotch eggs in flour to cover evenly all over, then quickly but thoroughly roll in the beaten egg and place in the bowl of breadcrumbs. Use your dry hand to sprinkle breadcrumbs over the top of the scotch egg, jiggle the bowl a bit and then turn the scotch egg around to completely coat in crumbs. Set aside and repeat with the rest of the eggs.

Heat a 6–8cm depth of fat or oil in a deep, heavy saucepan to 180°C; the pan should be no more than a third full. To check it is hot enough, add a cube of gluten free bread: it should turn golden brown in just less than a minute.

Lower a couple of scotch eggs into the hot oil – or all of them if your pan is big enough (the fat should just about cover them). Allow them to cook undisturbed for a minute and then turn gently every minute or so for 6–7 minutes, until the crumbs are evenly deep golden brown. Don't be tempted to crank up the heat or you will scorch the crumbs. Lift out carefully and drain on kitchen paper.

These scotch eggs are best eaten warm, when the coating is still crisp, but they'll be fine for a couple of days in the fridge. Eat them with a crisp salad and some cornichons.

chicken casserole with chestnut dumplings serves 4

This dark, flavoursome casserole, topped with fluffy chestnut dumplings, makes a delicious winter's evening meal. You can prepare it a day or two in advance, making the dumplings and baking them on top of the casserole when you come home from work. Gluten free white flour can be substituted for the potato starch, tapioca starch and rice flour, but the dumplings will be heavier and you may need a touch more water.

for the casserole
4 chicken thighs, boned
2 heaped tsp rice flour or gluten free
   white flour
3 tsp duck fat, lard or butter
70g pancetta or bacon lardons, diced
2 red onions, each sliced into
   8–10 wedges
2 garlic cloves, roughly sliced
1 tbsp tomato purée
2 bay leaves
3 strips of orange zest
200ml red wine
200ml chicken stock (see page 161)
   or water
350g mushrooms

for the dumplings
25g chestnut flour
15g rice flour
50g potato starch
20g tapioca starch
1 tsp ground psyllium husk
1 tsp gluten free baking powder
2 pinches of sea salt
25g ground almonds
40g unsalted butter, diced
50g full fat Greek yoghurt
1 medium egg
4 tsp water

equipment
Medium casserole dish

Cut the chicken into bite sized pieces and toss them in the flour to coat. (I retain the skin because it gives the sauce a velvety richness; if you're not a fan, leave it on during cooking and remove it later.)

Heat the fat in a large heavy-based saucepan, add the pancetta or lardons and fry gently until starting to take on a little colour. Now add the chicken to the pan and turn up the heat a little. Fry, turning as necessary to brown lightly all over. Remove all the meat from the pan with a slotted spoon and set aside for a few minutes.

Add the onions to the pan and fry gently, scraping up any caramelised meat juices, for about 10 minutes until they are translucent. Add the garlic and stir in the tomato purée.

Return the chicken pieces to the pan and add the bay leaves, orange zest, wine and stock or water. Bring to the boil and then lower the heat. Put the lid on and simmer gently for 30 minutes.

While the chicken is cooking, cut the mushrooms into quarters if small, or chunks if they are large. Add the mushrooms to the chicken and cook for a further 10 minutes or until they are soft.

Carefully tip everything into a casserole dish and discard the bay leaves and orange zest. If you want to remove the skin from the chicken thighs, do so now. (If preparing ahead, allow to cool completely, then refrigerate at this stage.)

To make the dumplings, sift together the flours, starches, psyllium, baking powder and salt into a large bowl. Tip in the ground almonds and stir to combine. Rub in the butter very roughly, keeping the butter in small pieces to ensure the dumplings will be light.

In a separate bowl, beat the yoghurt and egg together, using a balloon whisk. Pour into the flour mix along with the water, and mix with a fork to form a soft, sticky dough.

Place tablespoonfuls of the dough on an oiled sheet of foil or waxed paper; you should get 7–8 dumplings. If you flour your hands, you can lightly roll the mixture to make it look a little more dumpling-like, or shape it into quenelles with a couple of tablespoons. Leave to rest for 20 minutes.

Meanwhile, preheat the oven to 240°C/Fan 220°C/Gas 9.

Carefully pick up the dumplings and place them evenly on top of the casserole. Place in the oven and cook for 10 minutes to puff the dumplings up. Turn the oven setting down to 200°C/Fan 180°C/Gas 6 and cook for a further 20–30 minutes until the dumplings are cooked through and the casserole is bubbling.

yorkshire pudding makes 10

There are three secrets to successful gluten free Yorkshire pudding: sweet rice flour, allowing the batter to rest, and getting the fat in the tin to smelting temperature. If you do not have any sweet rice flour, you can try substituting white rice flour or potato starch, but without the amylopectin in sweet rice, you won't get quite the same puff.

200g eggs (about 4), lightly beaten
2 tsp liquid pectin
50g tapioca starch
40g sweet rice flour
30g rice flour
4–5 pinches of sea salt
180ml whole milk or goat's milk (or
   unsweetened almond or coconut milk,
   for a dairy free version)

5 tsp lard or softened beef dripping,
   or coconut oil

equipment
Muffin tray or small roasting tray
   (about 30 x 20cm)

To make the batter, lightly beat the eggs in a large jug, then beat in the pectin, tapioca starch, flours and salt, using a balloon whisk, to make a smooth paste. Add half the milk and whisk again until smooth. Whisk in the rest of the milk to make a smooth batter. Cover and set aside for 1–6 hours, or up to 24 hours in the fridge.

If you are having these with a roast dinner, get everything ready so that the puddings can bake in the oven while you rest your meat for 20 minutes.

Divide the fat amongst 10 holes of a muffin tray, or for one large pudding, put it into a roasting tray. Place the tray in the oven to heat up (along with the meat for the last 10 minutes of its roasting time).

When you take the meat out, turn the oven as high as it will go (ideally 250°C/Fan 230°C/Gas 10). When it reaches this temperature, take the tray out of the oven and place over a medium heat on the hob, trying to get an even spread of heat under the tin. Wait until the fat is starting to smoke. Meanwhile, give your batter a good whisk. Quickly and carefully pour the batter into the tray, dividing it evenly between the 10 moulds if making individual puddings. The batter will bubble in the hot fat as you add it.

Put the tray straight into the oven and turn the heat down to 240°C/Fan 220°C/Gas 9. Bake for 10 minutes, during which time the puddings should puff up into all manner of exciting and improbable shapes. Turn the oven down to 200°C/Fan 180°C/Gas 6 and bake for a further 10 minutes until the puddings are deep golden brown and crisp on top. Don't open the oven to check them at any point or they will collapse – just hold your nerve and get on with the gravy.

Eat the Yorkshire puddings right away, with your roast.

pudding

Forget fancy desserts with spun sugar baskets and intricate pastry work, pudding is all about buttery warmth, juicy fruit and silky custard. Wheat flour has a tendency to dull the flavours of other ingredients, but you only become aware of this when you bake with other flours and start noticing how much more chocolatey, lemony or spicy things taste.

Instead of trying to approximate the flavour and texture of wheat in these puddings, I have employed the mild hay tones of rice flour – to set lemon centre stage in a magic lemon pudding, the buttery richness of almonds in a peach crumble and the smoky sweetness of chestnut in a chestnut and orange cake. Sourdough breadcrumbs give the steamed marmalade pudding and Christmas pudding a depth of flavour that is incredibly moreish and often lacking in gluten free food.

Baked and steamed puddings are ideally served warm from the oven when gluten free flours are at their best, when the starches have gelatinised but not set, lending a moist, tender crumb and the crispest of crumbles. Once a pudding has cooled down, the starches will have set and a sponge will be less tender. However, it will still be good the next day if you warm it up and make a delicious sauce to pour over it before serving.

Ice cream is often a go-to gluten free dessert, but be sure to read the ingredients list on tubs of ready made ices, because cookie dough, biscuit pieces and barley malt can all sneak in there. In this chapter you will also find some dessert wafers, a little like tuiles, which you can flavour in various ways to serve with good vanilla ice cream as a lovely, simple dessert.

blueberry cheesecake serves 8

This recipe satisfies my lingering nostalgia for an uncooked cheesecake. Here, Greek yoghurt adds a tang that cuts through the richness of cream cheese without detracting from the wonderful creaminess. The base can also be made with gluten free digestive biscuits, but if you have time then I'd recommend using this homemade version.

for the biscuit base
100g white gluten free flour
⅓ tsp bicarbonate of soda
100g ground almonds
60g dark muscovado sugar
135g cold salted butter

for the cream cheese filling
200ml double cream
250g full fat cream cheese
100g full fat Greek yoghurt

1 tsp vanilla extract
50g icing sugar

for the blueberry topping
200g fresh blueberries
40g caster sugar
1 heaped tsp cornflour or arrowroot, blended with 2 tsp water

equipment
20cm springform cake tin

Preheat the oven to 180°C/Fan 160°C/Gas 4. Line the base of the cake tin and a baking tray with parchment.

For the base, sift the flour and bicarbonate of soda into a large bowl, add the ground almonds and sugar and mix with a balloon whisk. Rub in 65g of the butter with the tips of your fingers. Sprinkle on a little water and gently turn the mixture with your fingers. Incorporate enough water to give slightly damp crumbs (don't knead to a dough). Spread out on the baking tray and bake in the oven for 20 minutes. Leave to cool.

Melt the remaining butter gently in a saucepan and take off the heat. Break the crumble into crumbs with your hands or a wooden spoon, add to the pan and mix together well. Press into the cake tin and chill for at least half an hour.

Meanwhile, make the topping. Put the blueberries, sugar and 1 tbsp water into a small pan. Heat very gently until the juices start to run and the sugar has dissolved. Pour in the cornflour or arrowroot mixture and stir constantly as the mixture comes to the boil and thickens, then remove from the heat and set aside to cool.

For the filling, put the cream, cream cheese, yoghurt and vanilla into a bowl. Sift in the icing sugar. Whisk, using an electric whisk or balloon whisk, for 2–3 minutes until firm and airy. Spread the cream cheese filling over the chilled biscuit base and smooth the surface. Stir the cooled berry mixture and spoon over the cream cheese filling, easing it out to the edge. Chill for at least another hour, or if you have the patience, overnight.

honey and rose ice cream serves 6–8

This delicate ice cream makes a great dinner party dessert, served with the almond wafers on page 208; children will love it too. The subtle taste of rosewater fills out the flavour with a marshmallowy roundness, while the yoghurt has a pleasing sourness, which makes this lighter and more refreshing than standard ice cream.

4 large egg yolks
75g raw honey
360ml double cream
300g full fat Greek yoghurt
About 1 tsp vanilla extract

About 3 tsp rosewater
A handful of dried rose petals or
  2 tbsp rose petal jam (optional)
2 tsp lemon juice (optional)

Put the egg yolks into a large bowl with the honey and whisk, using an electric hand whisk, until the mixture is pale and thick. (You could do this by hand, but it would take rather longer.)

In a small saucepan, heat the cream to just below boiling. As soon as steam starts to rise from the surface, trickle it onto the egg yolks in a thin stream, whisking constantly as you do so. Return the custard to the rinsed pan and place over a low heat. Stir constantly until the custard is thick enough to coat the back of the spoon. Pour into a bowl, cover and allow to cool, then chill thoroughly.

Stir the yoghurt, vanilla, rosewater and rose petals or jam, if using, into the chilled custard. Taste to check it is sweet enough – if the yoghurt is really tart, you might need more honey, but don't make it too sweet. Add the lemon juice if you think it needs it. You might want to add a little more vanilla too, or a little more rosewater to taste. Don't be tempted to add too much rosewater – think marshmallow, not potpourri!

Pour the custard into an ice cream maker and churn until frozen. (If you do not have an ice cream maker, pour into a large shallow container and place in the freezer, stirring thoroughly every 15–20 minutes to break down the ice crystals, until frozen.)

If you are making the ice cream in advance, store it in a tub in the freezer and transfer to the fridge an hour or so before you plan to eat it. For a really smooth result, process it in a blender or food processor once it has softened a little. To serve, scoop into bowls and accompany with wafers, if you like.

dessert wafers makes about 20

These crisp, moreish wafers transform a simple bowl of vanilla ice cream or fruit fool into a dinner party dessert. *(Illustrated on previous page.)*

110g salted butter, softened
110g golden caster sugar
25g rice flour
45g tapioca starch
40g potato starch
40g ground almonds

2 tsp vanilla extract
60g (about 2) egg whites, beaten
  until frothy
Extra caster or demerara sugar
  for sprinkling

Preheat the oven to 180°C/Fan 160°C/Gas 4. Line a couple of baking trays with baking parchment. You will only get about 6 wafers per tray, so you can repeat the batches and reuse the same parchment when the first trays are baked.

Using a stand mixer or electric hand whisk and bowl, cream the butter and sugar until pale and fluffy, then beat in the rice flour, tapioca starch, potato starch and ground almonds – the mixture will look clumpy. Gradually beat in the vanilla extract and egg whites, in about four additions, until the batter is smooth and lump free.

Place heaped teaspoonfuls of the mixture on the prepared trays, about 10cm apart. Spread them out using the back of the spoon or an offset spatula and a circular motion, until you have a circle about 6–8cm in diameter. Hold the paper with your other hand as you shape them, so that it doesn't slide away from you.

Sprinkle with a little extra caster sugar, or demerara sugar for a crunchier top. Bake for 15–20 minutes until just golden brown at the edge, but paler in the centre and firm to the touch. Allow to cool a little before gently peeling the wafers off the paper and transferring them to a wire rack to cool. Repeat to use the rest of the mixture.

variations

almond wafers Use amaretto liqueur in place of vanilla, or add a couple of drops of almond extract to the vanilla. Sprinkle the wafers with caster sugar and flaked almonds.

anise wafers Use brandy in place of vanilla extract. Sprinkle the wafers with demerara sugar and anise seeds.

mimosa wafers Use orange flower water in place of vanilla extract. Sprinkle the wafers with finely grated orange zest and caster sugar.

poppy seed and lemon wafers Stir 25g poppy seeds and the finely grated zest of 1 unwaxed lemon into the mixture. Sprinkle the wafers with caster sugar.

summer pudding serves 6–8

Summer pudding is traditionally made with bread, but bought gluten free bread tends to disintegrate on contact with juicy fruit, so I use cake instead. Use any combination of soft fruit, keeping the total weight at 1kg. Serve the pudding with softly whipped cream.

for the cake

115g salted butter, softened, plus extra
    for greasing
90g light muscovado sugar
2 tsp rosewater (optional)
1 tsp vanilla extract
2 eggs, beaten
80g potato starch
2 tsp gluten free baking powder
80g ground almonds

for the fruit

1kg soft fruit (400g blackberries/
    blackcurrants/redcurrants, plus
    600g raspberries/strawberries/
    pitted cherries)
About 50g light muscovado sugar
50ml water

equipment

20cm cake tin and a 500g loaf tin

Make your cake a day ahead (or earlier and freeze it). Preheat the oven to 180°C/Fan 160°C/Gas 4. Line the base of the cake tin with baking parchment and butter the sides.

Using a stand mixer or electric hand whisk and bowl, cream the butter, sugar, rosewater and vanilla until light and fluffy. Gradually beat in the eggs, beating well between each addition. If it appears to be starting to curdle, add 1 tbsp potato starch and beat again.

Sift the potato starch, baking powder and ground almonds over the mixture and fold in gently, but thoroughly. Scrape the mixture into the prepared cake tin and bake for 25–30 minutes until golden and springy, and a skewer inserted into the centre comes out clean. Turn out onto a wire rack to cool.

Put the 400g fruit (blackberries and currants) into a saucepan with 50g sugar (or more if the fruit is very tart) and 50ml water. Heat gently until the juices run and just come to the boil. Take off the heat and let cool slightly. Mash about 150g of the 600g raw fruit and add to the cooked fruit. Halve large strawberries but keep the other raw fruit whole.

To assemble, line the loaf tin with cling film, leaving plenty overhanging the sides. Drizzle in a little juice from the cooked fruit. Cut the cake into 1cm thick slices. Line the base with a third of the cake slices and spoon on half of the cooked fruit (leave as much juice in the bowl as possible). Arrange half of the raw fruit on top. Repeat the cake, cooked fruit and raw fruit layers, then top with the rest of the cake. Snuggle it all into the tin gently with your hand. Drizzle the remaining juice over the pudding, then wrap the cling film over the top and press the pudding gently with your hand. Refrigerate overnight.

The next day, turn out the pudding onto a dish and slice with a sharp knife to serve.

blackberry and apple pie serves 6–8

Apple pie is good, but a couple of handfuls of blackberries make it amazing. Wild berries create less juice so you can add more of them without swamping the pastry. The nutty, malty flavours of the sorghum in the pastry sit so well with tart Bramley apples. Almond pastry is delicious too, but more delicate than shortcrust, so it can break up a little over the dish as it bakes, allowing the juices to bubble through enticingly.

1 quantity sweet shortcrust pastry
   (see page 128) or sweet almond
   pastry (see page 130), chilled
Tapioca starch for dusting

for the filling
6 large Bramley apples
3–6 tbsp light muscovado sugar,
   to taste

3 large handfuls of wild blackberries
   (or 2 handfuls of shop bought)
Milk or almond milk for brushing
Caster sugar for sprinkling

equipment
30cm round or oval pie dish

Preheat the oven to 200°C/Fan 180°C/Gas 6 if using shortcrust, or 180°C/Fan 160°C/Gas 4 if using almond pastry.

While the pastry is chilling, make the filling. Peel and core the apples, then cut them into chunks – not too small, or they will collapse early on baking and the pastry will flop. Taste the apples for sweetness and decide how much sugar to add. Tip the apples into a large bowl and add the muscovado sugar and blackberries. Toss gently, then pile into your pie dish.

Break off a small piece of pastry and roll it into a long thin sausage that will fit all around the rim of the pie dish. Wet the rim of the dish and press your pastry sausage to flatten onto the rim all around, joining the ends together.

Roll out the rest of the pastry between two sheets of cling film dusted with tapioca starch to about a 4–5mm thickness – not too thin or it will break when you lay it over the fruit. Peel off the top sheet of cling film and invert the pastry over the fruit.

Press the pastry down gently around the edge of the pie dish to seal and then use a sharp knife to trim the excess overhanging the edge of the dish. Use a fork or your fingers to crimp the edge. Make a couple of slashes in the pastry to allow steam to escape.

Brush the pastry lightly with milk and sprinkle generously with caster sugar. Bake for about 45–50 minutes until the pastry is crisp. If it looks like the pastry might become too dark, just lightly cover the top with foil.

Serve the pie warm, with lashings of cream.

plum buckle serves 6

So called because it groans under the weight of the fruit it contains, my version of this American pudding is a lemony pound cake, loaded with juicy fruit and topped with a nubbly crumble. Moist and pudding like in the centre, it is properly cakey at the edges and studded throughout with tart pieces of plum. It also works with other seasonal fruits, such as blueberries, blackberries, eating apples or peaches. Eat warm or at room temperature with a drizzle of single cream.

for the crumble
50g rice flour
50g tapioca starch
100g ground almonds
1 tsp ground psyllium husk
½ tsp ground cinnamon
50g light muscovado sugar
50g cold salted butter

for the cake
130g salted butter, softened
100g light muscovado sugar

100g white gluten free flour (or 50g rice flour and 50g potato starch)
50g ground almonds
2 eggs
2 tsp gluten free baking powder
1 tsp vanilla extract
Grated zest of 1 unwaxed lemon
2 tbsp lemon juice
550g plums, halved and stoned

equipment
20cm round deep springform cake tin

Preheat the oven to 180°C/Fan 160°C/Gas 4. Line the base and sides of the cake tin with baking parchment.

For the crumble, sift the flour, tapioca starch, ground almonds, psyllium and cinnamon into a bowl. Stir in the sugar and rub in the butter with your fingertips. Sprinkle over 4 tsp water and turn the mixture over with your fingers – to help the crumble absorb the water, without turning into dough. You may need to add another 1–2 tsp water to get the crumbs to form a crumble. You want big lumps, like granola, not breadcrumbs. Set aside.

To make the cake, beat all the ingredients except the lemon juice and plums together using a stand mixer or electric hand whisk until soft and fluffy. Beat in the lemon juice.

Cut each plum half into 6 pieces. Stir two thirds of the plums into the cake mixture and scrape it into the prepared tin. Cover with the remaining plums and then top with the crumble. Bake for 1¼ hours, then insert a skewer into the centre to check for any uncooked mixture. It's hard to tell if it is cooked because of the fruit, so if in doubt, give it another 10 minutes. Cover with foil if the crumble starts to darken too much.

Leave to stand for 10 minutes or so, then unmould and serve warm. Once cold, it can be kept in an airtight container for a day or two and reheated in the oven for 10–15 minutes.

peach crumble serves 4

Juicy peaches and cinnamon scented crumble make this pudding irresistible, but it is
also lovely with other fruit such as plums or apples, or pears with a handful of chocolate
chunks thrown in. For the crumble, you can use 60g of a gluten free flour blend in place
of the potato starch and rice flour if you like. The crumble is best served warm with
vanilla ice cream or custard. I like the crunchy bits where the juice has bubbled up and
caramelised on the crumble, while they are still a bit hot to touch – ouch, ouch, mmm...

for the crumble
150g ground almonds
75g light muscovado sugar
30g rice flour or sorghum flour
30g potato starch
1 tsp ground cinnamon
60g salted butter

for the fruit
800g ripe peaches, halved and stoned
25–50g light muscovado sugar, to taste
30g salted butter, diced
30g ground almonds

equipment
20cm round (or oval) pie dish

Preheat the oven to 180°C/Fan 160°C/Gas 4.

To make the crumble, put the ground almonds, sugar, rice or sorghum flour, potato
starch and cinnamon into a food processor and process until well mixed. Add the butter
and pulse until the mixture looks like delicious rubble. (Or you can do this by hand,
rubbing in the butter with your fingertips.)

Chop the peaches into chunks and put them into a small saucepan with the sugar and
butter. The sweetness of the fruit will determine how much sugar you need to add. Cook
the fruit over a medium heat until it is just starting to soften. Mix in the ground almonds
and spoon into the pie dish.

Scatter the crumble evenly over the top of the fruit almost to the edges and bake for
about 40 minutes until the top is golden brown. If it starts to look a little dark, turn the
heat down a notch and cover lightly with foil.

Leave to stand for at least 10 minutes before serving, to allow the crumble to cool down
a little and crisp up.

variation: **crumble in a jar**
Instead of baking the crumble on the pudding, you can cook it separately to keep on
hand for an instant dessert. Spread the crumble mixture out on a baking tray and bake at
180°C/Fan 160°C/Gas 4 for 25–30 minutes. Allow to cool and then store in a jar for up
to a week. It is particularly good sprinkled over chopped peaches, crushed raspberries
and vanilla ice cream, or chopped banana and Greek yoghurt.

magic lemon puddings serves 4

One of my mother's few culinary triumphs was magic lemon pudding. At some point during the baking, the pudding would separate into a fluffy cloud of sponge above and a layer of lemony curd below. I would often watch the oven, hoping to see the miracle happening in the glass baking dish, yet every time, my patience would fail and I'd return to find that I had missed the moment of transformation again. I like to make my version in individual cups, for a little refinement and portion control.

2 large eggs
125g golden caster sugar
40g unsalted butter, softened
40g rice flour
A pinch of sea salt
½ tsp gluten free baking powder

225ml whole milk
Finely grated zest and juice of 1½ unwaxed
  lemons (60ml juice)

equipment
4 large ovenproof teacups or small bowls

Preheat the oven to 200°C/Fan 180°C/Gas 6.

Separate the eggs and put the whites into a spotlessly clean mixing bowl. Set aside 50g of the sugar in a small bowl.

In a large bowl, cream the butter and the remaining 75g sugar until paler in colour, using an electric hand whisk or wooden spoon. Beat in the egg yolks, rice flour, salt and baking powder, then gradually incorporate the milk. The mixture will be slightly curdled, but don't worry, it will be fine.

Whisk the egg whites, using an electric hand whisk, until soft peaks form and then whisk in the reserved sugar, a tablespoonful at a time, whisking until you have a stiff meringue.

Stir the lemon zest and juice into the pudding batter, then gently fold in the meringue, without losing those precious air bubbles.

Gently pour the mixture into your teacups or little bowls, dividing it equally, and stand these in a roasting tin. (Don't butter the cups or the puddings will flop.) Pour boiling water around the cups to come at least halfway up the sides. Carefully transfer to the oven and bake for about 25 minutes, until the puddings are risen and golden on top.

Serve straight away, with a jug of pouring cream.

chocolate and chestnut fondants serves 4

Fondants were one of the first desserts I mastered after going gluten free. Oh my goodness, the joy of sinking a spoon into something that was both cake and sauce! Chestnut flour makes the little puddings seem more chocolatey. There is nothing tricky about these – just prepare your moulds carefully and keep checking on the fondants as they cook. You can prepare them up to 24 hours in advance and keep them in the fridge until you are ready to bake and serve – just add a couple of minutes to the baking time if cooking from chilled.

125g dark chocolate (60–70% cocoa solids)
125g unsalted butter, plus extra for greasing
Cocoa powder for dusting
4 medium eggs
75g light muscovado sugar

A pinch of sea salt
40g chestnut flour
25g gluten free white flour or rice flour

equipment
4 dariole moulds or small ovenproof teacups

Preheat the oven to 195°C/Fan 175°C/Gas 5.

Break the chocolate into small pieces, put into a heatproof bowl with the butter and set over a pan of gently simmering water, making sure the bowl is not touching the water. Leave until melted, stir, then set aside to cool a little.

Meanwhile, generously butter the moulds and dust the inside with cocoa powder to coat completely. Put into the fridge to chill.

Whisk the eggs, sugar and salt together, using an electric hand whisk or balloon whisk, until thick, pale and mousse-like. Add the melted chocolate mixture in a thin, steady stream, whisking constantly, until thick, smooth and glossy.

Sift the flours together over the mixture and fold in gently, using a spatula or large metal spoon, until fully incorporated. Pour the mixture evenly into the moulds.

Bake for 10–12 minutes until the fondants are risen and firm on the top, but still wobbly if pressed. The top should look like cake, not glossy at all. Check after 8 minutes just in case your oven is a little fierce.

Using a cloth to protect your hand, tip each fondant out onto a plate almost immediately and tuck in! Whipped cream is an excellent companion.

sticky maple toffee pudding serves 6

Dark, fudgy and irresistibly rich, this is a real winter treat. Take care to avoid overcooking the pudding, or you will lose the all-important sticky toffee sauce underneath. However, if you do give it a little too long, a generous drizzle of cream and a little more maple syrup should bring things right again.

for the pudding
150g dried stoned dates
100ml water
175g salted butter, softened, plus extra
  for greasing
75g dark muscovado sugar
2 tsp vanilla extract
3 large eggs, beaten
50g sorghum or white teff flour
75g potato starch
75g ground almonds
3 tsp gluten free baking powder

for the sauce
100g butter
100g maple syrup
25g dark muscovado sugar
25ml water

equipment
20cm round (or oval) deep
  ovenproof dish

A couple of hours before you plan to bake (or the night before), chop the dates and soak them in the water. Then cook in a small pan over a medium heat until the dates are just starting to absorb the water, mashing them against the side of the pan to help them to break down. Set aside to cool completely.

Preheat the oven to 180°C/Fan 160°C/Gas 4. Butter the sides of the ovenproof dish.

For the sauce, put the butter, maple syrup and sugar into a small pan, add the water and heat gently until the butter melts and the sugar dissolves. Pour into the prepared dish.

To make the pudding, cream the butter and sugar together in a large bowl, using an electric hand whisk, stand mixer or wooden spoon, until lighter in colour and fluffy.

Beat in the cooled date paste and vanilla extract. Gradually add the eggs, beating well between each addition. If the mixture threatens to split at any point, stir in a spoonful of the flour and carry on. Sift the flour, potato starch, ground almonds and baking powder over the mixture and fold in until just combined.

Spoon the mixture on top of the sauce in the dish, leaving a little gap around the edge for the sauce to bubble up. Bake for 30–40 minutes until well risen, deep golden and a skewer inserted into the middle comes out without any wet mixture on it.

Dig in as soon as the pudding is cool enough to do so. Serve with lightly whipped double cream, or single cream for pouring.

marmalade pudding serves 4–6

Sourdough crumbs give this rich, dark pudding the kind of depth that you just can't get from plain old bread (though of course, you can use it). A lovely alchemy occurs when dark muscovado, butter and bittersweet orange surrender to a long, gentle steam. For those who don't like a traditional Christmas pudding, this is a great alternative.

for the pudding
80g salted butter, softened, plus extra
   for greasing
60g dark muscovado sugar
70g ground almonds
20g rice flour
2 large eggs, beaten
100g sourdough breadcrumbs
Grated zest of 1 unwaxed orange
1 tsp vinegar

125g coarse cut marmalade
¾ tsp bicarbonate of soda
1 tbsp milk (or water)

for the sauce
2 tbsp coarse cut marmalade
Juice of ½ orange

equipment
1.15 litre pudding basin

Generously butter the pudding basin. Cut two discs of baking parchment 3cm larger than the diameter of the basin, place one on top of the other and make a small pleat across the middle (to allow for expansion). Pleat a slightly larger piece of foil in the same way.

For the sauce, mix the marmalade and orange juice together in a bowl. Pour into the bottom of the pudding basin and set aside while you make the pudding.

In a large bowl, beat the butter and sugar together with an electric whisk or wooden spoon until lighter in colour and fluffy. Beat in the ground almonds and rice flour, then add the eggs a little at a time, beating well between each addition. Beat in the breadcrumbs, orange zest, vinegar and marmalade.

Set a steamer on the hob, with plenty of water in the bottom. Alternatively, place a trivet or upturned saucer in the bottom of a large saucepan and put the kettle on.

Dissolve the bicarbonate of soda in the milk (or water) and stir thoroughly into the pudding batter. Working quickly now (as the bicarb will start to act), scrape the mixture into the pudding basin and level the top. Place the pleated parchment discs over the top and cover with the pleated foil. Secure with string, tying it under the rim of the bowl.

Put the basin into the steamer or lower into the pan and pour in enough boiling water to come halfway up the side of the basin, then set on the heat. Put the lid on and steam for 2 hours, checking the water level regularly. A gentle simmer is all you want.

Remove the foil and parchment. Turn out the pudding onto a plate and serve hot with orange segments, if you like, and custard, pouring cream or crème fraîche.

christmas pudding serves 6–8

Christmas puddings and cakes don't win any prizes for their looks, so I top mine with some glacé fruit, for a bejewelled finish. I secretly love glacé cherries – their succulence is brilliant in a Christmas pudding – and the fiery intensity of preserved ginger. The point is to pop something in the bottom of the bowl that makes the top of the pudding look dressed: you might also like to try roughly cut pieces of glacé peel, dried apricots, dried pear, Agen prunes or preserved orange slices. The pudding itself is a delight – dark, figgy, warmly spiced and redolent of roaring fires and sherry induced snoozing.

for the sherry soaked fruit
75g pitted prunes
75g dried figs (check they are not
   floured)
75g unsulphured dried apricots
50g natural glacé cherries, halved
75g raisins
100ml sweet sherry

for the pudding
Butter for greasing
100g natural glacé cherries
75g preserved stem ginger, chopped,
   plus a little of the syrup from the jar
2 large eggs
100g dark muscovado sugar
2 pinches of sea salt

Grated zest of 1 unwaxed orange
2 tbsp molasses
60g buckwheat or teff flour
1 tsp ground psyllium husk
1 tsp ground cinnamon
1 tsp ground mixed spice
1 tsp ground ginger
½ tsp allspice
100g gluten free breadcrumbs
   (sourdough are ideal, see page 101)
50g blanched almonds, roughly chopped
1 tsp gluten free baking powder
1 eating apple
150g unsalted butter, frozen

equipment
1.15 litre pudding basin

A day or two before you plan to make the pudding, snip the prunes, figs and apricots into pieces with scissors and put into a bowl. Add the halved glacé cherries and raisins. Pour in the sherry, mix well and cover. Leave to macerate, giving it a stir when you remember.

When you are ready to cook the pudding, generously butter your pudding basin. Cut a disc of baking parchment to fit the bottom of the basin and press this in. Arrange the whole glacé cherries and the chopped stem ginger neatly in the bottom of the basin and pour in a little of the syrup from the ginger jar, to taste.

Cut two circles of baking parchment 3cm larger than the diameter of the basin, place one on top of the other and make a small pleat across the middle. Pleat a slightly larger piece of foil in the same way. This allow for the expansion of the pudding on steaming.

(continued overleaf)

Set a steamer on the hob, with plenty of water in the bottom. Alternatively, place a trivet or upturned saucer in the bottom of a large saucepan and put the kettle on.

In a large bowl, beat the eggs, sugar, salt, orange zest and molasses together with a balloon whisk until frothy. Stir in the soaked fruit, flour, psyllium, spices, breadcrumbs, chopped almonds and baking powder until well combined.

Peel and grate the apple and stir this into the mixture.

Working quickly, grate a little of the frozen butter over the bowl and stir it into the mixture until thoroughly distributed. Grate in some more butter and then so on, until all the butter is in. (I find it easiest to grate it straight into the mix from a frozen 250g block and stop when the block weighs 100g.)

Scrape the mixture into the pudding basin. Place the pleated parchment discs over the top and cover with the pleated foil. Secure with string, tying it under the rim of the bowl (and leaving a length of string if you are cooking the pudding in a saucepan, to use as a handle to lift the pudding out).

Put into the steamer, or lower the basin into the pan and pour in enough boiling water to come halfway up the side of the basin, then set on the heat. Cover with a tight-fitting lid, bring back to the boil and then reduce to a simmer. Steam for 4 hours, checking the water level regularly.

Remove the parchment and foil and allow the pudding to cool completely. Wipe away the moisture from the foil and then store in a cool place until Christmas. If you don't peek and break the seal, it should be fine for at least 6 weeks like this.

Steam the pudding again, as before, for a couple of hours before you eat it. I like my pudding with a simple dollop of lightly whipped cream.

chestnut and orange cake serves 8

This cake has surprising depth, with a combination of sweet, slightly smoky chestnut, fragrant orange zest and warm vanilla. The crumb is moist, but with a pleasing melting quality, unique to chestnut, that ensures it is not heavy at all. Buy good candied orange peel from a deli that sells large pieces uncut; it does make all the difference. Instead of using a ring mould, you could bake the cake in a 23cm springform cake tin, but it may sink a little in the middle. The cake is best served a little warm.

200g soft unsalted butter (lactic butter is best), plus extra for greasing
100g chestnut flour, plus extra for dusting
250g light muscovado sugar
2 pinches of sea salt
150g gluten free white flour
3 tsp gluten free baking powder
150g full fat Greek yoghurt
1 tsp vanilla extract
Grated zest of 1 unwaxed orange
4 large eggs

150g candied orange peel, cut into smallish chunks
Icing sugar for dusting (optional)

for the orange yoghurt
400g full fat Greek yoghurt
Finely grated zest of ½–1 unwaxed orange
A little light muscovado sugar or honey, to taste

equipment
25cm ring mould (such as a savarin mould or Bundt tin)

Preheat the oven to 180°C/Fan 160°C/Gas 4. Butter the ring mould generously and dust with chestnut flour.

Cream the butter, sugar and salt together in a large bowl until soft and fluffy, using an electric hand whisk or wooden spoon.

Sift the flours and baking powder together over the mixture and beat in well, then beat in the yoghurt, vanilla and orange zest. Now add the eggs, one at a time, beating well between each addition. Finally stir in the candied peel.

Scrape the mixture into the prepared tin and let it rest for 15 minutes.

Meanwhile, make the orange yoghurt. Tip the yoghurt into a bowl, stir in the orange zest and sweeten to taste with sugar or honey. Cover and chill until needed.

Bake the cake for 45–50 minutes, until risen, firm on top, and a skewer inserted into the centre comes out clean. Leave in the tin for 5 minutes.

Invert the cake onto a serving plate and dust with icing sugar, if you like. Serve warm, with the orange yoghurt on the side.

teatime

Life can seem like a series of chores and deadlines, all hurry and no space. Teatime stops the hands of the clock for just a few minutes, welcomes you in and pulls out a chair. Whether you munch thoughtfully on a digestive with a cup of tea, or sink your fork gratefully into a cream-filled sponge, something delicious and homemade can set everything to rights again.

Gluten free cakes and cookies are every bit as wonderful as those made with wheat flour and they may be beaten as much as you like, as there is no gluten to toughen the batter. You could choose mild mannered rice flour to allow other delicate flavours to shine, or malty teff flour to bring a depth of flavour to a dark fruit cake. Potato starch can help make the lightest angel cake, while ground almonds lend a marzipan richness to brownies, muffins and teatime loaves. Regular bakers merely pick up a bag of plain flour, but gluten free bakers have a smörgåsbord to choose from.

Gluten free flours do tend to benefit from a little extra egg or some yoghurt, as they are inherently low in protein. They are also helped by a little more fat – unless there are ground nuts in the flour mix. If you are coverting a standard recipe to gluten free, flours may need time to hydrate, or a switch round in the method might be necessary, so the butter goes in before the liquid in order to avoid a grainy or gummy result. Some people add lots of baking powder to get the lift they are after, but I generally prefer to cream my butter or whip my eggs and avoid that characteristic tang when there is too much baking powder in the mix. I also use bicarbonate of soda in its place in some recipes. This is activated by acidity so it requires either vinegar or citrus juice to help it bubble (in recipes that contain cocoa or chocolate, no extra acid is needed, as cocoa is naturally acidic).

It's human nature to appreciate a little sweetness, but eating lots of sugar can have a disastrous effect on your body in the long run. Many of the cakes you'll find here are just sweet enough, allowing the other flavours to come forward: fruit, nuts, spices, good butter and the freshest of eggs. If you have a very sweet tooth, you may find you need to add a little more sugar than I suggest, to suit your taste. Cakes may be sandwiched with whipped cream or Greek yoghurt and/or crushed fruit in place of buttercream or chocolate ganache.

vanilla and blackcurrant
sponge serves 10

This moist, flavoursome cake is sandwiched with layers of tart blackcurrant and whipped
cream to create an impressive tiered cake. For a nut free version, replace the ground
almonds with 50g gluten free white flour – the cake will be a little drier, but still delicious.

200g gluten free white flour blend
100g cornflour
4 tsp gluten free baking powder
1 tsp ground psyllium husk
100g ground almonds
5 tbsp milk
1 tsp cider vinegar
350g salted butter, softened, plus
   extra for greasing
350g light muscovado sugar
2 tsp vanilla extract
6 large eggs

for the filling
Juice of 1 lemon
350g blackcurrant preserve
450ml double cream, whipped until thick

to finish
Icing sugar for dusting

equipment
2 x 20cm sandwich tins

Preheat the oven to 180°C/Fan 160°C/Gas 4. Line the base of the cake tins with discs
of baking parchment and butter the sides.

Sift the flour, cornflour, baking powder, psyllium and ground almonds together into a
bowl; set aside. Pour the milk into a small bowl and add the vinegar to curdle the milk.

In a large bowl, cream the butter, sugar and vanilla extract together using an electric
hand whisk or wooden spoon until light and fluffy. (Or use a stand mixer fitted with the
paddle attachment.) Beat in 1 egg, followed by 3 spoonfuls of the flour mix, beating well
between each addition until the mixture is smooth again. Repeat until the eggs are all in,
then beat in the rest of the flour mix. Beat in the curdled milk mix.

Scrape the mixture into the prepared tins and level the surface. Let stand for 15 minutes,
then bake for 28–30 minutes until golden, springy and a skewer inserted into the centre
comes out clean. Let stand for 10–15 minutes and then run a thin knife around the inside
of the tins. Turn out the cakes and place, right side up, on a wire rack. Leave until cold.

Using a serrated knife, slice each cake in half horizontally to make four layers. Stir the
lemon juice into the blackcurrant preserve. Place one cake layer on a plate, spread with
a third of the blackcurrant mixture and cover with a third of the whipped cream. Repeat
twice, placing the prettiest cake layer on top. Sift a little icing sugar over the top.

poppy seed cake serves 8

Browned butter, or *beurre noisette* as the French call it, gives this cake a distinctive flavour. It is simply butter cooked in a pan until it starts to turn golden; the solids in the butter caramelise as they cook, and the trick is to stop the cooking before they burn. The lovely caramel flavour and delicate crunch of poppy seeds give this simple loaf cake a surprising depth.

150g salted butter, plus extra for greasing
3 large eggs
150g light muscovado sugar
1½ tsp vanilla extract
70g tapioca starch
50g sorghum flour
115g ground almonds, plus extra for coating
3 tsp gluten free baking powder
30g poppy seeds

to finish (optional)
Greek yoghurt or browned buttercream (see page 236)
Poppy seeds for sprinkling

equipment
1kg (2lb) loaf tin

Melt the butter in a small saucepan and cook gently, stirring frequently until it starts to foam. Keep taking it off the heat and allowing the foam to recede a little so that you can see the golden silt forming on the bottom of the pan. Once it has turned golden and you can smell the caramel tones, plunge the bottom of the pan into some cold water to stop the cooking process (take care when you do this!). Cool until just warm.

Preheat the oven to 180°C/Fan 160°C/Gas 4. Butter the loaf tin generously and coat the inside with ground almonds, or line your tin with baking parchment.

Beat the eggs, sugar and vanilla extract together in a bowl, using an electric hand whisk or balloon whisk, until creamy. Drizzle in the browned butter a little at a time, whisking well between each addition. The mixture should look thick, paler and creamy. Scrape in all the sediment from the butter pan, to ensure you get all those flavoursome bits.

Sift the tapioca starch, flour, ground almonds and baking powder together over the mix and scatter over the poppy seeds. Fold in, using a large metal spoon, until just combined.

Scrape into the prepared loaf tin and gently level the surface. Bake for 40–45 minutes, or until springy to the touch and a skewer inserted into the centre comes out clean.

Leave to cool completely in the tin, then turn out onto a board. If you want to dress the cake up a bit, smother the top with yoghurt or buttercream and sprinkle poppy seeds generously over the top. This cake will keep in an airtight container for a few days.

rose and pistachio cake serves 8–10

A few teaspoonfuls of rosewater, a handful of pistachios and a scattering of rose petals elevate this simple cream filled sponge to something exotically redolent of a Persian flower garden. Some sugared rose petals are always gorgeous on any cake flavoured with rosewater: just paint the petals with egg white, toss them in a bowl of caster sugar and lay to dry on kitchen paper in a warm, dry place for 6–24 hours, until crisp.

230g salted butter, softened, plus
   extra for greasing
180g light muscovado sugar
4 tsp rosewater
2 tsp vanilla extract
4 large eggs, beaten
160g potato starch
3 tsp gluten free baking powder
160g ground almonds

for the filling and topping
225ml double cream
1 quantity rose buttercream (see
   page 236), or extra whipped cream
50g pistachio nuts, finely chopped
Fresh or crystallised rose petals (optional)

equipment
2 x 20cm sandwich tins

Preheat the oven to 180°C/Fan 160°C/Gas 4. Line the base of the cake tins with discs of baking parchment and butter the sides.

Cream the butter, sugar, rosewater and vanilla extract together in a bowl with an electric hand whisk or balloon whisk until light and fluffy. Gradually add the eggs, beating well between each addition. If it looks like the mixture is starting to curdle, add a couple of tablespoonfuls of the potato starch and beat again – it should come right.

Sift the potato starch, baking powder and ground almonds together over the mixture and fold in gently but thoroughly.

Scrape into the prepared tins and gently level the surface. Bake for 25–30 minutes until golden, springy to the touch and a skewer inserted into the centre comes out clean.

Leave in the tins for 10–15 minutes, then run a thin bladed knife around the inside of the tins. Turn out the cakes and place, right side up, on a wire rack. Leave to cool.

When the cakes are completely cold, whip the cream until thick, but not grainy. Put one of the cakes onto a plate and spread the cream almost to the edge. Place the other cake gently on top and twist it back and forth a little, just until the cream is peeking out between the layers.

Pipe or spread the buttercream over the top of the cake, or top with more whipped cream. Sprinkle with chopped pistachios and scatter over a few fresh or crystallised rose petals if you have them.

gooey chocolate cake serves 6-8

I remember having an amazing slice of chocolate cake at a friend's house as a child. It was dense and chocolatey, with ganache on top, and her mum told me that no one ever turned a slice down. This is my gluten free version. Here, I've added a lavish topping of chocolate curls but, of course, you can decorate it with Smarties and candles.

175g salted butter (or coconut oil)
60g dark chocolate (70% cocoa solids)
110g ground almonds
60g cocoa powder
60g tapioca starch
1½ tsp gluten free baking powder
2 tsp vanilla extract
150ml date syrup or honey
3 eggs, separated
A pinch of sea salt
125g coconut sugar or dark muscovado
    sugar
Finely grated zest and juice of
    1 unwaxed orange

for the chocolate ganache
200g dark chocolate (50-60% cocoa
    solids), finely chopped
200ml double cream
A pinch of sea salt
A knob of butter

for the chocolate curls (optional)
50g dark or milk chocolate, finely
    chopped

equipment
20cm round deep cake tin

Preheat the oven to 170°C/Fan 160°C/Gas 3. Line the base and sides of the cake tin with baking parchment.

Melt the butter or oil in a small pan. Meanwhile, break the chocolate into small pieces. Take the pan off the heat, add the chocolate and leave to melt and cool for a few minutes.

Sift the ground almonds, cocoa powder, tapioca starch and baking powder together into a bowl. Set aside.

Stir the chocolate mix until smooth and transfer to a large bowl. Using a balloon whisk, beat in the vanilla and date syrup or honey, then beat in the egg yolks, one at a time.

In a spotlessly clean bowl, whisk the egg whites and salt to soft peaks, using an electric hand whisk and squeaky clean beaters. Add the sugar in two or three lots, whisking well between each addition. Continue whisking until you have a fairly stiff meringue.

Add the sifted dry ingredients to the chocolate mixture with the orange zest and juice and beat until well combined. Working quickly now (as the baking powder will start to act), fold a quarter of the meringue into the chocolate mixture with a spatula or large metal spoon, to loosen it. Gently fold in the rest, just until no white is visible, keeping as much air in as possible. Scrape the mixture into the tin and gently level the surface.

Bake for 50–60 minutes, until a skewer inserted into the centre comes out with crumbs rather than raw mixture on it. The top will crack, but that will be fine. Leave the cake in the tin for about 10 minutes, then turn out onto a wire rack and leave to cool completely.

Meanwhile, make the ganache. Put the chopped chocolate into a large bowl. Heat the cream with the salt in a small saucepan until it is on the point of boiling, then pour it over the chocolate and leave to sit for a few minutes. Add the butter and stir gently but thoroughly until it is evenly combined and looks silky. Set aside, uncovered, to cool.

For chocolate curls, melt the chocolate in a bowl over a pan of gently simmering water. Spread on a marble slab or upturned baking tray and let cool until firm but not brittle. Hold a knife at a 45° angle to the surface and draw it towards you to make curls.

Spread the cooled, thickened ganache evenly over the top of the cake. If you have made chocolate curls, use a palette knife to lift them and arrange decoratively on the ganache.

coffee and walnut cake serves 8–10

Back when I was a wheat eater, I used to make Nigel Slater's deliciously moist coffee and walnut cake, whenever we felt the need for a proper cake – the sort you might find in a really good teashop. This is my homage to that excellent recipe.

200g salted butter
6 large eggs
300g light muscovado sugar
3 tsp vanilla extract
275g gluten free white flour
100g ground almonds
4 tsp gluten free baking powder
150g walnuts, roughly chopped

for the filling and topping
About 2 tbsp light muscovado sugar
A cup of strong black coffee
225ml double cream
1 quantity coffee buttercream
  (see page 236)
60g walnuts, chopped

equipment
2 x 20cm sandwich tins

Preheat the oven to 180°C/Fan 160°C/Gas 4. Line the base of the cake tins with discs of baking parchment. Melt the butter and set aside to cool slightly.

Using an electric whisk, beat the eggs, sugar and vanilla together in a bowl until tripled in volume and a thick rope of mixture falls from the whisk; this will take 6–7 minutes.

Drizzle in the butter a little at a time, whisking well between each addition. When it's all added, the mixture will be thick and paler, and the whisk should leave a trail when lifted.

Sift the flour, ground almonds and baking powder together over the mixture. Using a spatula or large metal spoon, fold in carefully but thoroughly until just combined. Finally fold in the walnuts.

Scrape the mixture into the prepared tins, dividing it evenly. Bake for 35–45 minutes, or until the cakes are springy to the touch and a skewer inserted into the centre comes out clean. Leave in the tin for 10–15 minutes and then run a thin bladed knife around the inside of the tins. Turn out the cakes and place, right side up, on a wire rack to cool.

For the filling, add the sugar to the coffee and stir until dissolved, then taste and add a little more sugar if you like. Turn the cakes over, pierce lots of holes in the bottom with a skewer and brush several times with the cooled coffee. Place one cake on a plate and brush the top twice.

Whip the cream until floppily thick and fold through 4 tsp of the sweetened coffee. Use to sandwich the cakes together. Top generously with coffee buttercream, or cover the top and sides with a thinner layer if you prefer. Sprinkle chopped walnuts over the top.

buttercream icing covers a 20cm cake (top and sides)

This is not as sweet as a typical buttercream. Choose a delicious organic butter, as this is the major flavour. I generally use salted butter because I like the way it balances the sweetness; if you use unsalted, add a pinch of salt to bring out the butteriness. Take the butter out of the fridge about 20 minutes ahead to soften a little, but no longer than 30 minutes, or you will end up with icing that is too soft to use.

150g icing sugar
100g salted butter, softened

1 tsp vanilla extract
4–6 tsp milk or almond milk

Put the icing sugar, butter and vanilla into a bowl and mash together with a wooden spoon until all the icing sugar is damp and the butter is broken down a bit. Swap to an electric hand whisk if you have one, otherwise continue to beat with the wooden spoon until the mixture is starting to lighten.

Add the milk, 1 tsp at a time, beating well between each addition. You may not need all the milk, so check after 4 tsp to see if you like the texture.

Use a palette knife to spread the buttercream onto your cake(s), or pipe it on if you prefer. Buttercream made with dairy milk needs to be eaten within 48 hours; if made with dairy free milk, it keeps a little longer.

variations

browned buttercream To make a buttercream with a salted caramel flavour, use browned butter (see page 229) instead of normal butter and chill it before using to make the buttercream.

coffee buttercream Make some really strong real coffee and let it cool. Use 6 tsp in place of the milk and add 2 or 3 pinches of finely ground coffee too. You could also use 1–2 tsp coffee liqueur in place of some of the coffee.

rose buttercream In place of vanilla, use about ½ tsp rosewater and the merest drop of cochineal if you like – go for the palest sugar pink rather than candy floss. Taste as you go – rosewater varies in strength and you may need less if you have a particularly strong one.

citrus buttercream Use the finely grated zest of 1 unwaxed lemon, orange or grapefruit and replace the milk with the juice from that fruit. Add the zest a little at a time, tasting as you go and stopping when it is zesty enough. Limoncello or Cointreau is a delicious addition too; use 2 tsp in place of some of the citrus juice.

luscious lemon cake serves 8

This is a particularly luscious lemon cake – moist, dark and drizzled generously with a sharp lemon syrup. A slice is lovely with a cup of tea, but you could serve it as a dessert, with some grilled plums or peaches and double cream. The recipe also works well with unsalted butter or coconut oil in place of the olive oil.

80g maple syrup
130g light muscovado sugar
3 large eggs
55g virgin olive oil
Grated zest of 2 unwaxed lemons
Juice of 1 lemon
125g ground almonds
85g rice flour
30g tapioca starch
½ tsp bicarbonate of soda

for the lemon syrup
3 tbsp light muscovado sugar
Juice of 1 lemon

equipment
20cm round deep cake tin or
   1 kg (2lb) loaf tin

Preheat the oven to 180°C/Fan 160°C/Gas 4. Line the base and sides of the cake tin or loaf tin with baking parchment.

Beat the maple syrup, sugar and eggs together in a bowl with an electric hand whisk or balloon whisk, until thick and creamy. Slowly trickle in the olive oil, beating all the time, until the mixture is paler and mousse-like. Beat in the lemon zest and juice.

Sift the ground almonds, rice flour, tapioca starch and bicarbonate of soda over the mixture and fold in gently.

Pour the mixture into the prepared tin and bake for 35–40 minutes until well risen, golden brown on top and slightly springy to touch; a skewer inserted into the centre should come out clean.

While the cake is in the oven, make the syrup. Put the sugar and lemon juice into a small pan over a low heat and heat slowly to dissolve the sugar. Don't let it boil as this will dull the sharp lemon juice flavour. Remove from the heat and set aside to cool.

Leave the cake to cool in the tin for at least half an hour and then pierce deeply all over with a skewer and drench with the lemon syrup. Leave in the tin until completely cold before removing.

rich christmas cake serves 12–15

There is something so comforting about soaking your favourite dried fruits in brandy. Once in the oven, this cake will fill the house with a brandied scent of goodwill. Don't be alarmed by the long list of ingredients – you can use whatever fruit you like as long as it makes up the same weight. The spicing is restrained, to allow the other flavours to sing, but feel free to add ground cloves or ginger, or grated nutmeg. If you do not have the listed flours, you can use a gluten free flour mix, but it won't hold together quite as well.

for the brandy soaked fruit
200g pitted prunes
150g dried figs
75g candied peel
75g preserved ginger in syrup, drained
150g currants
100g raisins
100g dried cherries
3 tsp vanilla extract
150ml brandy

for the cake
300g unsalted butter, softened, plus extra for greasing
275g dark muscovado sugar
150g ground almonds
100g teff flour or sorghum flour
100g buckwheat flour
2 tsp ground mixed spice
1 tsp ground cinnamon
2 tsp gluten free baking powder

4 large eggs
1 tbsp blackstrap molasses or black treacle (optional)
½ tsp sea salt
2 tsp psyllium husks
Grated zest of 1 unwaxed lemon
Grated zest of 1 unwaxed orange
100ml freshly squeezed orange juice
Extra brandy, for feeding the cake

to decorate
1 egg white (optional)
A large handful of fruit, such as physalis fruit, kumquats or grapes (optional)
Caster sugar for coating (optional)
3 tbsp apricot jam
Icing sugar for sprinkling
700g readymade marzipan

equipment
20cm round deep cake tin

A day or so before you intend to make the cake, you need to put the fruit to soak. Snip the prunes and figs with scissors into smallish chunks and chop the candied peel and preserved ginger. Put all the dried fruit, peel, ginger and vanilla extract into a bowl and pour over the brandy. Cover and leave to soak overnight, giving it a little stir occasionally.

Butter the cake tin and double line with baking parchment. To do this, cut two lengths of parchment to fit round the inside of the tin and extend 4–5cm above the rim. Lay one on top of the other, fold the bottom 2–3cm up and snip all the way along to create a fringe. Press this into the tin with the fringe circling the base. Top with two discs of parchment.

(continued overleaf)

Preheat the oven to 180°C/Fan 160°C/Gas 4.

Beat together all the rest of the cake ingredients, except the orange juice and extra brandy. You can do this by hand or in a stand mixer. If your butter is not very soft, cream it with the sugar and molasses first and then add the other ingredients.

Beat in the orange juice and stir in the soaked fruit, plus any boozy juices at the bottom of the bowl. Spoon into the prepared tin and gently level the surface.

Bake for 30 minutes, then lower the oven setting to 150°C/Fan 140°C/Gas 2 and bake for a further 2 hours, until the cake is firm to the touch and a skewer inserted into the centre comes out clean, covering loosely with foil if it seems to be browning too much.

Leave the cake to cool completely in the tin and then pierce all over with a skewer. Brush the top and sides of the cake with 50ml brandy. Once absorbed, wrap the cake in a fresh layer of baking parchment and a double layer of foil.

Ideally, allow your cake to mature for a couple of weeks. It should keep for at least a couple of months stored in a cool place. Feed it with brandy every week, brushing it all over, but don't feed it for at least a week before you want to decorate it.

To finish the cake, first prepare the sugared fruit, if using. Beat the egg white until lightly frothy and use this to brush the fruit all over. Dredge with caster sugar, shake off the excess and then set aside to dry for an hour or so. (If preferred, you can simply decorate the cake with sprigs of holly and berries, or bought decorations.)

Level the top of the cake if need be, using a sharp knife. Use a piece of string to measure from the bottom of one side of the cake, over the top and down the other side, cut the string and use this as a guide for the size to roll the marzipan.

Warm the apricot jam with 2 tsp water in a small pan over a low heat, then push through a sieve with a wooden spoon. Brush the bottom of the cake with a little of this apricot glaze before you set it on a board or plate. Brush the top and sides with the glaze and then set aside.

Dust the work surface with icing sugar. Roll out the marzipan into a circle, a little larger than your piece of string, dusting the rolling pin with icing sugar if it sticks. Loosely roll the marzipan around the rolling pin and unroll it over the cake. Press the marzipan gently down over the side of the cake, easing out any excess as you go, until the cake is snugly covered. Trim the marzipan around the base of the cake with a sharp knife. Dust with a little sifted icing sugar if you like.

Place the frosted fruit (or holly and berries) in the centre of the cake and serve. The marzipan, physalis fruit and kumquats will be fine like this for a week, but grapes will need to be removed if the cake is not eaten within 24 hours.

carrot and orange parkin serves 8

Parkin is a sticky, gingery treat that usually relies on oats to achieve a distinctly 'nubbly' texture. Here, I have married the fruity, tender crumb of carrot cake with the gingery stickiness of parkin, eliminating the oats along the way. When you've returned from a frosty walk, there's no better way to warm yourself than cradling a mug of tea with a thick slice of this parkin.

2 large carrots (200g), peeled
100g coconut oil (or 120g butter, softened), plus extra for greasing
75g dark muscovado sugar (or coconut sugar)
100g blackstrap molasses (or black treacle)
3 large eggs
Grated zest of 2 unwaxed oranges

150g ground almonds
70g tapioca starch
3 tsp gluten free baking powder
2–3 tsp ground ginger, to taste
1 tsp ground cinnamon
2 tsp vinegar

equipment
20cm square tin or 1kg (2lb) loaf tin

Preheat the oven to 180°C/Fan 160°C/Gas 4. Grease the sides of the cake tin or loaf tin and line the base with baking parchment.

Finely grate the carrots and tip into a large bowl; set aside.

In a food processor, or using an electric hand whisk, beat together the coconut oil (or butter), sugar and molasses (or treacle) until creamy.

Add the eggs, orange zest, ground almonds, tapioca starch, baking powder and spices – decide how gingery you would like it to be. Blitz until thoroughly combined, creamy and lighter in colour. Add the vinegar and blend well to incorporate, scraping down the sides.

Transfer the mixture to the bowl of grated carrot and beat with a wooden spoon, just until the carrot is incorporated.

Scrape the mixture into the prepared tin and gently level the surface. Bake for about 40 minutes if using a square tin, or up to an hour if using a loaf tin, until a skewer inserted into the centre comes out clean. Leave to cool in the tin.

Serve warm or at room temperature – it is delicious with double cream, or chilled thick coconut milk. Store the parkin in an airtight container and eat within a couple of days.

mocha muscovado brownies makes 8–10

These brownies are dangerously good. Coffee intensifies the chocolate flavour and teff flour has chocolatey notes and lends a silky texture that makes perfectly moist brownies. I've added a muscovado shortbread base that provides a contrasting biscuit texture. If you have a weakness for intensely chocolatey treats, you won't be able to resist these.

for the muscovado shortbread
80g ground almonds
60g rice flour
100g dark muscovado sugar
70g cold salted butter
1 tsp vanilla extract

for the brownie
200g dark chocolate (70% cocoa solids)
130g salted butter, softened
2 large eggs

175g light muscovado sugar
4 tsp very strong cold coffee or coffee
    liqueur
90g teff flour
1 tsp gluten free baking powder
100g coffee flavoured chocolate (or white
    or milk chocolate), cut into chunks

equipment
20cm square brownie tin

Preheat the oven to 190°C/Fan 170°C/Gas 5. Line the tin with baking parchment.

To prepare the shortbread, put the ground almonds, rice flour and sugar into a bowl and rub in the butter using your fingertips, until you have rough crumbs. Sprinkle in the vanilla and toss with your fingers to incorporate. Tip the mixture into the lined tin and press into an even layer. Bake for 10 minutes, then set aside to cool.

For the brownie, break the dark chocolate into pieces and place in a heatproof bowl over a pan of barely simmering water, making sure the bowl is not in contact with the water, and allow to melt. Take off the heat when it is almost fully melted and stir well. Scoop out 2 tbsp into a little bowl and set aside for the decoration. Add the butter to the rest of the chocolate and set aside until it has melted.

In a large bowl, whisk the eggs, sugar and coffee together, using an electric hand whisk or balloon whisk, until thickened and slightly lighter in colour (about 1 minute with an electric whisk, 2–3 minutes by hand).

Add a little of the melted chocolate and beat with the whisk until it becomes glossy again. Repeat until all the chocolate is incorporated and the mixture is thick and glossy.

Sift the teff flour and baking powder together over the chocolate mixture and then beat in until evenly combined and the mixture is smooth.

(continued overleaf)

Pour the mixture over the shortbread in the tin and sprinkle the surface with the chocolate chunks, pushing them in a little if any stand on the surface.

Bake for 30–40 minutes or until risen and fairly firm, and a skewer inserted into the centre brings out a little gooey crumb with it rather than uncooked mixture. Check after 25 minutes and err on the side of undercooking to get a truffley, dense brownie once chilled. If you prefer a cakey brownie, give it the full 40 minutes, but check 5 minutes before the end. Leave to cool in the tin for at least an hour.

Re-melt the reserved chocolate in a microwave or as above and drizzle decoratively over the top of the brownie. Leave for at least another couple of hours, to allow the brownie to set. Serve cut into squares – warmed, at room temperature or chilled. The brownies will keep for a week in an airtight container.

chocolate and coconut brownies makes 8–10

Chocolate and coconut were made for each other: the rich perfume of coconut brings out the best in dark chocolate, smoothing away any bitterness. My favourite way to cook these brownies is to let the edges bake to a cakey firmness, leaving the centre just over half cooked. Once chilled, the coconut oil does amazing things to the texture of the brownie, which will set into a dense truffle with that classic brownie crust.

115g virgin coconut oil
150g dark chocolate (70% cocoa solids)
2 large eggs
160g light muscovado sugar
½ tsp fine sea salt
¼ tsp bicarbonate of soda
2 tsp vanilla extract

55g ground almonds or coconut flour
40g buckwheat or teff flour
A handful of roughly chopped dark
   chocolate (or shredded coconut)

equipment
20cm square brownie tin

Preheat the oven to 190°C/Fan 170°C/Gas 5. Line the tin with baking parchment.

Put the coconut oil into a bowl over a pan of barely simmering water to melt and add the chocolate, in pieces. When almost melted, take off the heat, stir well and set aside.

Whisk the eggs, sugar, salt, bicarbonate of soda and vanilla extract together in a large bowl, using an electric hand whisk or balloon whisk, until thick and slightly lighter in colour (about 1 minute with an electric whisk, 2–3 minutes by hand).

Add a little of the melted chocolate mixture and beat with the whisk until it becomes glossy again. Repeat until all the chocolate is incorporated and the mixture is thick and glossy. Add the ground almonds and flour and beat until smooth.

Pour the mixture into the prepared tin and sprinkle the chopped chocolate or shredded coconut evenly over the surface.

Bake for 25–30 minutes, until risen and firm around the edges, and a skewer inserted into the middle brings out a little gooey crumb with it rather than uncooked mixture. Check after 20 minutes and err on the side of undercooking to get a truffley, dense brownie once chilled. If you prefer a cakey brownie, give it the full 30 minutes, but check 5 minutes before the end. Leave to cool and set in the tin for at least 3 hours.

If you've gone for a very truffley brownie, these are best chilled for maximum density, as the coconut oil sets at the lower temperature. If you've opted for a cakey texture, warm before serving to soften them a little. They will keep for a week in an airtight container.

cherry cupcakes makes 12

There's something delightful about a cake in miniature, complete with its own paper case, icing and decoration. I'm not much for sugary frosting or sparkly sprinkles though. For me, cupcake perfection is one that overspills the case a little, and is topped with a lavish spoonful of whipped cream or Greek yoghurt and some perfect jewel-like fruit. A single cherry tops these cupcakes, but they are also delicious made and topped with other fruit, such as raspberries in summer and blackberries in autumn.

300g fresh cherries
120g salted butter, softened
100g light muscovado sugar
300g ground almonds
100ml maple syrup or date syrup
70g maize flour or rice flour or millet flour
30g ground linseed

3 tsp gluten free baking powder
4 large eggs
Grated zest of 2 unwaxed lemons
Juice of 1 lemon
225ml double cream, to finish

equipment
12-hole muffin tray and paper muffin cases

Preheat the oven to 180°C/Fan 160°C/Gas 4. Line the muffin tray with the paper muffin cases.

Reserve 12 perfect cherries, with their stalks if possible. Stone and halve the remaining cherries and set aside.

Beat the butter and sugar together in a large bowl until smooth and creamy, using an electric hand whisk, wooden spoon or stand mixer. Beat in the ground almonds, syrup, flour, linseed and baking powder.

Add the eggs, one at a time, beating well between each addition until smooth. Continue to beat until the mixture looks a little lighter and creamier. Now beat in the lemon zest and juice. Finally, fold in the halved cherries.

Spoon the mixture evenly into the muffin cases, to about 1cm from the top, so that the cake will billow generously over the paper case as it rises. Bake for 30–35 minutes until risen, firm and golden brown.

Leave to cool in the tray for a few minutes and then gently detach any stuck bits and transfer the cakes to a wire rack to cool completely.

To finish, whip the cream until floppily thick, then spoon evenly on top of the cakes and spread it almost to the edges. Top each cake with a whole cherry. The cupcakes are best eaten within a few hours if topped with cream. Undecorated, they can be frozen or kept in an airtight container for a few days.

gingercake muffins makes 12

I use a combination of ground almonds and sourdough ferment to make these muffins moist and tender. Molasses gives the muffins a treacly flavour and crusty top – a little like Jamaican ginger cake. You can make the sourdough sponge a couple of days ahead and let it work slowly in the fridge. If you do not have a sourdough starter, use Greek yoghurt instead. I sometimes add chopped peel or preserved ginger in place of the fruit.

for the sourdough sponge
2 tbsp brown rice sourdough starter (see page 74) or full fat Greek yoghurt
50g buckwheat flour
50g rice flour
2 heaped tsp ground linseed
200ml tepid water

for the muffins
200g salted butter, softened
200g dark muscovado sugar
2 heaped tbsp blackstrap molasses

1 tsp bicarbonate of soda
2 large eggs, beaten
200g ground almonds
4 tsp ground ginger
1 tsp ground cinnamon
½ tsp ground allspice
4 tsp cider vinegar
2 large handfuls of currants or barberries

equipment
12-hole muffin tray and 12 paper muffin cases

At least 3 hours ahead, mix the ingredients for the sourdough sponge together in a bowl. Cover and leave at room temperature for 3–12 hours, or in the fridge for 24–48 hours.

Preheat the oven to 180°C/Fan 160°C/Gas 4. Put the muffin cases in the muffin tray.

In a large bowl, cream the butter with the sugar, molasses and bicarbonate of soda until smooth, using an electric hand whisk, wooden spoon or stand mixer.

Add the eggs gradually, beating well between each addition. If the mixture looks like it might split, add a couple of spoonfuls of the ground almonds and continue beating.

Beat in the ground almonds, spices and sourdough sponge, using a wooden spoon. Add the cider vinegar and currants or barberries and beat well to incorporate. Now, working quickly, spoon the mixture evenly into the cases and bake for 30–35 minutes, until the muffins are well risen and a skewer inserted into the centre of one comes out clean. Lift out onto a wire rack to cool.

Serve the muffins warm or at room temperature. They will keep in an airtight container for up to 3 days; they can also be frozen.

banana bread serves 8

This banana bread has a lovely light, yet rich crumb. I've added just enough sugar to make it treaty, but you could leave the sugar out altogether or replace it with finely chopped dates to make it a little less sweet – or go the other way and add extra sugar to make it more cakey. It is delicious sliced and slathered with butter, or made into French toast and sprinkled with cinnamon. A good blender is essential to break down the quinoa.

2 large ripe bananas
4 large eggs
100g cooked quinoa (follow cooking instructions on page 152)
175g ground almonds
30g tapioca starch
About 50g muscovado sugar
50ml olive oil
1 tsp vanilla extract
1 tsp ground cinnamon

2 pinches of sea salt
½ tsp bicarbonate of soda
½ tsp psyllium husks
Juice of ½ lemon
A handful of raisins or chopped pitted dried dates (optional)
40g flaked almonds

equipment
1kg (2lb) loaf tin

Preheat the oven to 180°C/Fan 160°C/Gas 4. Line the tin with baking parchment, leaving some overhanging the sides to make it easier to lift out the banana bread.

In a blender, whiz together all the ingredients except the lemon juice, raisins and flaked almonds. Scrape down the sides to make sure everything is well blended and the quinoa has broken down (you shouldn't be able to see much of its texture).

Taste the mixture and if it is not sweet enough, add a little more sugar. Add the lemon juice and blend well to incorporate. Stir in the raisins or dates, if using.

Immediately scrape the mixture into the prepared tin, gently level the surface and sprinkle the flaked almonds on top. Bake for about 1 hour, until well risen, golden brown and a skewer inserted into the centre comes out clean. Leave to cool in the tin for about 20 minutes.

Use the baking parchment to help you lift the banana bread out of the tin (it will have shrunk back a bit). Place on a wire rack and leave to cool completely, then carefully peel off the parchment.

The banana bread will keep for up to 3 days in an airtight container in a cool place, but don't let it get warm or the fruit sugars will attract mould. Alternatively, you can freeze it, sliced, for up to a month – freeze the slices on a parchment lined board before packing into a plastic box.

scones serves 12

In my wheat eating days, scones were a regular treat, but they do present problems for the gluten free baker. Those based on rice flour are too sandy, while wholegrain versions are too heavy and getting enough liquid into the dough makes it impossible to roll and cut. My solution is to shape a rustic scone round, break it into wedges after baking and split these to eat. Buttery, light, slightly sweet and a little bready, these scones are excellent with a dollop of cream and some homemade preserve. They do, however, need to be eaten straight away, or frozen on the day they are made.

150g ground almonds
150g potato starch
50g tapioca starch
50g rice flour
50g sorghum flour
4 tsp ground psyllium husk
4 pinches of sea salt
6 tsp caster sugar

100g salted butter, chilled and diced
2 eggs
140g full fat Greek yoghurt
2 tsp lemon juice
1 tsp bicarbonate of soda
A splosh of milk or fizzy water
Milk or beaten egg for glazing

Preheat the oven to 240°C/Fan 220°C/Gas 9. Line a couple of baking sheets with baking parchment.

Sift the ground almonds, potato starch, tapioca starch and flours into a mixing bowl. Add the psyllium, salt and sugar and mix to combine. Rub in the cold butter using your fingertips, until the mixture looks like fine breadcrumbs.

Using a fork, beat the eggs, yoghurt and lemon juice together in a bowl. Sift in the bicarbonate of soda and quickly beat it in, then immediately scrape the yoghurt mixture into the flour mix and work it in quickly using a fork or knife, so that the bubbles created by the bicarbonate are trapped in the dough.

Add a splosh of milk or fizzy water and briefly mix with the fork to make a soft dough. Cut the dough in half and then tip each half out onto a prepared baking sheet.

Using floured hands, form each portion of dough into a flattened round, approximately 3cm thick. Using a sharp knife, score each round deeply into 6 wedges. Brush with beaten egg or milk.

Leave for 15 minutes to allow the dough to hydrate and bubbles to form inside it and then bake for 15–16 minutes until risen, golden brown on top and cooked underneath.

Tear the scones apart, split in half and eat as soon as possible – still warm preferably! Any that don't get eaten straight away can be frozen or made into breadcrumbs and stored in the freezer (see page 101).

chocolate chip cookies makes 18

These are crisp on the outside and deliciously chewy inside. Make a roll of dough and keep it in the freezer for whenever the cookie urge strikes. You can be munching some freshly baked cookies – with melting chocolate chips and a gooey centre – in less time than it takes to go and buy a packet. Once baked, they will soften up after a day or so, but you can pop them back in the oven for a few minutes to crisp them up again.

115g salted butter, softened
150g light muscovado sugar
1 tsp vanilla extract
1 large egg, beaten
100g rice flour
40g tapioca starch

10g ground linseed
1 tsp gluten free baking powder
85g ground almonds
150g dark chocolate chips or chopped
    dark chocolate

In a large bowl, cream the butter, sugar and vanilla extract together with a wooden spoon until pale and smooth. Gradually add the egg, beating well after each addition.

Sift the rice flour, tapioca starch, linseed and baking powder over the mixture and tip in the ground almonds. Stir into the mixture to form a smooth dough and then add the chocolate chips. Knead in until evenly incorporated.

Place the dough on a sheet of cling film on your work surface and form into a sausage, about 6cm in diameter, wrapping it in the cling film. Twist the ends of the cling film to make a tight roll. Chill for 2–3 hours until firm. (Or freeze the dough roll, ready to slice off as many cookies as you need and bake from frozen, allowing a few minutes longer.)

Preheat the oven to 200°C/Fan 180°C/Gas 6. Line a couple of baking sheets with baking parchment.

Using a sharp serrated knife, slice the dough straight through the cling film into 1.5cm thick discs, removing the cling film from each one as you go. Place on the prepared baking sheets, leaving space in between.

Bake for about 10 minutes, until golden and firm to the touch at the edges, but still slightly soft in the centre – the cookies will crisp up a bit on cooling. Leave on the tray for 10 minutes to firm up, then transfer to a wire rack to cool.

Store the cookies in an airtight tin. They will stay crisp for about 24 hours and then start to soften a little. To crisp them up, return them to the oven (at the same temperature) for a few minutes.

bourbon biscuits makes 15–20

When I was small, we were allowed one biscuit after supper and Bourbons were my absolute favourite. I always twisted my Bourbon in half and scraped out the filling before dunking the biscuit part in a glass of milk. Commercial gluten free Bourbons tend to be too sweet and barely chocolatey enough for my taste, so I have made these just the way I like them – intensely chocolatey and sandwiched together with a rich buttercream. They are still sweet, but the cocoa knocks the edge off the sugar in a very grown up way.

for the biscuits
110g salted butter, softened
90g light or dark muscovado sugar
2 tbsp golden syrup
A pinch of sea salt
½ tsp bicarbonate of soda
100g sorghum flour
80g tapioca starch
60g cocoa powder
2 tsp ground linseed

for the filling
130g icing sugar
1 tsp cornflour or tapioca starch
8 tsp cocoa powder
75g salted butter, softened
½ tsp vanilla extract
1 tsp boiling water

equipment (optional)
Piping bag and a 1cm nozzle

Line a couple of baking sheets with baking parchment.

Put the butter, sugar, golden syrup and salt into a large bowl. Sift in the bicarbonate of soda and beat, using an electric hand whisk or wooden spoon, until pale and smooth.

Sift the flour, starch, cocoa powder and linseed over the mixture. Work in with a wooden spoon to form a smooth, semi firm dough. Knead the mixture a little to get it completely smooth, if necessary.

Divide the dough in half. Form each portion into a sausage, flatten slightly and wrap each loosely in cling film. Chill for about an hour until firm.

Preheat the oven to 180°C/Fan 160°C/Gas 4.

Roll out each portion of dough between two sheets of cling film to a strip, 6–7cm wide and 45–50cm long. Using a sharp knife or pizza wheel, trim the edges to neaten. Now slice the dough across into rectangles – the classic size is 6 x 3cm, but you can make them whatever size you like. Re-roll the trimmings to make a few extra biscuits.

Transfer the rectangles to the prepared baking sheets using a palette knife, leaving about 1cm between the biscuits. If they are too soft, chill them for 15–20 minutes first. Prick two rows of holes along each biscuit with a thin skewer or cocktail stick.

(continued overleaf)

Bake for about 12 minutes until fairly firm. To check whether they are ready, press one gently with a finger; if it leaves an impression the biscuits need a little longer. The colour won't change much, but they will crisp up on cooling.

Leave the biscuits on the trays to cool slightly and firm up and then transfer to a wire rack, using a palette knife. Allow to cool completely.

Meanwhile, make the filling. Sift the icing sugar, cornflour or tapioca starch and cocoa powder into a large bowl and add the butter, vanilla and the boiling water. Beat with a wooden spoon until all the icing sugar is moistened. Now, using an electric hand whisk, cream the mixture until it is soft, paler and completely smooth. A stand mixer also does the job brilliantly, but you still need to work the filling first to avoid clouds of icing sugar.

For a neat finish, transfer the filling to a piping bag and pipe a couple of rows of blobs on half of the biscuits. For a rougher finish, just smear the filling on, using a butter knife. Gently sandwich these together with the plain biscuits, pressing gently until the filling comes to the edge.

Chill the biscuits for half an hour to firm up the filling before serving. These Bourbons will keep for a few days in an airtight container at room temperature, or in the fridge for a firmer filling.

ginger snaps makes 20–30

As soon as the weather turns cold I crave the warm taste of ginger, which pairs well with dates and maple syrup. These biscuits are rolled thinly for a crisp snap, but you can adapt the recipe to make chewy centred cookies (see variation). As they are dairy free, grain free, refined sugar free and egg free, almost everyone should be able to eat them happily.

300g ground almonds or coconut flour
80g dried dates, finely chopped
2 large thumb sized pieces of peeled
   fresh ginger, roughly chopped
4 tsp ground ginger

A pinch of sea salt
120ml maple syrup

equipment
6–7cm biscuit cutter

Put all the ingredients except the maple syrup into a food processor and process until the dates and fresh ginger are incorporated, but don't let the nuts turn oily. (Or chop the dates and ginger together as finely as possible and beat everything together with a wooden spoon.) Add the maple syrup and pulse (or beat) until it forms a rough ball.

Scrape the dough onto a piece of baking parchment and flatten into a disc with your palm. Top with another sheet of parchment and place in the freezer for 1 hour.

Preheat the oven to 160°C/Fan 140°C/Gas 3. Line a couple of baking sheets with baking parchment.

Roll the dough out thinly between the parchment sheets to a 3–4mm thickness. Stamp out rounds with the cutter. (As this is a tacky dough, rinse and dry the cutter from time to time to prevent sticking. If the dough gets too sticky, put it back in the freezer for a while, between the parchment sheets.) Lay the rounds on the prepared baking sheets, leaving space in between. Re-roll the scraps and chill before cutting out more rounds.

Bake for 10 minutes, then lower the oven setting to 140°C/Fan 120°C/Gas 1 and bake for a further 20–30 minutes until the ginger biscuits are a pale nut brown colour – don't let them get too dark. If they are not crisp enough, return them to the oven for another 10 minutes, bearing in mind that they will crisp up further on cooling.

Leave the biscuits on the trays for a few minutes to firm up slightly, then transfer to a wire rack to cool. They will keep for a week in a jar.

variation: ginger cookies
For a soft centred, chewy cookie, roll the chilled mixture into walnut sized balls and place these on a parchment lined baking sheet. Flatten slightly with a fork dipped in water. Bake as above, until the cookies are firm on the outside but still have a little give. They may take another 10 minutes at the lower oven setting.

digestive biscuits makes 16

Digestive biscuits were originally so called because the bicarbonate of soda that gives them their characteristic flavour was thought to settle the stomach. I have made this version oat free, but you could use oat flour in place of ground almonds for a sturdier biscuit. These digestives have a buttery, wholesome flavour and fairly low sugar content, which makes them feel authentic. They are perfect with a cup of tea.

100g sorghum flour or teff flour
40g brown rice flour (or white will do)
80g tapioca starch
140g ground almonds
10g ground linseed
2 tsp ground psyllium husk
½ tsp sea salt

100g light muscovado or rapadura sugar
½ tsp bicarbonate of soda
160g salted butter, chilled and diced
3–4 tbsp milk

equipment
10cm biscuit cutter

Put the flours, tapioca starch, ground almonds, linseed, psyllium, salt and sugar into a large bowl. Sift in the bicarbonate of soda and mix to combine. Rub in the butter with your fingertips, until the mixture resembles breadcrumbs.

Sprinkle the milk over the surface and gently turn the mixture with your fingertips to incorporate. Use enough milk to give a slightly wet dough – it will firm up as it chills. (If you don't use enough milk, the linseed and psyllium won't be activated.)

Shape the dough into a ball, wrap in cling film and flatten it to a 2–3cm thick disc. Chill for a couple of hours, or overnight, until firm.

Preheat the oven to 200°C/Fan 180°C/Gas 6. Line a large baking sheet with baking parchment.

Divide the dough in half. Roll each portion between two sheets of parchment to about an 8mm thickness, working fast as the mixture will soon soften as it warms up. (Putting the dough into the freezer for a few minutes to firm up after you roll it out can help.) Cut out rounds with the cutter and use a palette knife to transfer them to the prepared baking sheets, leaving space in between.

Re-roll the extra dough from around the edges of the biscuits. If this is too soft to work with, roll out and freeze the sheet again, keeping the tray of cut biscuits in the fridge.

Using a fork or skewer, prick the biscuits a few times, marking a pattern if you like. Bake for 20–25 minutes until they are firm and golden brown.

Leave the digestives on the trays for 5–10 minutes to firm up slightly, then transfer to a wire rack to cool completely. The biscuits will keep in an airtight tin for up to a week.

sourcing gluten free ingredients

Check out the following websites for further information, or if you are having difficulty sourcing gluten free ingredients.

nutritionist resource (nutritionist-resource.org.uk)
A comprehensive database of UK nutritionists, who can help you sort out what to eat in order to thrive.

coeliac uk (coeliac.org.uk)
A good source of general advice on coeliac disease, which is especially helpful if you are newly diagnosed. Provides news, research updates and advice on products that are safe to eat.

foods matter (foodsmatter.com)
Excellent advice and articles on food intolerance in general, including product reviews. Hosts of the Free From food awards.

specialist suppliers
Most health food shops and many supermarkets stock a good range of gluten free products so you may well be able to source everything you need locally, but many food producers and retailers offer an online service. If you have friends who are avoiding gluten, consider getting together to buy ingredients in bulk and enjoy savings that way.

naturally good food (naturallygoodfood.co.uk)
An online supplier offering discounts for bulk purchase, stocking Infinity, Doves Farm, Sukrin and Tobia Teff brands, amongst others. Also a great place to buy ground almonds in bulk direct from the mill; these are not certified, but in my experience, this is a safe way to buy uncontaminated ground almonds. Also sells linseed and psyllium husk.

sussex wholefoods (healthysupplies.co.uk)
Supplier of Infinity and Bob's Red Mill products online. Be aware that they offer many brands that are not certified gluten free, but are inherently gluten free. If you are not coeliac, then you should be fine with the brands that are not certified; if you are coeliac, stick to the ones that are certified.

goodness direct (goodnessdirect.co.uk)
Sells a few flours from Bob's Red Mill, Doves Farm, Big Oz, Sukrin and others. Psyllium husk and linseed are available too. If you select 'gluten free', the site will show you only safe products.

nature's healthbox (natureshealthbox.co.uk)
Supplier of a wide range of Bob's Red Mill gluten free flours and grains, and Doves Farm gluten free flours.

auravita (auravita.com)
Sells a few flours from Bob's Red Mill, Doves Farm, Big Oz and other producers; not all are certified gluten free. They also sell linseed and psyllium husk.

real food source (realfoodstore.co.uk)
Supplier of ground almonds in various forms at reasonable prices and many other delicious nutty products, as well as cacao and coconut products. Not certified, but with a very clear chain of custody that should be fine for all but the exceptionally sensitive.

amisa (amisa.co.uk)
The gluten free brand of parent company Windmill Organics, selling certified polenta, oats and chestnut flour.

gluten free flours
When you are buying gluten free flours, look for the crossed grain symbol. In addition to the general retailers listed above, you can order gluten free flours from the following:

big oz (bigoz.co.uk)
A good source of reasonably priced brown rice, millet and buckwheat flour.

bob's red mill (bobsredmill.com)
An American company producing a wide range of certified gluten free speciality flours. Usually quite expensive, but worth investigating.

doves farm (dovesfarm.co.uk)
UK mill producing inexpensive rice flour, chickpea flour and flour mixes (this is the brand that I generally use for white flour). They also sell a range of more expensive gluten free wholegrain flours.

infinity (infinityfoods.co.uk)
Sussex-based retailer selling a range of organic gluten free flours, with lots of wholegrain options at reasonable prices.

koda farms (kodafarms.com)
A Californian company that grow their own heritage rice varieties and make flours from some of these. The sweet rice flour, which is labelled 'mochiko', is certified gluten free and very reasonably priced, although you may need to purchase in bulk.

rude health (rudehealth.com)
Good source of a variety of wholesome gluten free oat products and sprouted buckwheat flour.

shipton mill (shipton-mill.com)
UK mill that grind their own wholegrain flours in a dedicated gluten free facility. They produce brown and white rice flour, polenta, and a wide variety of flours including sorghum, chestnut, buckwheat, millet, teff, maize, chickpea, oat, sweet rice and quinoa. Although not currently displaying the crossed grain symbol, they do test their flours for gluten content to five parts per million, which is more stringent than many others.

sukrin (sukrin.co.uk)
An interesting range of low carb, low fat flours, made from peanut, sesame, almond and coconut. These are pretty expensive and won't work quite the same as ground nuts because they are defatted.

tiana (tiana-coconut.com)
The main available brand of coconut flour. It is reasonably expensive.

tobia teff (tobiateff.co.uk)
Reasonably priced white and brown teff flour direct from the supplier, who also sells 100 per cent teff bread.

quinoa
Quinoa is available in all good supermarkets and health food shops now, but it is a great idea to support UK growers of the grain. Try the following:
hodmedod's (hodmedods.co.uk)
british quinoa company (britishquinoa.co.uk)

chocolate
Most dark and milk chocolate is inherently gluten free, but it can become contaminated if it is processed in a facility which also processes products that contain gluten. The following brands are currently deemed to be safe, although it is always worth checking in case things have changed.

plamil (plamilfoods.co.uk)
Supplier of organic plain chocolate, chocolate chips, milk chocolate and dairy free milk chocolate.

montezuma's (montezumas.co.uk)
Great source of plain and unusual flavoured chocolates, chocolate buttons and chips.

organica (venturefoods.com)
For organic plain and flavoured dark chocolate.

callebaut (callebaut.com)
Supplier of high quality couverture chocolate.

the chocolate trading company (chocolatetradingco.com)
Sells a dizzying array of single estate chocolate bars, truffles and many other gluten free
chocolatey delights. You can call them to check whether the product you would like has
any traces of gluten in it.

meat products
Free range lard, duck and goose fat, bones for stock, gluten free sausages and old
fashioned cuts of meat are available from the following suppliers by mail order:
abel and cole (abelandcole.co.uk)
devon rose (devonrose.com)
eversfield organic (eversfieldorganic.co.uk)
green pasture farms (greenpasturefarms.co.uk)
peelham farm (peelham.co.uk)

dried fruit
If you are buying dried fruit, be aware that sometimes it can be coated in flour to
prevent it from sticking together – figs in particular. Most supermarkets and online
suppliers will be able to tell you if their products contain gluten or not, so identify a
reliable brand and stick with that.

crazy jack (crazyjack.co.uk)
Supplies a huge range of supermarkets, online suppliers and independent health food
shops with gluten free dried fruits and nuts.

yeast
If you want to buy fresh yeast online, check with the seller that it is coming direct from
the manufacturer to you and not via a bakery, where contamination often occurs.

planet organic (planetorganic.com)
Online supplier of fresh yeast.

acknowledgements

Where to start thanking the many people who have contributed to this book? Those early adopters of blogging, who were also searching for something wholesome and gluten free, became a virtual community for me in the early days. Shauna James Ahern, Carol Kicinski, Elana Amsterdam and Shirley Braden are amongst many others who supported and inspired me.

Thank you to the River Cottage kitchen team, who understand my obsession with 'gluten hygiene' and calmly weigh up bespoke flour mixes with barely a flicker of panic. Special thanks go to Andy Tyrrell for your unfailing support and to Ben Bulger for help with recipe testing.

Nothing happens at River Cottage without the amazing office team beavering away behind the scenes. Thanks to Jess Upton for suggesting me originally, Lucy Brazier for raising the book idea, and Jemma Moran for your virtual wizardry. Thank you to Hugh Fearnley-Whittingstall, Rob Love and Sally Gale for your confidence in me.

I have honed my recipes through teaching them, talking to chefs and pressing baked treats on anyone who comes to the house. If you have attended a course of mine or tried a recipe from my blog, you have been part of this process. Ali Sutch has been such a wonderful companion on my courses – I don't know what I would have done without you! I would also like to thank Darrin Hosegrove, whose passion for teaching is inspirational.

A book starts with an agent and I must thank Antony Topping for easing my anxiety about the process. Little did I know that the entire team at Bloomsbury would be so completely lovely! Thank you Natalie Bellos, Alison Cowan and Xa Shaw Stewart for your vision and enthusiasm for the project and to Marina Asenjo for masterminding the production. Many thanks also to Janet Illsley for editing the text with such care.

I do think that this book is even more beautiful than I imagined it would be, thanks to the gorgeous photography of Laura Edwards, thoughtful styling of Tabitha Hawkins, Gill Meller and Aya Nishimura, and Georgia Vaux's sensitive design. Photo shoots were unbelievably fun, with a brilliant soundtrack provided by Kendal Noctor.

Finally, I must thank Finn Devlin for your impressive ability to critique a portion of sourdough bread, and Nick Devlin for your faith that whatever I cook will taste good. I couldn't have done it without you both.

index

Bloomsbury Publishing
An imprint of Bloomsbury Publishing Plc
50 Bedford Square, London, WC1B 3DP, UK
1385 Broadway, New York, NY 10018, USA
www.bloomsbury.com

BLOOMSBURY and the Diana logo are trademarks of
Bloomsbury Publishing Plc

First published in Great Britain 2016
Text © Naomi Devlin, 2016
Photography © Laura Edwards, 2016
Foreword © Hugh Fearnley-Whittingstall, 2016

Naomi Devlin has asserted her right under the Copyright, Designs
and Patents Act, 1988, to be identified as Author of this work.

British Library Cataloguing-in-Publication Data
A catalogue record for this book is available from the British Library.

ISBN: HB: 978-1-4088-5847-9
         ePub: 978-1-4088-6366-4

2 4 6 8 10 9 7 5 3 1

Project editor: Janet Illsley
Designer: Georgia Vaux
Photographer: Laura Edwards
Food stylists: Aya Nishimura and Gill Meller
Prop stylist: Tabitha Hawkins
Indexer: Hilary Bird

Printed and bound in Italy by Graphicom

To find out more about our authors and books visit
www.bloomsbury.com. Here you will find extracts, author
interviews, details of forthcoming events and the option
to sign up for our newsletters.